HOW LIKE AN ANGEL
CAME I DOWN

HOW LIKE AN ANGEL CAME I DOWN

CONVERSATIONS WITH CHILDREN ON THE GOSPELS

by

A. BRONSON ALCOTT

Recorded by
Elizabeth Peabody

Edited and Introduced by
Alice O. Howell

Foreword by
Stephen Mitchell

LINDISFARNE PRESS

This edition of *Conversations with Children on the Gospels,* conducted and edited by A. Bronson Alcott is an edited and abridged version of the text first published in two volumes by James Monroe and Company of Boston in 1836 and 1837, and reprinted in a limited Library edition in 1972 by Arno Press Inc. in the series *The Romantic Tradition in American Literature.*

This edition ©1991 Lindisfarne Press

Introduction, Abridgement with Comments, Personal Observations and Applications ©1991 Alice O. Howell

Foreword ©1991 Stephen Mitchell

ISBN 0-940262-38X (paper)
ISBN 0-940262-398 (cloth)

Library of Congress Cataloging-in-Publication Data

How like an angel came I down: conversations with children on the Gospels / by A. Bronson Alcott: recorded by Elizabeth Peabody: edited and introduced by Alice O. Howell: foreword by Stephen Mitchell.
    p.   cm.
"This edition of Conversations with children on the Gospels, conducted and edited by A. Bronson Alcott is an edited and abridged version of the text first published in two volumes by James Monroe and Company of Boston in 1836 and 1837" — T.p. verso.
Includes bibliographical references.
ISBN 0-940262-39-8 $24.95. — ISBN 0-940262-38-X (pbk): $14.95
1. Bible. N.T. Gospels — Miscellanea. 2. Children — Religious life 3. Alcott, Amos Bronson, 1799–1888. I. Peabody, Elizabeth Palmer. 1804–1894. II. Howell, Alice O., 1922– . III. Alcott, Amos Bronson, 1799–1888. Conversations with children on the Gospels. IV. Title.
BS2555.5A43   1991
226'.0083—dc20   91-18878
                                                                      CIP

Published by Lindisfarne Press
RR 4, Box 94A-1
Hudson, NY 12534

Book design and typography by Studio 31

Printed in the USA

10 9 8 7 6 5 4 3 2

DEDICATION

To
the great lineage of teachers
with deep gratitude
and
to my colleagues and students
with much love

ACKNOWLEDGMENTS

I wish, first and foremost, to thank my very dear husband Walter A. Andersen for his unfailing efforts in helping me and supporting me in this work. Thanks also go to the Erlo and Ann Van Waveren Foundation for assistance and encouragement. To Douglass Howell I owe my first introduction to A. Bronson Alcott's biography many years ago thereby sparking my interest. Elizabeth Ferry and Judith Hayes helped greatly in procuring copies of Alcott's works — no easy task. My gratitude also goes to the Fruitlands Museum in Harvard, Massachusetts and to the most helpful and enthusiastic staff at the Orchard House Museum of Concord. To Alcott Allison, family descendant; to Christopher Bamford, friend and editor, who saw the worth in this forgotten treasure, and Nicky Hearon who retyped the Conversations with pleasure: all were inspirations to keep going. Last but not least, I thank my young granddaughter Jessie Elisabeth King, who cut her literary teeth at thirteen by giving excellent help in preparing the bibliography.

A.O.H.

WONDER

How like an Angel came I down!
How bright are all things here!
When first among his Works I did appear
    O how their Glory did me crown!
The World resembled his ETERNITIE,
    In which my Soul did walk;
And ev'ry thing that I did see
    Did with me talk.

The Skies in their Magnificence,
    The lively lovely Air,
O how divine, how soft, how sweet, how fair!
    The Stars did entertain my Sense;
And all the Works of God so bright and pure,
    So rich and great, did seem,
And if they ever must endure
    In my Esteem.

A Nativ Health and Innocence
    Within my Bones did grow,
And while my God did all his Glories show
    I felt a vigour in my Sense
That was all SPIRIT: I within did flow
    With Seas of Life like Wine;
I nothing in the World did know
    But 'twas Divine.

Thomas Traherne (1637–1674)

TABLE OF CONTENTS

FOREWORD
Stephen Mitchell
xiii

INTRODUCTION:
Education and the Soul of the Child
Alice O. Howell
xvii

THE CONVERSATIONS

CONVERSATION I: Idea of Spirit *(Evidence of Consciousness)*
1

CONVERSATION II: Testimony of Nature and Scripture to Spirit
(Nature and Scripture)
11

CONVERSATION III: Revelation of Spirit in Nature and Humanity
(Inspiration)
17

CONVERSATION IV: Testimony of Humanity to Spirit *(Inspiration)*
26

CONVERSATION V: Annunciation of Spirit to Paternity
(Paternal Sentiment)
38

CONVERSATION VI: Annunciation of Spirit to Maternity *(Chastity)*
51

CONVERSATION VII: Incarnation of Spirit *(Gestation)*
57

CONVERSATION VIII: Nativity of Spirit *(Family Relation)*
65

CONVERSATION IX: Marriage of Spirit *(Conjugal Relation)*
72

CONVERSATION X: Advent of Spirit *(Infancy)*
81

CONVERSATION XI: Consecration of Spirit to Self-Renewal
(Religion)
90

CONVERSATION XII: Adoration of Spirit by Hallowed Genius
(Infant Holiness)
97

CONVERSATION XIII: Apostacy of Spirit *(Malignity)*
106

CONVERSATION XIV: Genius of Spirit *(Childhood)*
113

CONVERSATION XV: Integrity of Spirit *(Filial Piety)*
123

CONVERSATION XVI: Organization of Spirit *(Corporeal Relations)*
132

CONVERSATION XVII: Spiritual Vision *(Blessedness)*
136

CONVERSATION XVIII: Spiritual Supremacy *(Self-Subordination)*
140

CONVERSATION XIX: Spiritual Supremacy *(Self-Control)*
147

CONVERSATION XX: Spiritual Reverence *(Humility)*
151

CONVERSATION XXI: Conciliation of Spirit *(Self-Sacrifice)*
155

CONVERSATION XXII: Inspiration of the Affections *(Faith)*
161

CONVERSATION XXIII: Spiritual Refinement *(Chastity)*
166

CONVERSATION XXIV: Instinctive Inspiration *(Enthusiasm)*
172

CONVERSATION XXV: Immortality of Spirit *(Resurrection)*
175

CONVERSATION XXVI: Analysis of the Human Spirit
(Human Nature)
179

CONVERSATION XXVII: Renovation of Spirit *(Regeneration)*
185

CONVERSATION XXVIII: Spiritual Union *(Faith and Love)*
190

CONVERSATION XXIX: Spiritual Intrepidity
(Courage and Pusillanimity)
194

CONVERSATION XXX: Spiritual Purity *(Holiness)*
197

CONVERSATION XXXI: Spiritual Worship *(Prayer and Praise)*
201

CONVERSATION XXXII: Quickening Agency of Spirit *(Reanimation)*
212

CONVERSATION XXXIII: Supremacy of Spiritual Force *(Awe)*
217

CONVERSATION XXXIV: Inspiration of Genius *(Divine Eloquence)*
223

CONVERSATION XXXV: Spiritual Influence *(Example)*
228

CONVERSATION XXXVI: Sensuality of Spirit *(Self-Indulgence)*
232

CONVERSATION XXXVII: Spiritual Invigoration *(Healing)*
239

CONVERSATION XXXVIII: Ministration of Spirit *(Philanthropy)*
245

CONVERSATION XXXIX: Apostacy of Spirit *(Impiety)*
252

CONVERSATION XL: Imitation of Spirit *(Discipleship)*
257

CONVERSATION XLI: Spiritual Instinct *(Superstition)*
264

CONVERSATION XLII: Resurrection of Spirit *(Spiritual Revival)*
272

CONVERSATION XLIII: Unity of Spirit (*Conscientiousness*)
279

CONVERSATION XLIV: Sabbath of Spirit (*Holy Time*)
284

CONVERSATION XLV: Spiritual and Corporeal Relations
(*Appetites and Passions*)
293

CONVERSATION XLVI: Foresight of Spirit (*Prophecy*)
302

Notes
308

APPENDICES

General Maxims
(A. Bronson Alcott)
317

Original Editor's Preface
(A. Bronson Alcott)
320

Personal Observations and Applications
(Alice O. Howell)
324

Bibliography
335

We have yet to learn that Wisdom and Holiness are of no Age; that they preexist, separate from time, and are the possession of Childhood, not less than of later years.

A. Bronson Alcott

The unconscious psyche of the child is truly limitless in extent and of incalculable age.

Carl Gustav Jung

FOREWORD
Stephen Mitchell

There are many things to admire in this fascinating book, and I am grateful to Mrs. Howell for rescuing it from oblivion. Who would have thought that we already had, as part of our American heritage, such a practical demonstration of Jesus' advice to become like little children? The book might be sub-subtitled *News from the Kingdom of Heaven*.

Bronson Alcott was obviously a fine teacher. At first that seems improbable, given his extreme Platonism. He is the classic *Luftmensch*, walking with his head in the stratosphere and constantly tumbling into the ditches of what he called the material world. But in these conversations we can feel his authority. The students recognize him as one of those rare adults, perhaps the *only* one, who speaks to them with complete sincerity and respect, not as mere children, but as equals.

The most fascinating element in the book, though, isn't Alcott's teaching, it is the children's responses. "Out of the mouths of babes and sucklings hast thou ordained strength." I don't want to comment on them, just to point. Here are my favorite passages:

MR. ALCOTT. *Now, does your spirit differ in any sense from God's spirit? Each may answer.*

CHARLES. (*10-12 years old*). *God made our spirits.*

MR. ALCOTT. *They differ from His then in being derived?*

GEORGE K. (*7-10*). *They are not so good.*

WILLIAM B. (*10-12*). *They have not so much power.*

AUGUSTINE (*7-10*). *I don't think our spirit does differ much.*

CHARLES. *God is spirit, we are spirit and body.*

JOSIAH (*5 years old*). *He differs from us, as a king's body differs from ours. A king's body is arrayed with more goodness than ours.*

EDWARD B. (*10-12*). *God's spirit is a million times larger than ours, and we come out of him as the drops of the ocean.*

* * *

MR. ALCOTT. *Jesus said he was the son — the child of God. Are we also God's sons?*

WILLIAM B. *Oh! before I was born — I think I was a part of God himself.*

MANY OTHERS. *So do I.*

MR. ALCOTT. *Who thinks his own spirit is the child of God?* (All held up hands). *Now, is God your Father in the same sense that he is the Father of Jesus?* (Most held up hands).

* * *

MR. ALCOTT. *Does Father and Son mean God and Jesus?*

CHARLES. *No; it means God and any man.*

* * *

MR. ALCOTT. *Do you think that were you to use all that is in your spirit, you might also be prophets?*

SEVERAL. *If we had faith enough.*

WILLIAM B. *If we had love enough.*

CHARLES. *A prophet first has a little love, and that gives the impulse to more, and so on, until he becomes so full of love, he knows everything.*

* * *

MR. ALCOTT. *Why did the angel say to Mary, "The Lord is with thee"?*

GEORGE K. *I don't know. The Lord is always with us.*

ARNOLD (?). *The Lord is with us when we are good.*

AUGUSTINE. *The Lord is with us when we are bad, or we could not live.*

* * *

ELLEN (10-12). *[mentions "Judgment Day"]*

MR. ALCOTT. *What do you mean by Judgment Day?*

ELLEN. *The last day, the day when the world is to be destroyed.*

CHARLES. *The day of Judgment is not any more at the end of the world than now. It is the Judgment of conscience at every moment.*

* * *

MR. ALCOTT. *Where did Jesus get his knowledge?*

MARTHA (7-10). *He went into his own soul.*

* * *

AUGUSTINE. *Heaven is in our spirits — in God. It is in no particular place. It is not above the sky. It is not material. It is wherever people are good.*

CHARLES. *Heaven is everywhere — Eternity. It stops when there is anything bad. It means peace and love. High and white are emblems of it.*

ANDREW (7-10). *Heaven is like a cloud, and God and Jesus and the angels sit on it.*

MR. ALCOTT. *Where is it?*

ANDREW. *Everywhere. Every person that is good, God looks at and takes care of.*

FREDERIC (10-12). *Wherever there is good.*

SAMUEL R. (10-12) *But in no place.*

FRANKLIN (10-12). *Heaven is the spirit's truth and goodness. It is in everybody; but mostly in the good.*

* * *

MR. ALCOTT. *Can you say to yourself, I can remove this mountain?*

[Now comes an astonishing rhapsody by the five-year-old Josiah Quincy.]

JOSIAH (burst out) *Yes, Mr. Alcott! I do not mean that with my body I can lift up a mountain — with my hand; but I can feel; and I know that my conscience is greater than the mountain, for it can feel and do; and the mountain cannot. There is the mountain, there! It was made, and that is all. But my conscience can grow. It is the same kind of spirit as made the mountain be, in the first place. I do not know what it may be and do. The body is a mountain, and the spirit says, be moved, and it is moved into another place. Mr. Alcott, we think too much about clay. We should think of spirit. I think we should love spirit, not clay. I should think a mother now would love her baby's spirit; and suppose it should die, that is only the spirit bursting away out of the body. It is alive; it is perfectly happy; I really do not know why people mourn when their friends die. I should think it would be a matter of rejoicing. For instance, now, if we should go into the street and find a box, an old dusty box, and should put into it some very fine pearls, and bye and bye the box should grow old and break, why, we should not even think about the box; but if the pearls were safe, we should think of them and nothing else. So it is with the soul and body. I cannot see why people mourn for bodies.*

MR. ALCOTT. *Yes, Josiah; that is all true, and we are glad to hear it. Shall someone else now speak beside you?*

[But Josiah's eloquence is like a mighty river; its momentum is such that he can barely restrain himself, and he is quiet only on condition.]

JOSIAH. *Oh, Mr. Alcott! then I will stay in at recess and talk.*

How interesting it would have been to stay in during that recess and listen to this five-year-old. (The great ninth-century Zen Master Chao-chou said, "If I meet a hundred-year-old man and I have something to teach him, I will teach; if I meet an eight-year-old boy and he has something to teach me, I will learn.")

It comes as no surprise when, at the end of one class, a student says to Alcott, "Every lesson is more interesting than the last!" Nor are we surprised at the following short exchange, which could serve as the epigraph for this book:

MR. ALCOTT. *Do you think these conversations are of any use to you?*

CHARLES. *Yes; they teach us a great deal.*

MR. ALCOTT. *What do they teach you?*

GEORGE K. *To know ourselves.*

INTRODUCTION

EDUCATION AND THE SOUL OF THE CHILD
Alice O. Howell

Education depends on its attitude toward the soul.
Elizabeth Peabody

Some Psychological Parallels

Gentle Reader (to begin as books often began in Bronson Alcott's day), you are holding in your hands a most precious and extraordinary book, truly an American heirloom, which has almost vanished from our ken. Yet, if its time to resurface is right, it may well affect you as profoundly as it did me when it fell into my hands. I cannot imagine anyone's attitude toward children not being altered by the perusal of this work. And I can imagine the child in us wishing wistfully, "Oh, that I might have had a teacher like Mr. Alcott!"

I remember the day we found the book. It was a sunny spring morning, and my four young children were hopping and skipping along the sidewalks under the shade of the great beech trees that are the glory of Newport, Rhode Island. We were headed for the Redwood Library, founded by Benjamin Franklin, which has a splendid children's section. We went in, passing the large replica of the Dying Gaul, and entered the dusky, hushed fragrance that only books can produce. Suddenly quiet, the children tiptoed under John Gilbert Stuart's portrait of George Washington, past the enormous tables laden with magazines, journals, and newspapers, to the intimate nooks of their destination. I knew the magic would last while I grazed with special permission in the stacks. Thus it came about that my eye lit upon three dusty volumes printed between 1835 and 1837. They were *The Record of a School* by Miss Elizabeth Peabody and *Conversations with Children on the Gospels* by A. Bronson Alcott.

Having recently read Odell Shepard's remarkable biography of Bronson Alcott, I was thrilled to have tracked down these rare volumes about Alcott's Temple School in Boston and so, gathering up the children, now laden with treasures of their own, I hurried back to my parents' house where we were vacationing. Once home, all five of us succumbed to the intense spell of the printed word and, within moments, I was transported to the city of Boston in the 1830's and into the archetypal, and therefore ever-repeated, theater of a schoolroom of children with fresh faces upturned to their teacher — and what a teacher this was! Since I was just beginning a career of teaching myself, I felt truly blessed by Alcott, and, indeed, vowed later to repay my debt someday by ensuring that these books and their precious contents would see the light again. I truly believe that any of us who have been exposed to these works cannot have failed to pass on some of their legacy to our students, and furthermore that they are of profound interest today to parents or anyone interested in appreciating and guiding children.

What was so special and unique about Bronson Alcott's views? It was his approach to the psyche of the child. Over fifty years prior to the concepts of Carl Gustav Jung, the great Swiss psychiatrist, Alcott, too, was convinced that the child was not a *tabula rasa* but entered this life imbued with inherent wisdom and insight, and that all that was necessary to summon these to consciousness was to appeal to each child with respect, trust, and affection. As a life-long student of the work and thought of Jung, I have been impressed again and again by how strikingly the two men bear each other out in their views concerning the true purpose of education: connecting it to the soul or psyche of the child by imparting to knowledge a spiritual relevance. In fact, Jung may have given us the *psychological* reason, framework, and terminology to redirect the course of public education, which at present is legally prevented from referring to or appealing to the spiritual nature of a child. Surely in separating church and state, this consequence was not what the Founding Fathers had in mind! We need desperately to distinguish the spiritual from the sectarian religious content which is the forbidden topic in today's schools. We must realize that we cannot eliminate the intrinsic need for meaningfulness simply by passing laws. The terrible void remains and we are facing the dire consequences.

Alcott pioneered the idea of a nonsectarian "spiritual culture" of children. We must not be deceived by the titles of his work into thinking that he was teaching Sunday School. He was not. He was applying a methodology of teaching used both by Socrates and Jesus Christ: the dialogue. For this Alcott was accused of both heresy and blasphemy. However, he was the first American teacher to have apprehended what Jung later was to call the "Collective Unconscious." "The world of the Spirit is the inward life of all things," is the way Alcott put it. And he felt that young children, not yet cut off, had ready access to it. For him, as for Wordsworth, the child came "trailing clouds of glory." Exposing them to those words of wisdom found in the works of the great philosophers and in the Gospels of the New Testament, he thought, would prove how we limit children by not grasping that the soul dwells, in part, always connected to that realm beyond time or space that we call eternity or what we recognize today as the *unus mundus*. The remarkable results of the experiment are the content of this book.

Prefiguring our understanding of the Collective Unconscious, Emerson, who acknowledged many an insight from Bronson Alcott, wrote the following words in his essay "History."

> There is one mind common to all individual men. Every man is an inlet to the same and to all of the same. He that is once admitted to the right of reason is made a freeman of the whole estate. What Plato has thought, he may think; what a saint has felt, he may feel; what at any time has befallen any man, he can understand. Who hath access to this universal mind is a party to all that is or can be done, for this is the only and sovereign agent.

Even today applying this approach to public education may seem radical. The prevailing attitude is that teaching applies only to the conscious mind (ego) of the student. The teacher gives information, and the student receives it, gets tested on it, and moves on to acquire more information. Children interviewed in high school invariably see the purpose of education to be fitting them for employment. The soul, or psyche, of the student is rarely seen as relevant, so the underlying importance of education to the individual child in terms of the universal mind doesn't even obtain. More often than not we grow up crying out with T.S. Eliot:

> Where is the Life we have lost in living?
> Where is the wisdom we have lost in knowledge?
> Where is the knowledge we have lost in information?
> The cycles of heaven in twenty centuries
> Bring us farther from God and nearer to the Dust.

Alcott was a Transcendentalist, to be sure, and profoundly influenced by the works of Wordsworth and Coleridge in England and, beyond them, the great Greek classics only recently translated into English by Thomas Taylor the Platonist. But Bronson was more than just an idealist; he sought to prove and to make practical a perennial wisdom that reaches far back in time. Emerson wrote of him: "The ideal world I might have treated as cloud-land, had I not known Alcott, who is a native of that country and makes it as solid as Massachusetts for me."

Over the years after I first read Alcott, I taught history and had ample occasion to notice a curious phenomenon: again and again, at crucial times when so-called paradigm shifts in collective consciousness have been at hand, a cluster of extraordinary people have been born in the same generation in the same culture. Often they have managed to meet, to cross-fertilize ideas and talents in various fields of endeavor — art, philosophy, literature, science, music, drama, and so forth, and their efforts have radiated out, slowly and subtly transforming their society with a new perception and expression of a constant and underlying truth. Just as a crystal conforms to an invisible lattice, humanity both collectively and individually seems to seek instinctively for a pattern of reality to which to be true. The perennial conclusion, which is rediscovered and then lost again, is that ultimate reality is spiritual. Psychologically speaking, Jung said that "in the end all reality is psychic reality." The reason is that each unique human psyche perceives its own reality.

We could therefore add to Descartes' *Cogito ergo sum,* the corollary *ergo scivio spiritus est.* (I think therefore I am; therefore I know spirit is.) Implicit in all Alcott's teaching is the idea that the purpose of consciousness is to recognize the spirit in all things, to see the sacred in the commonplace.

On the basis of this insight such revolutionary clusters of extraordinary individuals throughout history, have all had a spiritual rather than a dogmatic religious outlook in common, and as a consequence they have often been brought into conflict with a threatened status quo. We find such an outlook at different times in China, in India, in Palestine, in Alexandria, Greece and Rome; again in the Renaissance; and in the Romantic Movement in Germany, England, France, and Russia as well. Finally we find it appearing across the Atlantic in the early nineteenth century influencing yet another revolutionary cluster in New England: the company of Emerson, Hawthorne, Thoreau, Channing, Melville, and Alcott, to name but a few. And on the distaff side, Margaret Fuller and Elizabeth Peabody, among others.

The task of these Transcendentalists seems to have been to stem the tide of Puritanism with its rigid tripartite fundamentalism of a wicked earth caught between Heaven and Hell. Children, for instance, had been considered "limbs of Satan" literally to be whipped into shape. But Alcott's little scholars see themselves as intrinsically good, as angels come down. Much discussion ensues in the classroom as the children pursue the reasons that they themselves fall from grace. Yet as we read what they say in their childlike way, they seem spontaneously to agree with the mystics that the good, the true, and the beautiful in this world are "the Way" by which we get a reassuring connection to the Eternal, the *unus mundus*. "Spirit all in all — matter its form and shadow," wrote Alcott in his journal. We can understand how Wordsworth's *Ode: Intimations of Immortality from Recollections of Early Childhood* inspired much of what Alcott was attempting to do. In a way, these lines from the poem were this educator's manifesto:

Our birth is but a sleep and a forgetting:
The Soul that rises with us, our life's Star
    Hath had elsewhere its setting,
      And cometh from afar:
    Not in entire forgetfulness,
    And not in utter nakedness,
But trailing clouds of glory do we come
    From God, who is our home:
Heaven lies about us in our infancy!
Shades of the prison-house begin to close
    Upon the growing Boy,
But he beholds the light, and whence it flows,
    He sees it in his Joy;
The Youth, who daily farther from the east
  Must travel, still is Nature's priest,
    And by the vision splendid
    Is on his way attended;
At length the Man perceives it die away,
And fade into the light of common day.

In *The Platonic Tradition in English Religious Thought*, Dean Inge described concisely the tradition to which the American Transcendalists belonged:

> My contention is that besides the combative Catholic and Protestant elements in the Churches, there has always been a third element, with very honourable traditions, which came to life again at the Renaissance, but really reaches backto the Greek fathers, to St. Paul and St. John, and further back still. The characteristics of this type of Christianity are — a spiritual religion based on a firm belief in absolute and eternal values as the most real things in the universe — a confidence that these values are knowable by man — a belief that they can nevertheless be known only by wholehearted consecration of the intellect, will, and affections to the great quest —an entirely open mind towards the discoveries of science —a reverent and receptive attitude to the beauty, sublimity, and wisdom of the creation, as a revelation of the mind and character of the Creator — a complete indifference to the current valuations of the worldling.

It is worth comparing these words with Alcott's own "General Maxims for Teachers" in the Appendix. He took this philosophy, "Plato for thought, and Christ for action!" and tried to see if it resonated with children. Alcott knew that if a child retained a sense of Christ as Spirit Within (what Jung later termed the Self), then education would have a central reference point for meaning, and that the other academic disciplines (which also were taught) would be irradiated with deep purpose. This psychological centering is what is so sadly lacking today. Certainly parochial schools of the various religions make the attempt, but naturally they do it within the specific context of their own religious doctrines, and such an approach is forbidden, thanks to the O'Hare ruling of the Supreme Court, by our public school system today. But Alcott, even in his time, was far more ecumenical and universalist in his outlook — he felt that this method of education (*ex-ducere* —leading forth) transcended all sects. Despite the titles and the Christian content of his books, we find the universal stressed. His beloved Greeks were pagan; the great influx of Eastern philosophy was just reaching America, bringing with it new support for his theories. Was not the Atman another word for the same indwelling light?

Had depth psychology existed in his time, Alcott surely would have been delighted with its neutral terminology. He surely would have agreed that as human beings we all share a collective pattern of the human psyche, no matter what our color, culture, or creed: a conscious ego questing for an indwelling spirit. He would have rejoiced to know that a century later, some would perceive that the "one Way" or "only Way" described by the mystics and various founders of religions, east and west, is actually a name (or noun) pointing to the only psychological process or method of action (verb!) possible for human enlightenment and meaningful life. This way describes an inner process taking place within each of us. However, we tend to hear the word "way" as a road rather than a practice. So if Krishna and Christ, for example, say "I am the only Way", we assume that one must be right and the other one wrong. Understanding the "Way" to be a verb rather than a noun could lead, hopefully, in the future, to greater tolerance for the spiritual beliefs of others. Equally important would be the transmission to all children in all classrooms of the idea of their own dignity and importance as vessels of that inner light which Alcott called the Spirit Within.

Today, on the fringes of our culture, we are beginning to hear much of a spiritual goal behind "individuation" or "self-realization." It is considered by many the task of the incoming age. In this, we can see the Transcendalists as forerunners and prophets of our times. They saw the visible as witness to the invisible; and life in this world as a sacred metaphor.

Depth psychology points to a spiritual etiology. It maintains that we are born; that we become conscious with the help of an emerging ego with which, in time, we tend to identify. But we suffer through any identification which separates us from the unknown Self (Divine Guest, Atman, Christ Within) or the testament of love and beauty in nature and each other. We learn painfully with humility to sacrifice this identification; thus we awaken to the Quest, and with yearning heart we step into the "dark wood" of our own unconscious to find our perilous way home, carrying the treasure of our experience back to the Source.

Amos Bronson Alcott followed this pattern through his life more consciously than most. He kept a private journal for over fifty years. He came dangerously close to an inflated identification with what in his journals he called his "Imperial Self," discovered spontaneously through his own mystical moments of illumination. When he wrote, "ascending spine-wise, [we] traverse the hierarchy of gifts . . ." even his biographers deemed him close to mad. Today, yogis would venture that he experienced the kundalini, the uprushing of spiritual energy through the chakras or centers on the subtle spinal cord. According to yoga, an Eastern practice known for millenia, as the energy reaches each chakra it yields gifts of higher consciousness.

Bronson Alcott did not go mad, despite a lifetime of eccentric experiments in applied idealism. He never succeeded in making money, but he ended up dear, old, and wise. Perhaps he inspired his beloved friend Emerson to write:

The time is coming when all men will see that the gift of God to the soul is not a vaunting, overpowering sanctity, but a sweet, natural goodness, a goodness like thine and mine, and that so invites thee and me to be and to grow.

The Drama of the Conversations

I set out from the wide ground of Spirit. This is; all else is its manifestation. Body is Spirit at its circumference. It denotes its confines to the external sense; it individualizes, defines Spirit, breaks the Unity into Multiplicity and places under the vision of man parts of the great Whole which, standing thus separate, can be taken in by the mind — too feeble to apprehend the whole at once and requiring all save an individual thing to be excluded at a single view. — Infinitude is too wide for man to take in. He is therefore permitted to take in portions and spread his vision over the wide circumference by little and little; and in these portions doth the Infinite shadow forth itself, God in all and all in God.

Bronson Alcott's Journal
December 21, 1835

Amos Bronson Alcott was thirty-six years old and teaching his very young students at the Temple School in Boston when he wrote these words into the journal of his life that he was to keep for fifty years. Tall, fair, serious, and blue-eyed, he was a most extraordinary individual, almost a phenomenon, a saintly American Bodhisattva on the one hand, and an exasperatingly square peg on the other, with no hole to fit in, so contrary to the norm was he in his day. As Odell Shepard, his biographer, says of him, Alcott was almost always on the right track but earnestly headed in the wrong direction! At least from the materialistic point of view of the American rush to wealth and success. There is very little in his early environment to explain him. He just was. And because he was, we unknowingly are all the better.

Bronson Alcott was born on a farm on Spindle Hill in Wolcott, Connecticut, on November 29, 1799, to simple hardworking Yankee folk. Though his maternal grandfather was an Episcopal clergyman, Bronson was closer to his father's ways. He left school when he was thirteen, helped his father and paternal grandfather with farm chores, and read whatever books — and there were few to come by — that he could find. In his early twenties, he became one of many "Connecticut pedlars" and for several years traveled south to the Carolinas and Virginias with a tin trunk full of geegaws and trinkets. But he was no businessman — he ended up owing his father $600 and almost died of typhoid to boot. However, his charm and his interest in the Southern gentry led them to open their doors (and their libraries) to him, and he acquired quite naturally the courtly manners of the antebellum South. In one fling of extravagance he bought himself a fine suit of clothes to supplant his Yankee homespun. But then he ended up so broke he had to walk five hundred miles back north to arrive barefoot in New York. Still, he returned inwardly enriched. Among his experiences was a close contact with some Quaker folk in the Carolinas who taught him about the "inner light." This may have been the beginning of an increased awareness of his own inner Self.

He took up teaching posts in Connecticut, one in a cold, drab little schoolhouse with flat benches and a birchrod in the corner. Here he promptly spent his meager pay on making desks with benches, buying books and pictures for his young scholars, and —like the great Swiss educator Pestalozzi, whom he greatly admired — doing everything possible to make learning interesting and agreeable. To the horror of the parents, the children looked forward to going to school! There were flowers in the classroom, a space for dancing and clapping hands. This was something threatening, newfangled, and unheard of. Children were supposed to be whipped into shape, "no lickin', no larnin'," to suffer education as had their parents. They were to learn by rote, and never mind understanding too much. A rival school was set up along the old lines, and Alcott's school eventually closed. However, an influential man in the area, the Reverend Samuel J. May, heard of young Alcott. He invited him to visit and heard his views and encouraged him. So did May's sister Abigail, who eventually became Alcott's loving and at times (one cannot help but assume) long-suffering wife and the mother of his four daughters. (One of these, the stormy Louisa May, was to become famous as the author of *Little Women* and other still-beloved books.) Through connections, Bronson Alcott then made his way to Germantown, Pennsylvania where he taught at a school with William Russell, a graduate of Glasgow University. This friend not only loaned him many books but gave him an informal grounding in logic, philosophy, and literature, and imparted some structure to his thinking. All of this Alcott lapped up. It was as if he were reclaiming things he already knew deep within himself. So when the call to Boston came, and when he met up with the highly competent Miss Elizabeth Peabody, he was ready and poised to launch the new Temple School, where we find him at the time of the *Conversations*.

When Alcott first met Miss Peabody he did not like her that much. He confided to his journal that there seemed to be more man in her than woman. Today we would say that she must have had a very strong animus — a powerful challenging intellect. But as she was soon to learn, Bronson did not brook adult contradictions gracefully. In the Jungian sense, he most certainly was an intuitive-feeling type, the opposite of her thinking-sensation typology. It was a good match, however, in terms of a teaching partnership. Throughout her long life, according to her biographer, Elizabeth remained a warm, generous, practical and brilliant woman, kind and helpful to her parents, to her sisters, and to children everywhere. But equally opiniated.

All of the major Transcendentalists kept journals. They are the biographer's dream come true because their secret opinions are confided to the written page and are there to be contrasted and compared. Miss Peabody sometimes admired and sometimes despaired of Mr. Alcott, but she knew a great teacher when she saw one. (I think because it takes one to know one.) It was through Elizabeth that Alcott came to meet Ralph Waldo Emerson with whom she had studied Greek when she was nineteen. The two men began a very close friendship which lasted throughout their lives.

There are times, I confess, when I question the term "Transcendentalist." The word taken literally means "to rise above, to go beyond," but I believe they took it also in another sense. The word suggests that the Transcendalists were rising above and rejecting our ordinary world, when just the opposite was really the case. Actually, they viewed all of the natural world as being an embodiment of the divine filled with spiritual and symbolic meaning. They believed that there was a spiritual world hidden *within* this one and that access to it was possible if one knew how to look and to see with an inner eye, which in Mr. Alcott was certainly also a loving eye. A recorded incident from Mr. Alcott's schoolroom — when a ten-year-old boy touchingly paraphrases a line from a poem about a child's death —provides a fine example. The poem reads, "Yes, you are going home your Father's face to see." And the boy says that the line means "You are going within yourself your Father's face to see through your own spirit." It was the cultivation of that inner eye in each individual that Alcott and the other Transcendentalists were after. Convinced through experience, Alcott knew that each of us has a "Christ Within" (a Self, in Jungian terms) and he intended his young scholars to remember this presence and to honor it in all whom they encountered.

Alcott had no psychologist to analyze him or to warn him of the dangers of inflation attendant upon such a discovery, and so his personal life reflected the highs of inner certainty and arrogance, when his ego identified with that "Imperial Self," and the lows of utter humility, doubt, and despair — a sense of dismal failure when the feeling left him. Above all, however, Alcott was a great prophet of the value of "intuition," and among the Transcendentalists he was one of the few doers and one of the few testers of their ideals. His classroom was a psychological laboratory, no less. Emerson, fascinated, observed that while Thoreau moved the world by retiring from it, Alcott always believed and taught our social interdependence. Dorothy McCuskey, one of Bronson Alcott's biographers, writes: "Believing, too, in the inherent divinity and goodness of man, Alcott treated the children with the same reverence and courtesy the rest of the world accorded to a minister of the gospel." For Alcott, the schoolteacher held the greatest responsibility for molding the moral character of his pupils. This meant living and embodying his beliefs, not just mouthing them. He walked his talk, as our native American Indians say.

When, later, the scandal over the *Conversations* broke, Emerson was one of the few to defend Alcott and to offer him strength and comfort as well as financial assistance. This would not be the last time either, as Bronson Alcott seemed fated to walk through life as a Parsifal, eccentric, innocent, serene and idealistic — both foolish in the ways of this world and profoundly brave and wise in the world of the spirit. Many is the tale to bear this out, but for these the reader must turn to the biographies. Now, as we stand poised on the brink of the twenty-first century, we can see the tragic element in the life of a man filled with intuitions and insights so far ahead of his time, yet so misunderstood and rejected by most of his contemporaries. Alcott's ideas have not yet prevailed, though some have had their impact. Today, we certainly have attractive and pleasant schools and text-books, along with all kinds of colorful amenities. Alcott would rejoice in these, but he surely would grieve that the central idea of his teaching — the connecting of all education to the meaningfulness of life and the spiritual dignity and responsibility of each individual — is still so far off from being taught. "To teach with reference to Eternity," was one of the maxims of his educational credo.

Elizabeth Palmer Peabody was the oldest of the three Peabody Sisters of Salem. She was born in Billerica, Massachusetts on May 16, 1800. She could have been called Athena, for such was her nature. Her fragile and artistic sister Sophia was to marry Nathaniel Hawthorne, and her sister Mary married the educator, Horace Mann, founder of Antioch College. Their father was a dentist, but their more socially prominent mother insisted he was a physician. The family was often in financial straits, and it fell to the capable Elizabeth not only to support herself but to help out everyone else. She did this by diligent and enthusiastic study and by her very successful teaching of children in various schools. She was genuinely interested and excited by philoso-phy, theology, and history and was invited to give "Readings" on these subjects to groups of interested women. Soon people were clamoring for her own views, and in the new salons of Boston, Elizabeth Peabody became the first woman lecturer in the United States! Her conversations, in turn, inspired Alcott who many years later became a "pedlar" of civilized ideas throughout the as yet uncivilized West.

Though hampered in many ways by the social constrictions on "ladies," Elizabeth Peabody forged bravely ahead, breaking the ground for other women. She was just opening a school herself in Boston when she met Bronson Alcott. After hearing of his plans for opening a school which would include "Spiritual Culture," she immediately offered to bring her own pupils with her, volunteered to teach and to help manifest the new philosophy of education which she wholeheartedly believed in as well. Thus the Temple School was founded. Miss Peabody's *Record of a School,* a first account of the experiment, was well received. Heartened by this, she began the arduous task of taking down the *Conversations* verbatim to the best of her ability. Now Boston was about to see in Alcott "the like of a teacher they had never seen before — and the like of a teacher they would want never to see again."

Conversations with Children on the Gospels is an extraordinary book. We should treasure and honor it. And we should honor those involved in the drama surrounding its publication, coping as they had to with the puritanical prurience of Boston in the 1830's. The pure-minded and naive Bronson Alcott had no idea of what he would be up against. We should treasure the *Conversations* for the methodology and philosophy of education (if not the content) — which were far ahead of their time and might well remind us of what we could do or may have forgotten to do both at home and in public education. And we should treasure the book for what it reveals of the natural spirituality of children — it is such a delight, so full of the charm and humor, as well, that only the candor of the young can provide. These are little boys and girls between five and twelve years of age, little "proper Bostonians" struggling ever so hard to be both honest and "good." We can picture them wide-eyed, the boys in stovepipe trousers and and wide-collared shirts, the girls in dresses and pantalettes as in some tableau by Currier & Ives. This is the period of the early Dickens and the young Victoria across the Atlantic, the period of early American expansion and the first building of railroads, the period of sleighs and muffs, of horse carriages and stately brick houses around the Boston Common. It is impossible to forget five-year old Josiah Quincy, the little prophet, squirming with enthusiasm on his chair, or ringleted Emma Savage struggling with humility because she is naturally virtuous, or the practical and sturdy Charles Morgan, who, when asked what he thinks his mission in incarnating in this life is, responds: "I think the mission of my soul is to sell oil." All said and done, this is an important book, most worthy of rescue from obscurity, a chapter in the life of America which still must infuse and affect us, and as we follow the probing questions of the experimenting Bronson Alcott, faithfully set down by the redoubtable Miss Peabody (and later by her sister Sophia and by Margaret Fuller), we cannot fail to think how we ourselves would have answered such questions or how we would answer them as grownups today. In fact, if we we were to set some of the epigrams of these children off onto a separate page, it would be impossible to distinguish them from those of Socrates, Plato, or Descartes. In one Conversation on the relationship of Jesus to God, the root ideas discussed in the Councils of Chalcedon and Nicea emerge spontaneously and the same orthodoxies and heresies are solemnly though unconsciously debated. Here every child seems to have an inner theologian ready to jump out with an opinion! Some may argue that the children say what they think Mr. Alcott would like to hear. But is this not the basis of most education? However, we find Mr. Alcott trying so hard not to voice his own opinions that the children get exasperated with him at times. "What," they want to know, "do you think?"

According to my friend the Tibetan lama Tenzin Rinpoche, an approach similar to Alcott's is a given in the training of very young monks and lamas. The Tibetans, in keeping with their belief in reincarnation, assume a priori knowledge in all such children. It is interesting to note in Alcott's journal a similar conclusion. "All instincts are recollections of foregone lives." But he did not share this view with his pupils.

The mainly puritanical Christianity of those times is tempered in the *Conversations* by Alcott's personal ecumenism. According to Shepard, "He accepted no orthodox creed, belonged in an effective way to no church, and was quite devoid of what is usually regarded as piety, yet he was essentially a religious man." For him Christ was symbolic of the spirit within, and the life of Jesus a perfect paradigm of a life lived with full consciousness of that spirit. As Elizabeth Peabody expressed it:

Yet no sect of religion has asserted with sufficient distinctness the great truth that makes all this practical: namely that all other souls are potentially what Jesus was actually; that every soul is an incarnation of the infinite; that it will never think clearly until it has transcended time and space; that it will never feel in harmony with itself until its sensibility is commensurate with all beings; that it will never be fully alive till having finished the work given it to do.

For the two teachers this would be the highest goal of an ecumenical Christian education — "To teach, distinctive from all sinister, sectarian, and oppressive principles." Alcott and Peabody both felt that the soul needs no formal intermediary between itself and the Divine once their connection has been made conscious. This idea, of course, was not to stand in their favor with the ministers and clergy of Boston when the scandal broke. And yet their viewpoint prefigures much of our thinking today: that for any religion to be other than a significant social enterprise it must have a transformative effect within the individual psyche. Never before has it been more vitally important for us to understand and honor all religions in love and tolerance. As Mother Teresa puts it: "I believe in person to person and that God is in everyone." Mr. Alcott and Miss Peabody would have heartily concurred.

Throughout these *Conversations* Alcott is constantly looking for spontaneous evidence from the children for the innate existence of this "Christ Within" (the divine scintilla, the atman, or Jung's "Self") Alcott certainly felt an abiding love and deep reverence for the historical Jesus — but not in the doctrinal or orthodox sense. In fact, he shocked the Boston of his day by talking about Jesus not only on Sundays but on Mondays and Tuesdays as well and embarrassed people by emulating him, living simply (if not completely embracing holy poverty) and showing no interest whatever in the accumulation of outer wealth or the attainment of social position. Throughout his life, as his biographer remarks, it could be said of Bronson Alcott that he was a tremendous success at failure. (A comment leveled at Jesus, as well. Socrates and Plato, Pythagoras, Plotinus, Shakespeare, Milton, Coleridge and Wordsworth were other spiritual intimates). There is no doubt that he considered the entire external world as metaphor and symbol ("emblem", as he called it) of the inner one and perhaps he went too far in that direction, while today we generally reverse the emphasis. It is as if Mr. Alcott lived in the *unus mundus* while other people lived in Boston. He lived what he believed to an almost saintly degree; a traveling *hamsa* or wandering teacher monk in the Dark Ages could not have surpassed him; yet we can imagine that his wife and four daughters found the hardship trying at times. If only he had not been so lovable! A few years later, for instance, daring an attempt at utopian community life on a farm called Fruitlands (a true forerunner of our New Age communes), Alcott and several others banded together with the high purpose of doing manly outdoor work in the fields by day and gathering together to eat the raw fruits of the soil by the fire in the evening, there to talk of noble philosophies. It didn't work out that way. The men went out to the fields, but there they discussed the noble philosophies *ad infinitum* while the patient Mrs. Alcott and her four young daughters often ended up doing the work in the fields! On one occasion, Alcott got so caught up in a philosophical discussion that he walked aboard the Boston to New York ferry which sailed off with him aboard. A collection for his ticket had to be taken up among the amused passengers; there was no phoning home in those days to explain matters. No wonder Mrs. Alcott was to confide to her journal: "Give me one day of practical philosophy. It is worth a century of speculation and discussion."

I know that a teacher of any or no faith can find great wisdom in some of Alcott's methods if only at the psychological level, taking the Christ Within as archetype for the goal of the individuation, self-realization or questing process. It is a tradition common to the mystical side of every religion. That the child is not a *tabula rasa* Alcott proves without a doubt. As we read we rediscover that children are far more capable of philosophical insights and intuitions than we usually think, that indeed they take a delight in being taken seriously as individuals whose opinions are worthy of respect. All you need do is try asking children some of these questions today! I have — with astonishing results. Alcott's secret, and I believe, his success consisted in his approach to children; he worked from his own innermost center toward the same one he knew existed in each of them. A bond of trust, mutual respect, and affection was established at that level, so that the usual ego-to-ego tussle between teacher and student was avoided. "*Education,*" as Elizabeth Peabody remarked, "*depends on its attitude toward the soul.*"

Nowadays, certainly, there is hope at the level of the private school. Many of the ideas that occurred to Pestalozzi and Alcott also came later to such prominent educators as Rudolf Steiner (the Waldorf Schools) and Maria Montessori (a fine system for early childhood). Or take the "open classroom" experiment developed by the British. Alcott's Temple School had several features in common with the open classroom: for example, the division of the class into several groups doing different things at different times, necessitated by the number of students and the variety of their ages, four through twelve or thirteen. But the absolute discipline and silence that Mr. Alcott insisted upon would be considered unrealistic today.

In this country, the "spiritual culture" of a child can only be furthered in parochial or private school. The Supreme Court ruling prohibiting prayer - or even a moment of silence! - also rules out the opportunity for a child to center himself or herself with a moment of introversion. Our only hope is to put forward this need in psychological rather than religious terms. Something has to change! The following speaks for itself:

Each Day

* 2,795 teenagers get pregnant; 1,106 have abortions, 372 miscarry, 1,295 give birth, and 22 apparently "disappear" from the charts

* 689 babies are born without benefit of any prenatal care, 719 babies are born at low birth weight (less than 6 pounds), and 129 babies are born at very low birth weight (less than 4 pounds)

* 67 babies die within four weeks, 105 die before the age of one year

* 27 children die from the ravages of poverty, 10 die at the end of a gun barrel, 30 are wounded by guns

* 135,000 children bring guns to school

* 6 teen-agers commit suicide * 7,742 teenagers become sexually active, and 623 get syphilis or gonorrhea

* 211 children are arrested for drug abuse, and 437 more are arrested for drinking or drunk driving

* 1,512 teen-agers drop out of school and 3,288 children run away from home

* 1,849 children are abused or neglected

* 1,629 children are in adult jails

* 2,556 children are born out of wedlock, and another 2,989 see their parents getting divorced.

[To these statistics, presumably, we should add the number of children being born with or contracting AIDS.]

[Statistics from the *Children's Defense Fund* (Feb/Mar 1990)]

Given this current news — oh, Boston, where is your innocence now! — it is vitally important to examine a further comment of Miss Peabody's:

> The child comes [to school] to be intellectually trained. And this is his main object, it is true. But this is not to be accomplished by regarding his intellectual nature alone; for such a course produces a dismemberment, which is death to every form of life, aesthetic, intellectual, and moral.

Separation of church and state may be the law of the land, but the soul or psyche remains. It cannot be legislated out of existence. Since even a moment of silence is proscribed, we have left no time whatsoever in public school for introspection, for even reminding a child that he or she is a precious point of unique identity, a center, from which can be viewed the circumference of external events on any given day. Human consciousness, the prize of our planetary evolution has taken eons to develop, yet daily it is being thrown away by those wishing to escape a meaningless life. Drugs, alcohol, sex (often the search for love and human contact), are substitutes for the search for inner meaning and self-worth. Those resorting to them are getting younger and younger every day —middle schools and not only high school pupils. We are in a crisis situation!

So much of education consists in force-feeding more and more facts and information, and so little time is given to listening to the deeper needs of the psyches of children. I remember one of my own daughters, when she was twelve, banging her schoolbooks on the kitchen table and refusing to do her homework. "What's the point of going to school and doing stupid homework, when in the end we're all going to die anyway!" A very profound question! It echoes George Orwell's sad reflection that he never learned anything in the classroom that pertained to the ultimate meaningfulness of his own existence.

This irrelevance seems to have held true even in Alcott's time. But for the very first day at the Temple School, Elizabeth records the following:

> Mr. Alcott sat behind his table, and the children were placed in chairs, in a large arc around him; the chairs so far apart, that they could not easily touch each other. He then asked each one separately, what idea she or he had of the object of coming to school? To learn; was the first answer. To learn what? By pursuing this question, all the common exercises of school were brought up — successively — even philosophy. Still Mr. Alcott intimated that this was not all; and at last someone said "to behave well," and in pursuing this expression into its meanings, they at last decided that they came to learn, to feel rightly, to think rightly, and to act rightly. A boy of seven years old suggested, and all agreed, that right actions were the most important of these three.

Bronson Alcott, already the father of three of his four daughters (including Louisa May) was certain a change in education was needed. Perhaps naively and idealistically — sometimes even sentimentally —he was totally convinced of the intrinsic wisdom and purity of essence of all children. (For him all women were pure, as well!) He rejected the prevailing Lockian philosophy that all information comes to us from the outer senses. All he needed was proof that he was right. *The Conversations*, therefore, were to be an experiment, an extension of the intense study and note-taking observation of the first years of his daughters' lives, in which Alcott anticipated the scientific work of Darwin, Piaget, and Gesell. (The notes from the study of his children later grew and grew into a manuscript called "Psyche," which Emerson counseled against publishing. Alas, one of Alcott's failings was a stultifying propensity to lush and "phlogistical" prose! As one biographer puts it, he used words as would "a beserk pastrymaker"! Later when he did publish his *Orphic Sayings*, a critic commented that reading them was like watching fifteen boxcars go by with only one passenger in them!)

James Russell Lowell even went so far as mocking him in his *Fable for Critics* with the following lines:

> When he talks he is great, but goes out like a taper
> If you shut him up closely with pen, ink, and paper;
> Yet his fingers itch for 'em morning and night,
> And he thinks he does wrong if he don't always write;
> In this, as in all things, a lamb among men,
> He goes to sure death when he goes to his pen.

Mr. Alcott's system of discipline was considered fair and was agreed to in every instance by the children themselves, and when he resorted to the unusual practice of insisting that a naughty child strike *him* on the palm, the child demurred in horror and broke into tears. The task of running a class of thirty or so children of different ages single-handedly, as any teacher with the experience knows, is a challenge akin to directing a three-ringed circus, But Alcott succeeded through the voluntary cooperation of the children themselves. They agreed to suffer punishment in the full understanding, or so it seems, that it was for their own good. The worst punishment of all was banishment from story time or from the Conversations! And he made the good suffer with the naughty in order to make the point that personal behavior affects society.

If Alcott was overly idealistic, Elizabeth, the recorder, was anything but. She was a teacher of considerable experience already, and her little asides are realistic and show a warmth and a natural understanding of the limits of children's virtue and self-control. One knows that she has strong opinions herself and there are times when she does not agree with the master and lets him know it.

The Conversations is presented after the manner of a play, the cast consisting of Mr. Alcott, the Recorder (Miss Peabody), and the various children. The setting is the one large room and the smaller anteroom of the Temple School, fortuitously set on Temple Street in Boston on the upper floor of a large, cold building belonging to the Masonic Order. The classroom was high and wide and carefully furnished with four precious busts of Socrates, Plato, Scott, and Milton. There was a bas-relief of Jesus Christ behind the master's desk, a statue of a child aspiring, and the figure of the god of silence. Each little scholar had his or her own desk facing the wall and was equipped with slate and notebook. While one age group was busy with a subject, other children would draw up their chairs *very quietly* to sit in an arc before the teacher. His imposing desk and various other materials were bought at Elizabeth Peabody's expense, and it should be noted here that despite promises to the contrary, she never received a salary. She also paid for the publication of *The Record of a School* out of her own pocket, and when the warehouse of the publisher — with the rest of the copies in it — burned down, she bravely bore the loss.

Light fell through handsome Gothic windows into the schoolroom, but the only heat came from a single stove. The cold required heroic fortitude from the children and from poor Elizabeth, who, trying to keep up with the recording, sometimes had to write with gloves on. Mr. Alcott taught reading, writing (each child kept a journal), spelling (with each word discussed at length as to its meanings on various levels), and geography. Latin and arithmetic were taught by Miss Peabody, and a few also studied geometry under her supervision. These Conversations took place only once a week.

The time of the drama was 1835-1837.

* * *

Before proceeding any further, let me sketch the historical context so that the "play" can be followed with some sense of dramatic irony. Boston, a city founded by Puritans for Puritans, was at Alcott's time in the throes of theological ferment. On the one hand Puritanical Calvinism was beginning to lose its grip; and on the other Unitarians, Universalists, Baptists, Presbyterians, Swedenborgians, Episcopalians, Methodists, Quakers, Roman Catholics, and Free Enquirers were all thriving. All of these, excepting the Quakers and Catholics, were represented by the twenty-nine boys and eight girls in the Temple School. ("Just enough [girls] to ensure that 'purity' which the teacher considered so important, but enough, alas, to make it seem particularly horrible that the teacher himself should have allowed and even promoted the discussion of themes about which 'female children,' at any rate, should never speak, never hear, and never even think.") The formidable Unitarian Dr. William Ellery Channing, then the dominating personality of Boston, positively worshiped by Miss Peabody, had given the idea of the school his approval. Emerson was preaching and lecturing, and the first news of Oriental philosophy had reached the newly independent American states, giving rise to Transcendentalism and (eventually) to Christian Science. Boston, in brief, was rapidly becoming "the hub of the universe" and considering itself very proper indeed. Feelings against the South were rising, feelings against slavery, and various demonstrations and riots were erupting. Inferring a connection between the ingestion of whole wheat flour and longevity, Dr. Graham was starting the granola generation of his time. Literary salons and discussion groups were active, and women were both attending and conducting them for the first time. And the railroads, though still viewed sceptically by many, were just beginning to push westward. However, no matter how busy and prospering and full of new ideas Boston was, it still remained true to its puritan heritage of "morality and decent behavior."

Thus it was not surprising that, no sooner were the *Conversations* published in 1836, than all hell broke loose. The press and the pulpit alike denounced Alcott (Miss Peabody foreseeing the storm had prudently resigned), soon succeeding in closing the school down and virtually terminating the teaching careers of two of the finest and most committed teachers the country had ever known! Though each went on eventually to better things and expanded horizons, the pain of such revilement and rejection must have been devastating. Two years previously, Elizabeth had recorded Alcott's words to the children on the death of Socrates. They were to become prophetic.

> There was never a great benefactor to man, who was not accused of being opposed to the very objects he had at heart. And it is so in common life most frequently. The noble souled are misunderstood. Martyrs, and even discoverers of science, have been uniformly traduced by people around them. The greatest benefactors of the present age are all of them slandered grossly. The best people I know are the most slandered. Have you faith enough to bear slander then? For if you have not, you will not keep your faith.

Alcott kept his faith. He had a good model in his friend Jesus and he bore his own cross. Always poor, he became poorer, and in the end he had to sell even the beloved busts of Plato, Scott, and Milton (it seems he kept Socrates) and his own small library of books, including his most precious copy of Plato translated by Thomas Taylor! He was reduced to a basement room with only six students — three of them his own children, two the children of a close friend, and the sixth a little black girl, daughter of an escaped slave. He was offered more students if he were to dismiss the black child. True to his beliefs, he refused. He deserves to be honored as one of the first Americans ever to attempt desegregation in a school.

In the end, the remaining copies of the *Conversations* were sold at 5 cents a pound to a trunkmaker for lining luggage. Thus the number of volumes comes down to a precious few. But they are living seed.

You may well ask, even after reading all the *Conversations*, what on earth the people of Boston could have objected to? Why would one critic cry out from his pulpit that the book was "one third absurd, one third blasphemous, and one third obscene"?

Elizabeth Peabody had heard the rumors in advance and tried to warn her friend, but he was not in the habit of listening to her. In desperation, she resorted to writing him a letter, which has survived, he having carefully copied it into his journal. Obviously embarrassed, she wrote clumsily at first but gathered speed in her urgency:

Dear Sir:

The very day after my letter to you I received a communication from a friend; by which I learn that much more extensive than either you or I were aware of is the discussion of such subjects as it is known were discussed in connection with the birth of Christ censured even by friends of your system and of yourself, and that something of an impression was gratuitously taken up that I left the School on that account — an impression for which I can in no ways account, except it was thought I ought to leave it. For I have been very wary what I said about it — generally leading off from the subject when it was mentioned, but turning attention upon your purity of association being so much like that of children. For I always wanted the plan to succeed in this particular of it especially, so sure I am that it is impossible to keep children ignorant and that it is better to lead their imaginations than to leave them to be directed by idle curiosity. And yet I do not think I should ever have ventured so far myself. And a great many questions I thought were quite superfluous, and what was to be gained by them was not worth the risk of having them repeated and misunderstood abroad. A great deal is repeated, I find, and many persons, liking the school in every other respect, think it is decisive against putting female children to it especially.

I have told you this in the spirit of friendship, and hope you will not despise it. I am conscious of the effect of a few week's freedom from the excitement of being a part of the School, all taking down that exaggerated feeling which made every detail of it seem so very important to the great cause of Spiritual Culture; and I never was under half the illusion in this respect that you were.

But with respect to the Record: whatever may be said of the wisdom of pursuing your plan as you have hitherto done in the school-room, where you always command the spirits of those around you (only subject to the risk of having your mere words repeated or misinterpreted) I feel more and more that these questionable parts ought not to go into the printed book, at least that they must be entirely disconnected from me.

In the first place, in all these conversations where I have spoken, I should like to have that part of the conversation omitted, so that it may be felt that I was entirely passive. And I would go a little farther: there is a remark of Josiah Quincy's about the formation of the body out of "*the naughtiness of other people*" which is very remarkable. Please to correct that in my record. But if you wish to retain it, you can add a note in the margin saying:'the Recorder omitted Josiah's answer in this place 'which was &c. &c.' — putting Josiah's answer in your note.

There are many places where this might be done, and thus the whole responsibility rests upon you. I should like, too, to have the remarks I made on the Circumcision omitted. I do not wish to appear as an interlocutor in that conversation either. Besides this, I must desire you to put a preface of your own before mine, and express in it, in so many words, that on you rests all the responsibility of introducing the subject, and that your Recorder did not entirely sympathize or agree with you with respect to the course taken, adding in (for I have not the slightest objection), that this disagreement or want of sympathy often prevented your views from being given full justice to, as she herself freely acknowledges. In this matter yourself also is concerned.

Why did prophets and apostles veil this subject in fables and emblems if there was not a reason for avoiding physiological inquiries &c? This is worth thinking of. However, you as a man can say anything; but I am a woman, and have feelings that I dare not distrust, however little I can *understand them* or give an account of them.

Yours, etc.

E.P. Peabody

Today one cannot help smiling at this anxiety, feminist though she was, of an unmarried spinster of thirty-six. Alcott's response was to remove some of the offending passages into an appendix, [I have restored them to their places] where, of course, they attracted more attention! Fearing for her own reputation, Miss Peabody left the school before the book's publication. She knew her Boston and she was right. The very idea that the subject of the physical births of St. John and Jesus should come up in a classroom of mixed boys and girls was too much! As tactfully and beautifully as Bronson Alcott circumvented the basic facts, only hinting that mothers had something to do with it, this section of the *Conversations* was considered obscene. We can only assume that for two hundred years the reproduction of Bostonians must have proceeded more miraculously even than those in the New Testament.

Here is what Alcott said:

The deliverance of the spirit is the first thing. . . . The physiological facts, sometimes referred to, are only a sign of the spiritual birth. You have seen the rose opening from the seed with the assistance of the atmosphere. This is the birth of the rose. It typifies the bringing forth of the spirit by pain and labor and patience. . . . And a mother suffers when she has a child. When she is going to have a child she gives up her body to God, and He works upon it in a mysterious way and, with her aid, brings forth the child's Spirit in a little Body of its own; and when it has come she is blissful.

Emerson, and Elizabeth, ever a staunch and loyal friend, rose to his defense, as did James Freeman Clarke, and Orestes Brownson. Papers, journals, and reviews attacked and counterattacked. Alcott was hooted at in the streets, a mob action was threatened, as was a Grand Jury. Through it all, Alcott kept his peace, cutting out the reviews and pasting them without comment into his journal. His young students were taken away from him. One cannot help wonder what they thought about it all. As Odell Shepard comments, there is no way of telling what impact Alcott's teaching had upon the world. One can only speculate that some of his message was carried by the children and imparted to their children in turn.

The Conversations and *The Record of a School,* however, were well received in England and inspired an Alcott House in Surrey. Emerson paid Bronson's way to England to visit there. But the English applications of his ideas were eccentric in the extreme. There he found a boardingschool run by three peculiar misogynists who believed in adding a Spartan regime of cold baths and uncooked vegetables, and who denounced marriage and family life. Intrigued by some of these notions (he was already a rabid vegetarian), Alcott was to return with two of the Englishmen to found the ill- fated Fruitlands in Harvard, Massachusetts. A silent struggle for Bronson's soul then ensued between the grim English Charles Lane and the loving and enduring Abby May Alcott, now nursing her fourth baby. Fortunately for the world, Mrs. Alcott won out!

Lane retreated in disgust to a Shaker colony, leaving Alcott close to a suicidal nervous breakdown, torn as he was between his love of God and his deep faith in the sanctity of family. For days and nights he lay on his bed, facing the wall, refusing sustenance, confronting yet another failure in his life. And again his loving wife and the girls rallied around him and chaffed him back to life. It was his dark night of the soul.

Bronson Alcott struggled on until his old age, never deviating from his deepest convictions, and he left a legacy of some golden seeds of truth. Those things that are true tend to endure and to resurface when they are most needed. Teaching is a sacrificial profession: no teacher ever sees the harvest. But Alcott lives on in my own students unbeknownst and surely in others, and in this book perhaps some of his ideas can return in a totally different social and psychological context. He is calling on us across a century and a half to care enough not to forget the reality of the invisible and determining psyche in children and in ourselves; he is calling on us with the message that to be good parents and teachers we must as well be curators of souls.

We need to thank and bless them — the well-meaning Mr. Alcott and Miss Peabody, two dear souls, two forerunners of our present age, for having transplanted from other cultures the seeds that have taken vigorous root in our world of today. Elizabeth Peabody, many years after the debacle of the Conversations, traveled to Germany to learn more about Friedrich Wilhelm Froebel's novel idea for children called "Kindergarten." She returned and singlehandedly promulgated the idea in the United States. Every primary school in the country owes her this debt. A stout old lady with white curls and crinkly smiling eyes, who sometimes solved her luggage problems by traveling with her nightie under her dress and her toothbrush in her purse, she stomped across the country spreading the word. In the end, they dubbed her "the Grandmother of Boston."

Alcott himself could be called the Grandfather of Workshops. A phenomenon of our times is the increasing number of broadly educational Centers, and the number of classes open now to adult education, to which eager students of all ages apply themselves, many of which have a non-denominational spiritual goal: the psychological involvement with inner growth and personal development, something Jung termed the individuation process. In his time, Jung deplored the fact that just when people were ready and eager for further education, education ceased. As one who has traveled the world giving lectures and seminars myself, I used to consider St. Paul the patron saint of workshops. Today, I see Bronson Alcott as another forerunner. Ten trips he made between 1853 and 1860, stopping at town after town to "converse" on spiritual and philosophical ideas. He spoke in over a hundred towns in Missouri, Iowa, Kansas, Wisconsin, Illinois, New York, Indiana, and Ohio, to say nothing of New England. These "conversations" were not lectures but true dialogues about ideas intended to get people thinking profoundly on the meaning of the personal life. Many were deeply affected and went on to affect others.

In the beginning, however, it was rough going. Here is Louisa May's account of her father's return:

We were waked up hearing the bell. Mother flew down crying "My husband!" We rushed after, and five white figures embraced the half-frozen wanderer who came in hungry, tired, cold, and disappointed, but smiling bravely and as serene as ever. We fed and warmed and brooded over him, longing to ask if he had made any money; but no one did till little May said, after he had told all the pleasant things, "Well, did people pay you?" Then, with a queer look, he opened his pocket-book and showed one dollar, saying with a smile that made our eyes fill, "Only that. My overcoat was stolen and I had to buy a shawl. Many promises were not kept, and traveling is costly; but I have opened a way and another year shall do better." I shall never forget how beautifully Mother answered him, though the dear hopeful soul had built much on his success; but with a beaming face she kissed him, saying "I call that doing very well."

Against this background, we can now begin the reading of the *Conversations with Children on the Gospels* with some understanding of where Bronson Alcott was coming from. He was not teaching a sectarian Sunday School class. As he explains on the very first day: he does not know all that he will say, and they do not know yet what they will say, but something wonderful, wise, new, and fresh may come up — "a thought I never thunk before", as the song goes. So now let us steal into Mr. Alcott's classroom on a cold day in Boston and sit on the visitors' couch and eavesdrop on a magical moment in the history of education.

THE CONVERSATIONS

MR. ALCOTT'S SCHOOL-ROOM
(Courtesy of the Concord Free Public Library)

QUARTER CARD OF DISCIPLINE & STUDIES IN MR. ALCOTT'S SCHOOL FOR THE SPRING TERM CURRENT 1836

The tuition and discipline are addressed in due porportion to the threefold nature of childhood.

THE SPIRITUAL FACULTY (Means of its Direct Culture)	THE IMAGINATIVE FACULTY (Means of its Direct Culture)	THE RATIONAL FACULTY (Means of its Direct Culture)
Listening to Sacred Readings Conversations on the Gospels Writing Journals Self-Analysis & Self-Discipline Listening to Readings from works of Genius Motives to Study & Action Government of the School	Spelling & Reading Writing & Sketching from Nature Picturesque Geography Writing Journals & Epistles Illustrating Words Listening to Readings Conversation	Defining Words Analyzing Speech Self-Analysis Arithmetic Study of the Human Body Reasonings on Conduct Discipline

TIME	MONDAY	TUESDAY	WEDNESDAY	THURSDAY	FRIDAY	SATURDAY
IX	Studying Spelling & Defining & Writing in Journals	Studying Geography & Sketching Maps in Journals	Studying the Gospel & Writing in Journals	Studying Parsing Lesson & Writing in Journals	Paraphrasing Text of Readings & Writing in Journals	Completing of Account of week's studies in Journals
X XI	Spelling with Illustrative Conversations on the Meaning & Uses of Words	Recitations in Geography with Picturesque Readings and Conversations	Readings & Conversations on Spirit as displayed in the Life of Christ	Analyzing Speech Written & Vocal on Tables with Illustrative Conversations	Readings with Illustrative Conversations on the Sense of the Text	Readings from Works of Genius with Applications and Conversations
	RECREATION ON THE COMMON OR IN THE ANTE-ROOM					
XII I	Studying Arithmetic with Demonstrations in Journals	Drawing from Nature with Mr. Graeter	Conversations on the Human Body and its Culture	Composing & Writing Epistles in Journals	Studying Arithmetic with Illustrations in Journals	Review of Journals, Week's Conduct & Studies
	INTERMISSION FOR REFRESHMENT AND RECREATION					
III IV	Studying Latin & Writing in Journals	Studying Latin with Recitations	Recreation & Duties at Home	Studying Latin with Recitations	Studying Latin & Writing in Journals	Recitations and Duties at Home

EDITOR'S NOTE

The Conversations are in the original sequence but have been renumbered for convenience. A few were ommitted since the ideas presented in them consisted of either review or ideas more eloquently expressed elsewhere. Some of the Conversations have been condensed to save repetition. Those parts excerpted by Miss Peabody have been restored to their places. Spelling and punctuation remain (with few exceptions) as in the original text. The present editor has added a few comments. These are initialed in the notes.

A.O.H.

THE CAST

Mr. Amos Bronson Alcott, 37, master teacher

Elizabeth Palmer Peabody, 36, recorder and assistant teacher

Children under 7

Josiah Quincy, 6, grandson of the mayor of Boston. Emerson wrote of him: "A child having something wonderful and divine in him. A youthful prophet." Josiah stuttered.

Edward J., John Davis, Frank A., Edward C., Nathan, Samuel, Tuckerman, Hales, Corinna

7-10 years old

George Kuhn, grew up to attend Harvard but died of consumption while a student there. Martha Kuhn, his sister, grew up to be a distinguished linguist.

William C., Andrew, Lucy E., Alexander, Welles, Joseph, Lemuel (a deaf boy), Susan, George B., Augustine, Lucia, John B., Herbert, Francis, William, Augustus

10-12 years old

Charles Morgan, son of a New Bedford whale oil merchant, boarder at the Alcott home; always practical and tenderhearted

Edward B., Emma Savage (revered by her peers for her virtue and wisdom), Samuel R., Ellen (has a sweet tooth), William, Bliss, Franklin, Frederic, Alfred, George

An Arnold and a Hillman attend, but no ages are specified.

CONVERSATION I

* * *

IDEA OF SPIRIT:

Evidence of Consciousness

MR. ALCOTT. We are now going to speak of the Life of Christ. If any of you are interested to understand how Jesus came into this world; and lived; and acted; and went back to God; and will try to give me your whole attention, and not let your minds wander, you may hold up your hands. (*Many did so.*) Some of you, most of you, will sometimes let your thoughts wander; but you will all try, I hope, to keep them as steady as possible; for only by doing so, can we have interesting conversations. The best thoughts do not lie on the surface of our minds. We have to dive under for them, like pearl fishers. This morning I am going to ask some questions, that I may prove to you, by your own answers to them, that you are all, every one of you, capable of thinking on this subject; and of having thoughts come from your minds, which will interest all, teaching yourselves to know yourselves, and teaching me.[1]

We are going, all of us, to study the life of Jesus, the Christ. As often as it is studied, it is better understood, and suggests new thoughts. I do not know all I am going to say, for I shall have new thoughts, that I never had before. Still less do you know all you are going to say; for you have not thought so much of the subject as I have. But if we will all think, and all say what we think, not repeating the words and thoughts of others, we shall teach each other.

CHARLES. But sometimes several of us will have the same thought, of ourselves.

MR. ALCOTT. Then you can say so, and there will be no repetition.

(The Recorder then said, that she was going to keep a record of the conversations, not of the same kind as before, when she was making a picture of the school; but, in the first place, to preserve Mr. Alcott's thoughts, as far as they were expressed; and, in the second place, to preserve their thoughts, when they seemed sincere.

1

All expressed great pleasure in the coming lessons, were very ready to promise attention; and seemed perfectly to understand what was meant by sincere conversation.)

MR. ALCOTT. Now, when I ask a question, each one may think of an answer to it, and as soon as he has one, hold up his hand. I shall then ask any one I please to speak; perhaps I shall ask every one to give an answer to some of my questions, so that I may compare your answers. Let no one speak without I ask him, but only hold up his hand. *(After a pause, during which there was a profound silence of expectation on the part of the children.)* Have you a clear feeling, idea, of something, which is not your body, which you never saw, but which IS — which loves, which thinks, which feels? *(All gradually held up their hands.)* Now what are your proofs? *(Many hands fell.)* Those who have proofs may answer in turn.

LEMUEL. I am sure of it, but I do not know why.

ALEXANDER. I have heard *you* say so.

MR. ALCOTT. You have trusted to me? Well! That is faith in testimony.

WILLIAM C. I cannot prove it, but I feel it.

MR. ALCOTT. You and Lemuel have the evidence of consciousness. You cannot think otherwise.

GEORGE K. I thought of my mind as my proof.[2]

ANDREW. I thought of my conscience; when I do right I feel that I have one.

WILLIAM B. I thought and I felt. That is Spirit.

CHARLES. I felt your question working within me, and that was my proof.

EDWARD B. Conscience is my proof. I feel when I do right and wrong, and that is my soul.

LUCY. I have proof, but I cannot express it.

EMMA. I knew before I was asked.

MR. ALCOTT. It is a sentiment with you and Lucy.

JOSIAH. Self-government.[3]

EDWARD J. Conscience. *(Some other answers were repetitious.)*

MR. ALCOTT. So you all think there is something, which is not body. But have you seen it; who has seen conscience? *(All made the negative sign.)* Then your eyes, it seems, did not tell you of this being, which is not body. *(All shook their heads.)* Nor your ears?

GEORGE K. I have heard my father and mother talk about conscience with my ears, and so I believed it was.[4]

MR. ALCOTT. What believed? Your ears? Or was it the conscience within you that understood what your father and mother meant by conscience?

GEORGE K. Yes, that was the way. But our ears do a little good.

MR. ALCOTT. Yes, the spirit uses the organs of sense, though it is something else than these organs. *(Pause)* What do you call those faculties or functions, which see, hear, touch, taste, and smell?

JOSIAH. The senses.

MR. ALCOTT. You may name the organs of sense.

LEMUEL. The tongue is the organ of taste.

FRANCIS. The eye is the organ of sight.

WILLIAM C. The hand is the organ of feeling.

LEMUEL. No; the nerves feel.

SUSAN. The hand is the organ of touch.

MR. ALCOTT. Yes; I should like to have feeling kept for the spiritual act.

SEVERAL. The ear is the organ of hearing.

EDWARD B. It only *seems* as if our senses themselves saw, and heard, and smelled; but it is the mind which is really doing those things with the eyes and ears for its instruments.

MR. ALCOTT. Now in all this, what are your senses after? What is it, that this something within you wants, when it uses your eyes, ears, and other organs of sense; what does it go out after?

JOHN D. When we use our tongue, the spirit goes after our food.

LEMUEL. When we look, it wants something to see; and when we listen, it wants something to hear; and when we taste, it wants something to eat and drink.

ALEXANDER. When we look, the spirit comes to help.[5]

WELLES. When we hear, the spirit is after instruction.

CHARLES. The senses are a kind of feelers, to show forth what the spirit within wants.

MR. ALCOTT. When you see an infant, you observe that its little body is full of motion. It seems to be constantly seeking after something. Do you think the spirit within it feels, and tries to express its feelings and wants through the senses?

(Charles assented.)

EMMA. The spirit goes out through the senses after outward things.

MR. ALCOTT. After what outward things? *(Emma did not answer.)* Josiah, what is your answer?

JOSIAH. My mind sees through my eyes.

EDWARD J. The spirit comes out to see and hear.

JOSEPH. The senses are to help keep the mind good and the body good.[6]

MR. ALCOTT. Do they always keep all good?

JOSEPH. When we let them.

MR. ALCOTT. What hinders them sometimes?

JOSEPH. Anger.

MR. ALCOTT. What lets them make us good at other times?

JOSEPH. Love.

MR. ALCOTT. Are the senses intended to keep the mind and body good?

FRANKLIN. The senses see wrong things which make us bad.

JOHN D. When a baby goes into his mind to feel, he feels after wisdom and goodness.

MR. ALCOTT. The infant goes inward, then, for wisdom and goodness; and outward for food for the body, and for knowledge?

ANDREW. When we have done right, the spirit comes out in our eyes; and when we have done wrong, it comes out and makes us ashamed to show our face.

MR. ALCOTT. Is there any conscience in shame?

ALL. Yes.

WILLIAM B. The senses are made so that your spirit, and soul, and mind, may get knowledge, and be kept alive; for if you had no senses you could not be very wise; and you need the senses to communicate to others, what you gain from the use of your senses.

MR. ALCOTT. Where does life come from, William?

WILLIAM B. From the spirit.

MR. ALCOTT. Your answer implies that life comes from without, through the senses; for you speak of the spirit's being kept alive by them, as if there was something that came from objects of sense to keep it alive.

WILLIAM B. Oh, I do not mean that; I mean that one person, by means of the senses, is able to keep alive the spirit of others.

EDWARD B. I think the spirit goes into the eyes, ears, &c. after knowledge. But I think the soul would have some wisdom, even if we had no senses at all — were blind, deaf, and all.

(Mr. Alcott again asked, What is wisdom?)

LEMUEL. Wisdom is the spirit's knowledge.

MR. ALCOTT. What other knowledge is there?

LEMUEL. Worldly knowledge.

MR. ALCOTT. What is worldly knowledge?

ELLEN. Knowledge about the body.

CHARLES. About geography and material things.

MR. ALCOTT. What power of spirit gathers knowledge?

LEMUEL. Reason and conscience get wisdom. [7]

WILLIAM B. I think people who had no senses might be good, but could not be very wise.

MR. ALCOTT. What is wisdom? *(A pause.)* Does not wisdom stand for all that the spirit gets from itself? The senses gain knowledge of outward things; the spirit feels, judges of, disposes, uses this knowledge and makes it an instrument, and this is wisdom, is it not? Is not this the distinction?

EDWARD B. A person who has great knowledge has greater means, sometimes, of being bad and unwise.

MR. ALCOTT. Do you remember the two trees in Paradise? The tree of knowledge and the tree of life — of wisdom perhaps?

LUCY. We ought to have some senses to tell us when we do right, and how.

LUCIA. There are senses in the spirit for that!

MR. ALCOTT. What other senses have we but the body's senses; what are the names of the spirit's senses?

GEORGE K. The mind has senses, which it puts into the body's senses.

MR. ALCOTT. Has the mind any other senses than those which it puts into the body's five senses?

GEORGE K. Yes, a sense of good.

MR. ALCOTT. Has the mind a sense about right and wrong?

SEVERAL. Yes; conscience.

MR. ALCOTT. How many of you have this inward, this spiritual sense of right and wrong? (*A pause.*) What are the senses that do not go out, but inward?

LUCIA. Conscience is one.

MR. ALCOTT. There is a man to whom I owe some money, perhaps, I must pay him.

FRANKLIN. Honesty is an inward sense.

MR. ALCOTT. Sense of Justice, and the sense of Duty, of Right. And here is a man very sick and unhappy.

MARTHA. Compassion is one of the inward senses.

MR. ALCOTT. Yesterday one of the boys behaved wrong and was punished. When he came into school, yesterday morning, his eyes looked large and bright. When he comes into school to-day, his eyes are half shut; why is this?

SEVERAL. Conscience.

THE REST. The spirit's senses.

WELLES. Shame is one of the spirit's senses.

MR. ALCOTT. The boy I have been speaking of may rise and show himself. (*Several rose.*) Well! I thought of one; but conscience, it seems, has thought of many more.

LUCY and OTHERS. The spirit's senses.

GEORGE K. The eye is the looker and conscience is the seer.

JOSIAH. No; The soul is the looker, and the spirit the seer.

MR. ALCOTT. What is the Listener?

SEVERAL. Spirit.

GEORGE B. Conscience.

MARTHA. The soul.

FRANKLIN. Jesus Christ.

MR. ALCOTT. What do you mean by that, Franklin?

FRANKLIN. I mean the same as the spirit, when I say Jesus Christ.

JOSIAH. Mind is the listener.

MR. ALCOTT. Do you mean different things, Josiah, by mind, soul, and spirit, or the same thing, acting in different ways?

JOSIAH. I think it is the soul that acts upon the senses, while the spirit is acting inwardly; and the mind has something to do with the senses too; the mind does all about hearing and the soul all about seeing.

MR. ALCOTT. What is the name of the Knower?

JOSIAH. The heart.

CHARLES. God.

MR. ALCOTT. What do you mean by that?

CHARLES. Why God and the spirit are one, and when the spirit is so perfect as to know everything, it is God.[8]

LEMUEL. Reason is the knower.

WILLIAM C. Mind. (*Others agreed.*)

FRANKLIN. Jesus Christ is the knower.

LUCIA. The understanding knows.

JOSIAH. It takes the spirit and everything that is in it, to know; the reason, the understanding, and all the faculties. The spirit sees that all these go on rightly.

GEORGE K. Conscience knows.

GEORGE B. The soul is the knower.

MR. ALCOTT. When you use these various words, I want to know whether you mean different things, different powers, or different ways in which the one power of spirit acts.

FRANKLIN. I mean spirit when I say Jesus Christ, for I am tired of saying spirit. But I mean the same thing.

MR. ALCOTT. Have any of you said some word, because you were tired of saying the word which was the simplest and truest? (*None assented.*) How many mean something acting differently when they say heart, conscience, &c., from what they mean when they say spirit? (*All raised hands.*) What is the name of the Feeler, not the Toucher?

SEVERAL. The spirit.

CHARLES. The heart is the spirit that feels.

JOSIAH. Mr. Alcott, I think a little of the mind and a little of the soul go down and form a body, and that body feels.

MR. ALCOTT. What is the name of the Believer?

SEVERAL. The spirit.

OTHERS. Conscience.

OTHERS. The heart believes.

MR. ALCOTT. When you use these words, do you mean different powers separate from spirit?

SEVERAL. Not separated.

CHARLES. But different powers.

MR. ALCOTT. What is the Actor, Willer, the *I*

SEVERAL. The spirit. (*All agreed.*)

MR. ALCOTT. What is the Obeyer?

SEVERAL. Spirit.

CHARLES. The body is the obeyer of the spirit.

ELLEN. No; the body is the instrument, by which the spirit obeys.

OTHERS. Conscience obeys.

CHARLES. I meant what Ellen said.

MR. ALCOTT. What, or where is the Chooser?

SOME. Conscience chooses.

OTHERS. Spirit is the Chooser.

MR. ALCOTT. Did you ever hear of persons placed in the midst of beautiful things, in a beautiful place, charming to their sense, where they could gather food for the spirit also; with nothing but kindness around them, to protect them from pain and sorrow, and to teach them not to indulge too much in eating and drinking, and yet who chose to disobey?

CHARLES. Yes; it was in the Garden of Eden.

FRANKLIN. I have done it myself.

GEORGE K. I was in that garden when I was a baby.

SEVERAL. So was I.[9]

MR. ALCOTT. When did you first taste the forbidden fruit?

WILLIAM C. When I began to do wrong.

MR. ALCOTT. What did wrong?

WILLIAM C. My body.

LUCIA. My appetites and passions.

MR. ALCOTT. Where did the evil begin?

LUCIA. In my Will.

MR. ALCOTT. What is the tree of knowledge?

FRANKLIN. Indulgence.

GEORGE K. Temptation.

MR. ALCOTT. The outward world, perhaps; and what is the tree of life?

FRANKLIN. The spirit.

MR. ALCOTT. Why have I asked you these questions about the

Taster, Looker, Knower, Feeler, Believer, Seer, Listener, Actor, Willer, Obeyer, and Chooser?

CHARLES. To show us that the beginning of all action and all movement is within us.

MR. ALCOTT. Yes; I have been endeavouring to lift your vision above the organs, the senses, the understanding, the reason, into Spirit, the origin and cause of all your actions. *(Pause)* Such of you then, as think there is something within you which is no part of your body, but which moves your body, acts in it, and is better than your body, and your body lives upon it, may hold up your hands. *(All held up hands.)* How many think a good name for this is mind? *(Several held up hands.)* Or soul, or God, or intellect, or conscience, or spirit? *(Most agreed upon God as the best name. One said Spirit was the best; another said God and Spirit were the same.)* I prefer the word SPIRIT. And soon we shall begin to talk of a particular Spirit that came into the world and took a body; and acted in the world; and we shall inquire what became of it when it left the world. What Spirit are we going to talk about?

ALL. Jesus Christ.

MR. ALCOTT. How many of you will always know hereafter what I mean by the word *spirit*, when I use it? *(All held up their hands.)*

ANDREW. I think the word conscience would be a better word than spirit.

MR. ALCOTT. *Conscience* is spirit acting on duty; *Mind* is spirit thinking; *Heart* is spirit loving; *Soul* is spirit feeling; *Sense* is spirit inquiring into the external world; *Body* is the instrument and organ of spirit. The action of these is divided between consciousness and conscience.

CONVERSATION II

* * *

TESTIMONY OF NATURE
AND SCRIPTURE TO SPIRIT:

Nature and Scripture

MR. ALCOTT. What was the conclusion to which we came, after the conversation of Wednesday last?

SEVERAL. That there was a Spirit.

MR. ALCOTT. Did each of you conclude and feel it proved *in your own heart,* that there is a Spirit? *(All held up hands.)* What do you understand by an *inward proof* of Spirit?

CHARLES. What one feels, and thinks.

MR. ALCOTT. Are there *outward evidences* of Spirit?

CHARLES. Actions, any actions, outward actions, an earthquake, the creeping of a worm.

GEORGE K. Moving, the creeping of a baby.

LEMUEL. The moving of a leaf, lightning.

ANDREW. A waterfall, a rose.

FRANK. Walking.

SAMUEL R. A tree.

EDWARD C. A star.

SUSAN. The sun.

GEORGE B. A steam engine.

MR. ALCOTT. Where does the spirit work in that?

GEORGE B. In the men that work it.

CHARLES. No; in the steam.

EDWARD J. In the machinery, and the steam, and the men, and all.

MR. ALCOTT. You perceive then what I mean by outward evidence of spirit?

CHARLES. Things, external nature.

MR. ALCOTT. And this will be our subject in part to-day. Do

smaller things prove greater things, or greater things smaller things? How many do not understand me? (*Several held up their hands.*) Does an acorn prove there has been an oak, or an oak prove there has been an acorn? (*Some said one and some the other.*) Which was first in time, an acorn or an oak?

GEORGE K. Sometimes one is first and sometimes the other. In the woods, oaks grow up wild; and you can plant acorns and have oaks.

SAMUEL R. I think God made oaks first, and all the other oaks there have ever been, came from the acorns of those first oaks.

MR. ALCOTT. Does light prove darkness, or darkness light?

SEVERAL. Each proves the other.

MR. ALCOTT. Can nothing prove something?

ALL. No.

MR. ALCOTT. But darkness is mere absence of light. Is darkness any thing to your spirit?

SEVERAL. No.

CHARLES. I think darkness is something.

MR. ALCOTT. Is darkness any thing to your senses?

ANDREW. No; it only seems so.

MR. ALCOTT. What does it seem to be?

ANDREW. It is the shadow of light.

MR. ALCOTT. Does the egg foretell the chick, or the chick the egg? (*They first said one, and then the other, and then both, and some referred to God who could make either.*) Which has most meaning, a bud or a flower?[10]

SEVERAL. A flower.

SUSAN. A bud, because it is going to be a flower, and makes you think of it.

EDWARD J. Perhaps the bud will be picked.

MR. ALCOTT. Accidents are always excepted. (*He then asked like questions about many things, among the rest a brook and the ocean, the cradle and the grave, and similar answers were returned. He remarked that their answers showed which minds were historical and which were analytic. He then went on:*) Which is the superior, spirit or body?

ALL. Spirit.

MR. ALCOTT. Lemuel, will you give me a reason?

LEMUEL. Because the body decays, and the spirit cannot decay; and the spirit is not seen; and when the spirit is gone the body cannot do any thing.

MR. ALCOTT. Is it the invisibleness and the undecaying nature of the spirit, which makes it superior, then? Have you ever seen any perfect visible thing?

GEORGE B. Yes; a rose.

MR. ALCOTT. Did it remain perfect?

GEORGE B. No.

MR. ALCOTT. What thing is perfect and remains perfect?

GEORGE K. Jesus' body was perfect, for it ascended into heaven.

MR. ALCOTT. Is there proof that his body ascended?

GEORGE K. The Bible says so.

CHARLES. The Bible says the disciples saw him ascend.

MR. ALCOTT. Yes, they saw him ascend; yet not perhaps his body; and besides, Jesus' body suffered pain; and was it perfect, while it was suffering pain? (*No answer.*) Can you say that your bodily senses are perfect, that they have never deceived you? (*None held up hands.*) When you look round the world, and see no perfect, visible thing, what do you feel? (*No answer.*) Is there not something within you which measures all imperfection?

CHARLES. Yes, the thought of Perfection.

MR. ALCOTT. By what do you measure your thought of Perfection?

CHARLES. By God.

MR. ALCOTT. Is the imperfection in the outward world a proof of something perfect within? (*No answer.*) For instance, you tell me that you have seen a person do something wrong: now, what do you make the standard? How do you know it is wrong?

CHARLES. By Reason.

LEMUEL. No; Judgment judges.

EDWARD J. We measure by the spirit.

MR. ALCOTT. What is in the spirit; a sense of — what?

LEMUEL. A Sense of Good — of Perfection.

MR. ALCOTT. Where is all proof, then?

LEMUEL. In Conscience and in God.

MR. ALCOTT. And when Jesus utters the divine injunction, "Be ye Perfect, even as your Father in Heaven is Perfect," he does but reannounce the sentiment of Duty in every conscience, which ever utters the same words. Now, do perfect things prove imperfect things, or imperfect things prove perfect things?

GEORGE K. They prove each other.

MR. ALCOTT. Does your spirit prove there is a God, or because there is a God, must your spirit be?

CHARLES. Each proves the other.

MR. ALCOTT. All proof then is in God, spirit being its own proof, because there is more of God in it, than in any thing outward. As an acorn reminds you of an oak, so does the spirit within remind you of God. Your spirits, like the acorns (if you choose to carry on the figure), drop off from God, to plant themselves in Time. Once they were within the oak, but they come out individual differing acorns, the seeds of new oaks. The other things mentioned are proofs of the same kind. Spirits are born out of the Supreme Spirit, and by their power of reproducing spirit, constantly prove their own existence from his existence, and his existence from their own. —That there is a spirit in us all you have proofs, as you have shown. There are yet other proofs of spirit, especially the Life of Jesus Christ, which we are going to study. He took a body and came into the world almost two thousand years before we did. He was seen, and those who saw and knew him — his friends — wrote down what he said and did; and their words make what are called the GOSPELS. Luke was one of these friends. He began an account of Jesus — the Gospel of his life, that is, the Good News of his life —in these words:

THE GENERAL PREFACE TO THE GOSPELS

Forasmuch as many have taken in hand to set forth in order a declaration of those things which are most surely believed among us, even as they delivered them unto us, which from the beginning were eyewitnesses, and ministers of the word; It seemed good to me also, having had perfect understanding of all things from the very first, to write unto thee in order, most excellent Theophilus, that thou mightest know the certainty of those things, wherein thou hast been instructed. (Mark 1:1, Luke 1:1-4.)

MR. ALCOTT. You perceive that Luke wrote this Gospel for a particular friend. He had himself learned most of the facts from others, for he was not an eyewitness from the beginning. Now I suppose that you can place entire confidence in these words, which are called the Gospels. You doubtless believe that they have a meaning, all of them, worth finding out; and you feel sure that they are all true.

GEORGE K. There are some things I think *truer*. I believe those words, but I am more sure of some things.

MR. ALCOTT. Of what?

GEORGE K. Why — that the stove is in the room.

CHARLES. I do not believe that those words are the same as Luke wrote down.

MR. ALCOTT. Luke wrote in Greek; and these words are translated. But the Greek words are yet preserved, and those are the very words of Luke, as can be satisfactorily proved; for great care was taken of so valuable a writing by the earliest Christians.

(Some more conversation ensued on this subject, in which Charles was told that there had been a great deal of dispute concerning these writings in the early ages; and that it was now an undisputed fact — except by an individual here and there — that these writings all belonged to the persons by whom they were said to be written. And that this was a subject he might examine for himself when he was older.)

MR. ALCOTT. As many of you as think you have as high evidence, that these words of the written Gospels are a true record of what Jesus Christ did, as you have of any thing that is put into language, may rise. *(All rose.)* As many as think they have as high evidence that Jesus Christ lived, as that they live themselves, may rise. *(All rose.)* How do you know that this Record of Jesus Christ's action is true?

CHARLES. Because the principles and truths of the Gospel are acted out every day; and when we do the same kind of things Jesus did, we have proofs within ourselves that it is as Jesus said. I feel perfectly sure that Jesus lived and did just as it says there.

SEVERAL. So do I.

SUSAN. I am sure of it, because Luke would not say so, if it was not true. There are a great many things that are said there, which we know are true, because we find them out in ourselves.

MR. ALCOTT. You mean by experience?

SUSAN. Yes; and so we believe that all the rest of the things said there are true.

CHARLES. And we see there is nothing there, that does not happen every day, and so there is no reason why we should not believe.

MR. ALCOTT. Is Lazarus raised, and are demons cast out every day?

CHARLES. There is resurrection, as we know in other ways, every day, and men are possessed by appetites and passions; and their demons are cast out by faith, and love, and truth.

MR. ALCOTT. There are many men among us, Charles, who do not feel this evidence that you speak of. Yes; some ministers, I fear, go into the pulpit and preach, who do not.

CHARLES. Then they have not risen from their graves — the graves of their bodies.

MR. ALCOTT. As many as are perfectly convinced, and cannot doubt, that there is a Spirit within you, may rise. *(All rose up.)* Yesterday I saw a man who said he knew of no evidence of spirit.

ELLEN. How large a man?

MR. ALCOTT. A grown up man, and learned.

CHARLES. Why did you not talk to him and tell him?

MR. ALCOTT. Faith and knowledge of spirit is something which cannot come by the hearing of the ear; it comes by living, by a pure and holy life. You may now tell me what has been the subject of to-day's conversation.

LEMUEL. Outward Evidences of Spirit.

CHARLES. In Nature.

OTHERS. And in the Gospel.

MR. ALCOTT. And the Evidence for the Gospel Record.

CONVERSATION III

* * *

REVELATION OF SPIRIT
IN NATURE AND HUMANITY:

Inspiration

MR. ALCOTT. Another friend of Jesus, who wrote Good News of his life, was John. His Gospel is very interesting. He seemed to understand, how and why Jesus said and did things, better than the other disciples. The others seem to know what he did; John seems to know why he did it. Jesus loved John especially, because his spiritual vision was clearer than the rest, perhaps. And this spirituality made him understand Jesus better than the rest did. See how he begins his gospel.

THE INCARNATE WORD

In the beginning was the Word, and the Word was with God, and the Word was God. The same was in the beginning with God. All things were made by him; and without him was not any thing made that was made. In him was life; and the life was the light of men. And the light shineth in darkness; and the darkness comprehended it not. (John 1:1-5:)

MR. ALCOTT. Give me the history of a word — who is a wordmaker?

CHARLES. God.

MR. ALCOTT. How do words first come to you?

SEVERAL. By hearing. By thought.

MR. ALCOTT. What are words?

LEMUEL. Thoughts expressed.

MR. ALCOTT. What word is large enough to spread over all that is in Conscience, and that opens out all in the Outward World?

JOSIAH. Creation.

MR. ALCOTT. Creation is made known to us through it. It is the light that comes forth from God, &c. It is Revelation.

SEVERAL. I never heard that word.

MR. ALCOTT. God reveals himself in Reason; in Imagination, in the Outward World; in the Bible; in Moses; in David; in the Prophets; in the trees; in the flowers; in oceans, &c. Does God reveal himself in you?

MANY. Some.

NATHAN. A very little.

JOSIAH. God does not reveal himself in me, but only in Jesus Christ.

NATHAN. We should not live if God did not act through us.

MR. ALCOTT. What is the darkness that does not comprehend the light?

LEMUEL. Intemperance.

SEVERAL. The appetites.

NATHAN. Laziness.

CHARLES. Ignorance.

MR. ALCOTT. Now those who have some dim idea of what the words of our reading mean, may hold up their hands. (*Several did.*) Now, those who think they have a clear sense of their meaning. (*Several hands fell.*) Now, let each who can express it tell what idea these words convey to him.

JOSIAH. They seemed to me to mean that there was nothing without God.

JOSEPH. Nothing ever would have been without God.

EDWARD B. God made every thing that was and would be.

AUGUSTINE. There could be no life without God, for all life comes from God. He is the fountain of life.

WILLIAM B. God is in every thing.

GEORGE K. God was the first thing, then he made things. If he had not been first, there would have been no other things.

CHARLES. God made every thing, is in every thing, and will continue in every thing to the end.

MR. ALCOTT. I wish you would all of you give me an emblem of Creation.

HERBERT. A little child beginning to speak.

MARTHA. A little child.

SAMUEL R. A bud beginning to open.

GEORGE B. A plant coming out of the ground.

ELLEN. A little child beginning to exist.

(Mr. Alcott spoke of Incarnation generally.)

LUCIA. There must have been spirit before there was any thing else. There must have been spirit to make the world before there could be any world.

ALEXANDER. Every thing was God, first.

WILLIAM B. Every thing is God, now.

JOSIAH. I think all spirits are emblematic of God. Just as images of stone are copies of men's bodies, so the souls of men are copies of God. I mean all good souls.

FRANK. I think the body is the shadow of the spirit.

LEMUEL. If, as Josiah says, all good spirits are emblems of God, what must bad spirits be the emblems of?

MR. ALCOTT. We will not begin on that subject now, Lemuel. It will come bye and bye.

LUCIA. God must have thought within his mind before any thing could be made, and it was his thought that shaped things.

MR. ALCOTT. Was his thought the word then?

CHARLES. First there was God; then he thought, then he spoke the thought in a WORD; and so there was a World.

MR. ALCOTT. And did Moses intend to express the same Idea in the account of the Creation: God said let things be — let things come out of me. How many of you have heard the words, "In him we live, and move, and have our being"? (*All held up hands.*) When you speak, what goes out of your mouth?

JOHN D. Sound.

MR. ALCOTT. What makes sound?

LUCIA. Spirit.

MR. ALCOTT. What does the spirit make of sounds?

LUCIA. Words.

MR. ALCOTT. What action of spirit makes words?

CHARLES. Thought.

MR. ALCOTT. How many of you think your spirits are God's breathings? (*Several held up hands.*) And if our spirits should think out, and utter God's breathings, would our utterance be the Word of God? (*Several assented.*) Was Jesus Christ's Spirit a pure breathing or inspiration of God's Spirit, and may what he said justly be called the pure Inspired Word of God? (*All held up their hands.*) Are our spirits also, the Word of God; the breathings of God; an Inspiration of God? (*They generally held up hands.*) And is the Outward World also a Word of God; the Manifestation of God; God in Things; the Shadow of God, as Frank said; an Emblem of God, as Josiah said? (*They held up hands.*) And besides the word of God within, which is CONSCIENCE; and the word of God in the outward world, is there also a word here, written out to our sense? (*He laid his hand on the Bible. They all held up hands.*) How is Conscience a word of God?

NATHAN and CHARLES. Because it tells right and wrong.

MR. ALCOTT. How is Nature a word of God?

JOSIAH. Because it shows forth God's works, and how they are made, to our eyes.

MR. ALCOTT. When God's word comes through Conscience, what faculties does it address?

JOSIAH. Why, even then, sometimes it addresses the eye; for when I walk out, and every thing is very beautiful, and I have been doing something wrong, I think I feel it.

MR. ALCOTT. And what when you are doing right?

JOSIAH. Why, then everything seems pleasant.

MR. ALCOTT. Who is the most perfect emblem of god?

ALL. Jesus Christ.

MR. ALCOTT. What other person?

GEORGE. Socrates.

MARTHA. Mary, the mother of Jesus.

FRANCIS. I think you are a little like Jesus Christ.

MR. ALCOTT. Who was the most perfect Image, Representation, Emblem, Revelation of God? Who showed forth God most completely?

ALMOST ALL. Jesus Christ.

FRANK. I first thought of Moses. Was he not as good a picture of God as Jesus Christ?

JOSIAH. I first thought of the angels.

MR. ALCOTT. And if God revealed himself in Jesus, would he not also in all men? Or was Jesus different from all others? Had he something within him which you have not? Such of you as think that Jesus had something within him which you have not in you, may rise. (Ellen and Corinna rose.) Do the rest think that you have all the faculties that he had? (They assented.)

NATHAN. We have conscience as much as he.

MR. ALCOTT. Is it because you have not cultivated what is within you faithfully, that you are not like Jesus Christ? (All but Ellen assented.) Why, then, have you not done as much, and why are you not as spiritual as Jesus, when he was twelve years old?

JOSIAH. Because I have not used my powers so much.

MARTHA. Because I have indulged my passions and spoiled my powers.

CHARLES. Because I have not attended to cultivating my powers as I ought.

LEMUEL. Because I have indulged myself.

SAMUEL R. I have done wrong, and have not brought out my powers.

MR. ALCOTT. How many of you think you have God within you to be brought out?

JOSIAH. I think I have every thing Jesus had, only he had more.

WILLIAM B. He had more power.

CHARLES. He had more power because he had more faith.

WILLIAM B. I think all his power flowed out of his love.

LUCIA. We have a great deal in us, but Jesus had more and used it better.

MR. ALCOTT. Yet you all appear to think that you have something within you godlike, spiritual, like Jesus, though not so much, and what is this?

SEVERAL. Spirit. Faith. Goodness. Conscience.

MR. ALCOTT. Now, does your spirit differ in any sense from God's spirit? Each may answer.

CHARLES. God made our spirits.

MR. ALCOTT. They differ from His then in being derived?

GEORGE K. They are not so good.

WILLIAM B. They have not so much power.

AUGUSTINE. I don't think our spirit does differ much.

CHARLES. God is spirit, we are spirit and body.

JOSIAH. He differs from us, as a king's body differs from ours. A king's body is arrayed with more beautiful garments than his subjects. And God's spirit is arrayed with more goodness than ours.

EDWARD B. God's spirit is a million times larger than ours, and we come out of him as the drops of the ocean. [11]

GEORGE K. God's spirit is a great deal larger and has more power.

MR. ALCOTT. You seem to think, generally, that the difference of God's spirit and yours is not in kind but degree. But now tell me in what conscience and God are alike.

ALEXANDER. God can love and so can we.

MR. ALCOTT. Are any of you able to describe any difference between God, who is conscience, you say, and conscience in you?

ANDREW. Conscience is God within us.

(There was a slight movement of inattention.)

MR. ALCOTT. Oh! What if I should call upon some Spiritual Power to descend from heaven into visible presence, and take the supervision of you all, and write down in his book what passes within your minds!

SEVERAL. I should like it!

MR. ALCOTT. And do you not say that such a Power has descended? Is not Conscience such a superintendant, keeping a record? He is not visible, with a shining countenance and glistening wings, to your body's eyesight, but is he not to the Spirit within you?

(They all responded, smilingly.)

ALEXANDER. Our conscience is God's Child.

AUGUSTINE. Our conscience is God acting.

FRANKLIN and FREDERIC. God has more — and uses it more —but ours is of the same kind.

SAMUEL R. God is better.

WILLIAM B. God has more power.

MR. ALCOTT. What is the nature of that power?

WILLIAM B. It is inward — spiritual.

LUCIA. Our consciences are young; God is their Father.

MR. ALCOTT. The parental idea comes to your minds. How did Jesus signify his connexion with God?

EDWARD B. He said God was the Father, and he was the Son.

MR. ALCOTT. Does the relation of father and son express something better, deeper, more spiritual than that of king and subject? (*All said yes.*) — Jesus said he was the son — the child of God. Are we also God's sons?

WILLIAM B. Oh! before I was born — I think *I* was a part of God himself.

MANY OTHERS. So do I.

MR. ALCOTT. Who thinks his own spirit is the child of God? (*All held up hands.*) Now, is God your Father in the same sense that he is the Father of Jesus?

(*Most held up hands.*)

GEORGE K. Jesus was more the Son of God than we are.

LEMUEL. He had more of that same.

MR. ALCOTT. Was Jesus Christ perfect?

(*All held up hands but two.*)

CHARLES. Because Jesus had a body, he could not be perfect.

GEORGE K. Jesus was not perfect, because he was made by God. God is perfect, because he made himself.

MR. ALCOTT. Then he was imperfect only in that he drew his existence from God?

GEORGE K. Jesus did not make the world, so he was not so perfect as God.

RECORDER. Which do you think is the greater work; to make a spirit pure and perfectly good; or to make an outward world?

GEORGE K. It would be harder to make a world.

MR. ALCOTT. Would it be harder to make a material world than a spiritual world? And which is the best?

GEORGE K. The spiritual world is the best. But I am sure I could not make a world — and I could — (*He stopped.*)

RECORDER. Could you be perfect? (*He still paused.*)

MR. ALCOTT. So you think it would be hard to manage the earth and rocks and marble, mountains and ocean.

GEORGE K. Yes; for I know I could not in any way make a world; but if I tried as hard as I could, and tried all the time, I could be perfect. I know it is very hard to be perfect — to love all the time and never be angry and never do wrong; but we can — we ought to be perfect, and so we can be. It would be necessary to be perfect in the first place, to make a world. It was because Jesus was perfect he could work miracles.

MR. ALCOTT. Could you work miracles, if you were perfect?

GEORGE K. If I was perfect I could. It is the spirit that makes bodies, and if my spirit was perfect it would know all that spirit could do, and how to do it.

MR. ALCOTT. Do you know how Jesus worked a miracle — cured the withered arm, for instance?

GEORGE. I suppose he told the man's spirit to go into his arm, and make it what it ought to be.

MR. ALCOTT. Make bones and muscles whole?

GEORGE. Yes; the spirit makes bodies — made them in the first place.

RECORDER. So, if your spirit was perfected, you think you could make a whole world?

GEORGE K. Oh yes, easily.

RECORDER. Was it Jesus' spirit that made the bones and muscles of that withered arm whole, or the man's own spirit?

GEORGE. It was the man's own spirit.

MR. ALCOTT. How could he command the man's spirit?

FRANK. I suppose he made him feel faith.

MR. ALCOTT. What have we been talking about this morning?

SEVERAL. The Spirit. Spirit in God. Spirit in Christ. Spirit in Ourselves.

MR. ALCOTT. Almost all have expressed that they think, God is revealed in everything; in Jesus Christ, in Good Men, in the Outward World, even in Yourselves; and that the only reason why we are not all like Jesus Christ is because we do not use every thing that we have within us; excepting Ellen. Now let me ask you a new question. Do you think the opinions you have expressed are those which grown up people generally have?

CHARLES. I do not know what other people's opinions are, but I should think they were like mine.

MR. ALCOTT. How many think your opinions are your own, and not derived from others? (*All rose.*)

ELLEN. My parents may influence me some.

MR. ALCOTT. Who else think their parents have influenced them?

CHARLES. I have not the least idea what my parents think, any more than what you think.

(*Here some conversation ensued as to what Mr. Alcott thought, and all expressed their ignorance as to what he thought of the various subjects on which themselves differed. Some wished he would tell them; some not, lest it should influence their opinions.*)

CONVERSATION IV
* * *
TESTIMONY OF HUMANITY TO SPIRIT:
Inspiration

Mr. Alcott recalled the subject of the last conversation, and then read the lesson for the day:

JOHN THE HERALD OF JESUS

There was a man sent from God, whose name was John.

The same came for a witness, to bear witness of the Light, that all men through him might believe. He was not that Light, but was sent to bear witness of that Light. That was the true Light, which lighteth every man that cometh into the world. He was in the world, and the world was made by him, and the world knew him not. He came unto his own, and his

own received him not. But as many as received him, to them
gave he power to become the sons of God, even to them that
believe on his name. Which were born, not of blood, nor of
the will of the flesh, nor of the will of man, but of God. And
the Word was made flesh, and dwelt among us (and we beheld
his glory, the glory as of the only begotten of the Father), full
of grace and truth. John bare witness of him, and cried,
saying, This was he of whom I spake, He that cometh after me
is preferred before me: for he was before me. And of his fulness
have all we received, and grace for grace. For the law was
given by Moses, but grace and truth came by Jesus Christ. No
man hath seen God at any time; the only begotten Son,
which is in the bosom of the Father, he hath declared him.
(John 1:6-18.)

MR. ALCOTT. What thoughts does this suggest to your minds?

WILLIAM B. I thought that Jesus was better than John; and that
John only came to announce him.

FRANKLIN. John was the sign of truth; Jesus the truth.

GEORGE K. The Light was Jesus. John came to tell that it was
coming.

LEMUEL. John was the sign of the Light; Jesus the Light.

WELLES. John came to convince the people that somebody was to
be sent from God to teach them.

MR. ALCOTT. How many of you think that I might say with truth,
that a star appeared when each one of you was born?

(All smiled and held up hands.)

CHARLES. I like to have Jesus alone have a star.

EMMA. I think it might be so for all.

CHARLES. The spirit of a baby is a star.

MR. ALCOTT. When the spirit first came into your body, was it
star-like, and did it stand over the place where the body lay?

CHARLES. Yes.

MR. ALCOTT. Did any Wise Ones worship there?

CHARLES. Only our father and mother.

JOSIAH. I thought the same as some of the rest said. The only thought I have now is, that John was the shadow of Jesus.

MR. ALCOTT. What is the "Light that lighteth every man," &c.?

GEORGE K. The Spirit.

MR. ALCOTT. Give some manifestations of that light.

GEORGE K. Love, gratitude, faith, hope.

MARTHA. The Bible.

LEMUEL. Repentance enlightens.

MR. ALCOTT. Yes; after we have become dark, but what enlightens act first?

EMMA. Conscience.

CHARLES. Reason, Imagination.

MR. ALCOTT. Yes; Reason is light, and love is warmth. When we speak of that faculty which sends forth light, what do we call it?

EMMA. The understanding.

CHARLES. Reason.

MR. ALCOTT. But whence comes the warmth?

CHARLES. From the heart. And warmth is more valuable than light. I should rather have it.

MR. ALCOTT. Who have more light than warmth; think more than they feel? (*None rose. He reversed the question and all rose.*)

NATHAN. John came down first to tell that Jesus was coming.

LUCIA. Moses taught by the law and tried to make people good by that; but Jesus taught by goodness, by being good himself; and John came to prepare the people for Jesus.

(*Mr. Alcott asked what Moses appealed to, the head, or the heart.*)

CHARLES. The head.

JOSIAH. John lighted the candle. Jesus was the light.

MR. ALCOTT. "There was a man sent from God." How?

NATHAN. Sent down from Heaven.

MR. ALCOTT. Do all think so? (*All held up hands.*)

SEVERAL. Every body came down from heaven. (*They corrected themselves.*) No! every *spirit* did.

(*Mr. Alcott read the expression of Nathan, "sent down from heaven."*)

CHARLES and LEMUEL. The expression "send down from heaven" is too external.

GEORGE and MARTHA. Once I had that outward view only, but I am just taking the inward view.

ANDREW. It is impossible for me to help having this image.

MOST. The first thought is the outward, the sky, &c.; but it is corrected by the next thought.

SEVERAL. We like the image, and do not like to give it up.

CHARLES. It is a perfect emblem.

MR. ALCOTT. Did you come from heaven just as John did? (*Several responded affirmatively.*) Where is heaven?

FRANCIS. In our spirits.

HILLMAN. Every where.

ANDREW. Wherever there is goodness, not in body, but in spirit.

GEORGE. Wherever there is love and gratitude.

CHARLES. Wherever there is Perfection.

EMMA. Everywhere, but most in spirit.

LEMUEL. Wherever there is goodness.

MARTHA and GEORGE B. In our thoughts.

MR. ALCOTT. Why has the sky become the emblem of heaven?

MARTHA. Because it is above, and God is above.

CHARLES. Because it is beautiful and full of stars.

GEORGE. Because we feel that God, who is above us, is more pure and beautiful than we are, and so is the sky.

CHARLES. And you cannot see the end of it, that is, it is infinite.

EMMA. And it is over and around every thing.

WILLIAM C. We think God is better, and ought to be above us.

GEORGE B. I know that heaven is within, but I imagine it in the sky.

CHARLES. I once thought it was in the sky, and was happy in my ignorance, for I was not perplexed.

MR. ALCOTT. Do any of you feel that were the sky and earth to pass away, heaven would remain, so sure are you that it is in the Spirit, and that the outward heavens are but the emblem of it?

(Most of them rose.)

LUCIA. God made John and put power into him.

GEORGE K. God made him and sent an angel to carry him to earth.

LEMUEL. His spirit was brought down by angels and put into a body.

ALEXANDER. God sent one of his angels into a body.

MR. ALCOTT. I should like to know what you each think angels are.

MARTHA. I think some angels have had bodies and some not.

GEORGE K. I think angels were good people that have lived here.

EMMA. Angels are God's messengers, like our thoughts; they bring us our thoughts.

MR. ALCOTT. So you think that they are not ourselves, but bring us thoughts. Is there any thing human in them? Can you become angels? Have you been angels? *(Almost all rose.)*

GEORGE. My spirit was an angel when I was a baby.

MR. ALCOTT. What change happens to an angel when it takes a body?

CHARLES. It becomes human.

GEORGE K. Angels are good spirits; once they were in bodies and did good with their bodies.

FRANK. Very good spirits that have been in a body.

LUCIA. Spirits in heaven, before they have ever had a body, are angels.

MARTHA. Angels are good spirits with or without bodies.

CHARLES. I think some angels have lived in bodies, and some are going to be born.

EDWARD B. The spirits of the bad are the devil's angels.

MARTHA. Bad spirits ought not to be called angels.

LEMUEL. They ought to be called demons.

MR. ALCOTT. Do you think that you were angels before you were boys and girls? (Many.) Do you think that you shall be angels when you die? (Many.) Some people live only in the body. They are body folks. Some feel that they have lived before they were in the body, and are sure that they shall live after they leave the body.

CHARLES. I think that Jesus Christ was Adam, and that Adam was an angel first.

FRANCIS. It says in the Bible that Adam was the Son of God.

MR. ALCOTT. As many as think John was an angel before he was sent, signify. (All held up hands but Josiah.)

JOSIAH. God at first only had one angel, but he wanted more, and so he determined that when people died, they should become angels.

MR. ALCOTT. People, then, were not angels first?

JOSIAH. No, they were made at the time they began to live on earth.

MR. ALCOTT. How many of you think you were angels, before you were boys and girls?

(All thought so but Josiah.)

EDWARD B. I think our ideas of God and divine things are faint remembrances of our angelic life.

MR. ALCOTT. Can you remember any instances of Jesus referring to his angelic life?

CHARLES. No; but I like the idea very much, and it is a new one to me; I never had it before. [12]

MR. ALCOTT. Who else are pleased with this idea?

(All rose, and Mr. Alcott asked them to reproduce the idea, and they did in so many words. Mr. Alcott remarked that Plato thought so, and added that Plato taught how we were born into this world, and Jesus how we were to be born out of the body.)

CHARLES. Did Plato live before Jesus?

MR. ALCOTT. Yes; a great while.

CHARLES. How could he know then about Spirit? I should have thought that he would have been a prophet, or an apostle.

MR. ALCOTT. And was he not? Christians who seek depth to their knowledge read Plato, and learn from him as well as from the Bible, the nature of Spirit. Before Jesus came, Plato revealed spiritual things; and all spiritually minded people loved him. I do not know that Jesus ever read his works, but he might have done so. He seldom speaks of the books which he had read; he seldom quoted books.

CHARLES. Oh, I wish he had; we might then have known what to read ourselves.

MR. ALCOTT. I do not mean that all who entertain the sentiments of Christianity read Plato, but people who would understand the Idea that Christianity gives of Spirit, find that Plato sheds light upon it.

EMMA. Some people who believe that the Spirit is to live after the body dies, do not believe that it lived before the body was born.

MR. ALCOTT. Yet they may not understand, fully, what they feel or believe?

EMMA. They only think they do, perhaps.

CHARLES. How came they, in those times, to believe in Moses?

MR. ALCOTT. They had been taught to believe in him; but they did not understand even Moses, or they would have believed Jesus. Moses did not address the heart. He addressed the head, and the heart may, but does not always, follow that. Why did John come to bear witness?

LUCIA. If they did not know Jesus was coming, they would not have believed him when he did come.

WILLIAM B. They would not have believed John was a prophet.

MR. ALCOTT. What is a prophet?

LUCIA. A man who tells things that are going to happen.

MR. ALCOTT. How does he know these things?

SEVERAL. Because he has more faith than we have.

MR. ALCOTT. Do any of you think you have in your souls, what makes a prophet? (*Several.*) Do you think that were you to use all that is in your spirit, you might also be prophets?

SEVERAL. If we had faith enough.

WILLIAM B. If we had love enough.

CHARLES. A prophet first has a little love, and that gives the impulse to more, and so on, until he becomes so full of love, he knows every thing.

MR. ALCOTT. Do prophets look within or without to find out what is going to happen without?

SEVERAL. Within.

JOSIAH. But I don't think so.

MR. ALCOTT. Where do you think they look?

JOSIAH. To God.

MR. ALCOTT. Is God within or without?

JOSIAH. He is in heaven.

MR. ALCOTT. Is heaven within? What do you mean by within?

SEVERAL. Within the spirit.

MR. ALCOTT. Do things happen first within or without the spirit?

SEVERAL. Within.

(*Mr. Alcott said the prophet looked both within and without. He asked whether he did not look in for the Idea, and outward for the means of expressing it. He then spoke of the moral conditions of prophecy.*)

MR. ALCOTT. He that understands a seed can see the tree in it. A little baby opens out into a man or woman. Thought and Love seem to be the seeds of all things. A prophet, finding out what goes on within the spirit, can tell what will happen without. They are called Seers, not outseers. Their sight is insight. Who is the universal prophet?

ALL AT ONCE. God.

MR. ALCOTT. How long does God prophesy an event, before it happens?

LEMUEL. He always knows.

MR. ALCOTT. Is there more foresight than backsight, or is it insight, spreading over all time and space?

CHARLES. Either eternity has an end, or God's sight is within eternity.

MR. ALCOTT. A little child once said that "Eternity was God's life time."

CHARLES. Oh, that is beautiful; it is a precious gem to be put by the side of Edward B.'s thought upon the remembrances of our angelic life.

EMMA. Charles said that eternity must have an end; but if it did, it would not be eternity.

MR. ALCOTT. Eternity is the abolition of all Time. No dial plate can measure it.

EMMA. A dial plate marks off Time.

MR. ALCOTT. The flow of Eternity shall not cease, though centuries are marked off endlessly.

LEMUEL. Eternity has no hours, no spaces.

GEORGE K. I cannot imagine it.

MARTHA. I cannot imagine any thing without an end.

LEMUEL. There is no thing without an end.

CHARLES. My mind is too small to imagine any thing without an end.

MR. ALCOTT. What does an acorn prophesy, or intimate?

ALL. An oak.

MR. ALCOTT. What does a child suggest?

SEVERAL. A man.

MR. ALCOTT. What does a caterpillar foretell?

ALL. A butterfly.

MARTHA. It is impossible to have prophets now.

MR. ALCOTT. Do you think it impossible to have prophets now? (*Some held up hands.*) Who think it is possible to have prophets? (*Several held up hands.*) Now, let me hear those who think it impossible tell their reasons.

GEORGE K. Because there is no need of them. There have been enough to teach people. Now fathers and mothers and others, who can read the prophecies and Gospels, can teach their children, and make them good.

EDWARD B. I think the spirit has gone away from men now, because there are no men good enough to be prophets.

CHARLES. Ever since Jesus was crucified, people have been growing worse and worse, because the goodness that was in the world has been lost, and so there is not faith enough to make a prophet.

MR. ALCOTT. Do any of you think you could get faith enough to make a prophet?

(*Some held up hands. Mr. Alcott made some remarks on prophecy. He then read all the verses that have the word LIGHT in them. What does the light mean? Who was the brightest and most shining spirit that ever took a body; the most full of truth, faith, and love?*)

SOME. Jesus.

SOME. John.

OTHERS. God.

MR. ALCOTT. Has God a body?

SEVERAL. No.

CHARLES. He has a great many bodies.

MR. ALCOTT. What do you say to this — the Universe is the body of God; God has the Universe on him as we have our bodies on us; His spirit supports, feeds, renovates it.

CHARLES. I thought of that, but I did not like it, and so I did not say it.

MR. ALCOTT. How does Jesus light every man?

JOSIAH. We may be compared to candles, and John may be compared to a large candle in the middle of all the rest. And Jesus comes to light all the candles. [13]

WILLIAM B. Jesus is the fire which kindles.

MR. ALCOTT. (*Reading*) "Who was in the world, and the world knew him not?"

SEVERALLY. God. Jesus. John.

MR. ALCOTT. How is God in the world, and the world does not know him?

JOSIAH. The sense is, God is in our spirits, yet cannot be seen, because he is a spirit, which cannot be seen by our outward eyes.

CHARLES. God is in our spirits, but he is nothing to our senses.

MR. ALCOTT. There are some people who think that nothing is to be believed but what is evident to the senses.

CHARLES. Why, that is just the same thing as denying that there is a God.

MR. ALCOTT. (*Reading*) "He came to his own;" to whom?

SEVERALLY. To men. To his own dominion. To our spirits. To both the outward and the inward world.

MR. ALCOTT. (*Reading*) "And his own received him not."

LUCIA. His own family did not believe in him.

SEVERAL. Men did not believe in him.

MR. ALCOTT. What is meant by "Sons of God"?

SEVERALLY. Angels. Our spirits. [14]

MR. ALCOTT. What is meant by "will of the flesh"?

LEMUEL. Appetite.

MR. ALCOTT. What by the "will of man"?

LUCIA. Thought.

MR. ALCOTT. What is the "will of God"?

SEVERALLY. Goodness. Spirit.

MR. ALCOTT. When God's will is in action, what is it called?

CHARLES. Creation.

MR. ALCOTT. What does he create?

SEVERALLY. Happiness, Goodness, Holiness.

MR. ALCOTT. How was the "Word made flesh"?

EMMA. Spirit took a body.

MR. ALCOTT. When was the Word made Flesh in you?

CHARLES. About eleven years ago.

LEMUEL. About nine years ago in me.

MR. ALCOTT. What did we call the Word the other day?

ALL. Spirit.

MR. ALCOTT. What did we call flesh?

ALL. Body.

MR. ALCOTT. How does our spirit manifest to the eyes its existence on earth?

FRANKLIN, LUCIA, &C. By the body.

MR. ALCOTT. Then the use of the body is to show that a particular person exists on earth? And how does this person manifest that love exists in his spirit?

CHARLES. By expression.

SEVERAL. Of the eyes; of the countenance.

MR. ALCOTT. How does kindness show itself to the eyes?

WELLES. By actions; kind actions.

FRANKLIN. By caresses.

MR. ALCOTT. The spirit of Jesus, born of God and having taken a body, is called the only begotten Son of God.

FRANCIS. That means the best.

CHARLES. It was conscience, but our conscience is not the only one.

MR. ALCOTT. Only God can beget conscience, so conscience is called the only begotten of God; and here it speaks of the Word's dwelling among men. Does the Word dwell among you?

CHARLES. Yes; our spirits are the Word.

MR. ALCOTT. What is meant by the Son, "in the bosom of the father"?

FRANCIS. Jesus; in God's love.

MR. ALCOTT. Bosom is then —

LUCIA. An emblem of God's love.

MR. ALCOTT. How many of you think your spirits are in the bosom of God? *(Several do.)*

FRANCIS. If we love God.

MR. ALCOTT. Who has declared God?

ALL. Christ.

MR. ALCOTT. What in you declares God?

SEVERAL. The spirit.

MR. ALCOTT. Have you all this spirit assuring you that God is in you and loves? *(They held up hands.)* Do any of you think so because your parents, teachers, or ministers, say so? *(Many held up hands.)*

ANDREW. I feel it.

MR. ALCOTT. Our subject today has been inspiration, as it was in our last conversation. In our next, we shall speak of outward facts. We are coming to the history of the appearing of spirit on the earth in a body — to its advent.

CONVERSATION V

* * *

ANNUNCIATION OF SPIRIT TO PATERNITY:

Paternal Sentiment

MR. ALCOTT. What has been the subject of our conversations since we began the study of the Gospels?

WILLIAM B. Our spirit.

FRANKLIN. Christ's spirit.

LUCIA. God's spirit.

GEORGE K. Spirit.

WILLIAM B. We spoke of the parts of spirit.

MR. ALCOTT. What were some of its parts?

WILLIAM B. Faith and Love.

GEORGE K. Faith and Love are not parts; they are in Spirit; they are Spirit.

CHARLES. They are not Spirit; they are Truth and Faith.

MR. ALCOTT. There is a word which I have not told you, attributes, qualities.

CHARLES. I was going to say qualities, but I thought it was wrong.

MR. ALCOTT. You might also use the word features; features of spirit.

FRANK. Goodness.

EDWARD B. Truth.

ANDREW. Conscience.

LUCY. The spirit's senses.

MR. ALCOTT. In these four conversations we have spoken of the Ground, Foundation, Idea, and Evidences of Spirit — of the External and Internal Evidences of Spirit. I am now going to read how that spirit — John's spirit, which you have decided came from God — took a body. It was about two thousand years ago, in the country of Judea. See the Map. It was governed by a king called Herod.

VISION OF ZACHARIAS

There was in the days of Herod, the king of Judaea, a certain priest named Zacharias, of the course of Abia: and his wife was of the daughters of Aaron, and her name was Elisabeth. And they were both righteous before God, walking in all the commandments and ordinances of the Lord blameless. And they had no child, because that Elisabeth was barren, and they both were now well stricken in years. And it came to pass, that while he executed the priest's office before God in the order of his course, according to the custom of the priest's office, his lot was to burn incense when he went into the temple of the Lord. And there appeared unto him an angel of the Lord standing on the right side of the altar of incense. And when Zacharias saw him, he was troubled, and fear fell upon him. But the angel said unto him, Fear not, Zacharias: for thy prayer is heard; and thy wife Elisabeth shall bear thee a son, and thou shalt call his name John. And thou shalt have joy and gladness; and many shall rejoice at his birth. For he shall be great in the sight of the Lord, and shall drink neither wine nor strong drinks and he shall be filled with the Holy Ghost, even from his mother's womb. And many of the children of Israel shall he turn to the Lord their God. And he shall go before him in the spirit and power of Elias, to turn the hearts of the fathers to the children, and the disobedient to the wisdom of the just; to make ready a people prepared for the Lord. And Zacharias said unto the angel, whereby shall I know this? for I am an old man, and my wife well stricken in years. And the angel answering said unto him, I am Gabriel, that stand in the presence of God; and am sent to speak unto thee, and to show thee these glad tidings. And behold thou shalt be dumb, and not able to speak, until the day that these things shall be performed, because thou believest not my words, which shall be fulfilled in their season. And the people waited for Zacharias, and marvelled that he tarried so long in the temple. And when he came out he could not speak unto them: and they perceived that he had seen a vision in the temple: for he beckoned unto them and remained speechless. And it came to pass, that, as soon as the days of his ministration were accomplished, he departed to his own house. And after those days his wife Elisabeth conceived, and hid herself five months, saying, thus hath the Lord dealt with me in the days wherein he looked on me, to take away my reproach among men. (Luke 1:5-25.)

(Mr. Alcott then asked the children to tell, what thoughts had entered their minds while he was reading.)

JOSEPH. I couldn't see how Zacharias could tell whether an angel had come or not — for an angel is invisible — and is not to be seen outside, but within.

MR. ALCOTT. Do you think Zacharias made a mistake?

JOSEPH. No, but I don't see how he knew.

GEORGE K. I think Zacharias fell into deep thought, very deep, and an angel came into his thoughts.

CHARLES. He fell into a dream of delight; such as the child did in the "Story without an End," when he saw the image of his unknown parents float before him in mystery.

MR. ALCOTT. What kind of delight did he feel?

CHARLES. Parental delight. I wonder whether Elizabeth knew that she was to have a child.

MR. ALCOTT. Both Zacharias and Elisabeth had prayed to have a child; Elisabeth believed, but Zacharias thought of outward things.

CHARLES. I thought he saw the angel. But I could not understand how it came.

GEORGE B. I thought Zacharias ought to have believed the angel's words.

ALEXANDER. I don't see why the angel made him dumb, except he did not wish Zacharias to tell the people he was going to have a child.

CHARLES. The angels made him dumb because he wanted faith.

GEORGE K. I think his punishment was too great.

MR. ALCOTT. Your sense of justice is violated.

ANDREW. I thought that man wanted to have a child, so he prayed for it, but he did not believe the angel, because he could not see how the angel could know God was going to give him one.

FRANKLIN. I thought he dreamed it.

MR. ALCOTT. Is a dream a reality?

FRANKLIN. Sometimes. It was in this case.

MR. ALCOTT. Franklin may tell me what he means by reality; did Zacharias see reality in his thoughts?

FRANKLIN. I mean the dream came to pass.

CHARLES. All good and holy dreams are real.

MR. ALCOTT. What makes the holy dream? Should you say a bad man could have holy dreams?

CHARLES. A bad man could not have good dreams, for we have often heard that Conscience tormented the bad in their dreams. But these were real dreams, because there is Conscience in them.

MR. ALCOTT. Have any of you had that come to you in dreams which afterwards took place in your life?

(Most held up hands. Others responded to the reverse.)

CHARLES. When I have done something wrong, I have dreamed of punishment, and the punishment came when I was awake.

MR. ALCOTT. Have any of you felt that the dream itself was a punishment, that the foresight of conscience is the retribution of conscience, that the dream punished you? *(Some held up hands.)* I see most of you think so.

CHARLES. Sometimes I have cried out loud, and thought it was real, even while it was a dream.

MR. ALCOTT. I am not aware of any nation on earth which does not believe in dreams — believe that they are prophetic. There are persons who do not, but I never knew of any nation.

CHARLES. There are dreams about outward things.

MR. ALCOTT. There are fancy dreams; but we are not talking of the dreams of superstition.

FRANKLIN. There are some people now who believe in holy dreams.

CHARLES. I do not think that there are such good dreams as there used to be in old times, because men were better then.

MR. ALCOTT. Do any of you think that you are good enough to interpret your own dreams? *(None answered.)* Do any believe there are dreams in which Conscience seems to foretell happiness or punishment? *(Some held up hands.)* Sometimes you expect to go somewhere or see some one, and in your dream you are there and see your friend and have the most delightful time.

FRANKLIN. Sometimes I get up in my sleep.

CHARLES. Sometimes I hug people in my dreams. I did when I came to New York.

SAMUEL R. I dreamed just before Vacation, that I was already at home, and was very much disappointed when I awoke.

MR. ALCOTT. Yes, your heart was singing all the time, "father, mother, brothers, sisters;" and when you went to sleep, your heart's song continued, it still went on, "father, mother, brothers, sisters."

EMMA. I thought last night that mother had got home.

GEORGE K. I dreamed of a visit that I was going to make, that I was there, but when I awoke I found it rained, and I could not go.

NATHAN. I never had any Conscience dreams.

MR. ALCOTT. And I am sorry for it.

CHARLES. It is one way in which my mother punishes me, to talk to me of what I have done that is wrong before I go to sleep, so that my dreams may punish me.

MR. ALCOTT. Dreams are retrospective and prospective. Our thoughts doubtless go on in our sleep. The Soul is ever active.

EDWARD B. I did not see why the angel made Zacharias dumb. I don't wonder he did not believe; he could not tell but it was an evil spirit come to tempt him.

MR. ALCOTT. Do you believe in evil spirits?

EDWARD B. I don't see why evil spirits should not come as well as good ones.

MR. ALCOTT. Have you any such difficulty as Edward has?

CHARLES. No; for he said he was Gabriel.

MR. ALCOTT. But you know evil spirits can tell a lie.

NATHAN. Evil spirits know nothing about God.

FRANKLIN. They don't like to speak of him.

MR. ALCOTT. They are pretty good at language.

NATHAN. Evil spirits could not make little babies come.

CHARLES. No; for babies are all good.

EDWARD J. I don't see how it was right for God to make Zacharias dumb, for God must have made him disbelieve.

EMMA. I should not think the disbelief came from God. God certainly gave Zacharias power to believe.

GEORGE K. Now, Mr. Alcott! Do you think it was right for God to make Zacharias dumb?

MR. ALCOTT. Why do you think it was wrong?

GEORGE K. I don't think Zacharias was wrong in not believing in the angel on the angel's own word. God ought to have convinced Zacharias that it was a good angel. It is not always wrong to doubt. Zacharias, perhaps, could not believe such good news, because he might have thought he was not good enough to have the child. Very good people often think they are worse than they are. I think the angel ought to have explained to Zacharias.

EMMA. Zacharias did not entirely doubt. He asked for a sign, and a sign was given.

EDWARD B. Gabriel made him dumb, not to punish him, but to give him a sign of God's power, and convince him that God could make old people have children, or do any thing.

CHARLES. God always does what is right; but we are not always able to understand it.

MR. ALCOTT. Zacharias' doubts perhaps closed his mouth; so he was not fit to speak.

CHARLES. Yes; but God made him dumb.

MR. ALCOTT. Do you all see it now?

CHARLES. I don't understand it, but I believe it, for my understanding brings up nothing against it.

MR. ALCOTT. Much that appertains to birth, it is impossible to understand, therefore all are dumb upon this subject.

CHARLES. Zacharias could not speak at all.

MR. ALCOTT. He certainly could not speak on that subject. (*Returning to Edward B.'s comment*) But why should not old people have children?

ONE. Because they would not live long enough to bring them up.

LUCIA. Zacharias asked for a sign. His being dumb was a sign.

MR. ALCOTT. *(Reading verse)* "Walking in all the commandments and ordinances of the Lord blameless." What is blameless?

CHARLES. "Blameless" is obedient to conscience.

MR. ALCOTT. How do commandments and ordinances differ?

EDWARD B. A commandment is express, and one will be punished who does not obey. An ordinance is more free; baptism, and Jesus's feasts are ordinances, that may be followed or not.

MR. ALCOTT. *(Reading)*. "His lot was to burn incense." For what?

CHARLES. To carry up the prayers.

SOME. As an emblem.

MR. ALCOTT. What are prayers?

WILLIAM B. Asking God not only with your mouth, but with your heart and spirit, to take care of you, and give you what you need.

MR. ALCOTT. What goes up?

WILLIAM B. Your spirit in faith; your heart in love.

MR. ALCOTT. Is that prayer?

EMMA. You should thank him besides.

MR. ALCOTT. Prayer is the soul, doing what?

EMMA. Communing with God.

MR. ALCOTT. Suppose that in the middle of this room was an altar of marble, and on the altar stood a censer, and in that censer was fire and sweet wood burning, and the sweet incense rose up and went through the temple.

GEORGE. The incense is an emblem —

MR. ALCOTT. — of the aspiration of the soul in prayer. I should like to have that emblem here; it would be very beautiful.

MR. ALCOTT. "And there appeared unto him an angel." Have any of you seen an angel?

FRANKLIN. I have seen one in my soul, but not with my outward eyes.

SEVERAL. So have I.

WILLIAM B. I never saw one in my soul, till I saw Greenough's group.

MR. ALCOTT. Where did that beautiful group of Greenough's first exist?

GEORGE K. In his thought.

MR. ALCOTT. Have all of you seen angels like Franklin? Those may rise who never have seen one even so.

(Joseph, Andrew, and others rose.)

MR. ALCOTT. Andrew, have you seen angels since that time? Did not you rise just now?

ANDREW. Yes.

MR. ALCOTT. Well, I am glad that you have made progress.

CHARLES. Those angels of Greenough's were the most beautiful I ever saw.

MR. ALCOTT. Now I should like to know where the men who make all these beautiful angels first find them. An artist says, Now I will shape a beautiful angel — how must it look? It never was seen. Then he shapes it in his thought; his hands go to work, his thoughts still lingering about it. At last it comes out in the marble. It is very beautiful. It never was seen before.

GEORGE K. It came from his thought.

MR. ALCOTT. The marble statues were not in his thought. Which was in his thought, the marble-angel or the thought-angel?

CHARLES. The thought-angel.

EDWARD B. I think there can be spirits without bodies, but they can only be seen by miracle, as Zacharias saw this one; and such miracles do not happen in these times.

MR. ALCOTT. Do such miracles happen now? *(Several held up hands.)* You may tell what was the miracle in that instance.

CHARLES. That Zacharias thought so much about the little baby that it came when he was old.

MR. ALCOTT. Can you conceive that when God sends a message, a thought into the soul, the mind of the person may give a shape to the message? *(Some thought they could, others, not.)* Might not the Angel, or God's message, be real though invisible, and the mind of

Zacharias give it shape? (*There was a difference of opinion.*) "Thy prayer is heard." What prayer?

SEVERAL. For a child.

(Some conversation ensued on the reasons for joy at the birth of a child. Mr. Alcott described a festival to be held on the birth of a child, emblematic of the causes of our joy in its birth, and suggested thoughts appropriate for that occasion. They all expressed great pleasure in his picture.)

MR. ALCOTT. What does it mean by his being "filled with the Holy Ghost"?

GEORGE K. That he should be full of goodness, love, faith, truth.

MR. ALCOTT. What does Holy Ghost mean?

LUCY. Here it means the word of God.

WILLIAM B. It means, he should believe in the word of God.

AUGUSTINE. Our spirits are the Holy Ghost.

FRANK. A man that has a great deal of truth and goodness is one.

MR. ALCOTT. Are there any holy ghosts in Boston?

FRANK. No *very* holy ghosts here.

MR. ALCOTT. What is meant by his "turning the hearts of the fathers to the children"?

FRANKLIN. The children should turn the hearts of their fathers from idolatry by their goodness.

MR. ALCOTT. How could children turn the hearts of their fathers? How is that possible? Did any of you ever turn the hearts of your parents, by a kind look, a kind action?

CHARLES. I don't think people should say so.

MR. ALCOTT. I have heard of children who have done it; and I am sure I never look upon a baby, without thinking how much better I should probably become could my thoughts linger about it. Could every one have children, they would be better for it; I mean if they took care of them. Perhaps some of you make your parents better. They go out into the world and are tempted, and when they come home and see you, who are not tempted, it makes them better, perhaps.

CHARLES. I can see how little babies have that effect. Parents see that these little babies are perfectly happy because they are perfectly good, and they know they are not happy themselves, and they compare their own conduct with the innocence and purity of their children.

MR. ALCOTT. Are there any idolaters in Boston?

AUGUSTINE. A great many. They worship money.

MR. ALCOTT. Do any of you worship money? (*George B. and Nathan rose.*)

GEORGE K. Was it not George B. who asked, when Jesus overturned the tables of the money changers, what became of the money?

GEORGE B. Yes. I had five cents in copper once, and father took out five cents in silver, and I preferred to take the silver.

MR. ALCOTT. It looked pretty. I have often known a boy to change a rusty cent for a bright one. Imagination affects this subject, and if money were a disagreeable object to the senses, there would not be such a love of it.

FRANKLIN. I often go into a shop with an old fourpence-halfpenny, and exchange it for a bright five-cent piece.

FRANKLIN. Gluttons are idolaters.

EMMA. Their bodies are their idols.

CHARLES. The spiritually minded may make idols of their spirits and neglect their bodies.[15]

MR. ALCOTT. How does Gabriel stand in the presence of God?

FRANK. That means to be good; but I don't see how Gabriel could stand in God's presence, when he had made Zacharias dumb just because he did not believe him.

MR. ALCOTT. You see Frank persists in thinking Zacharias did not make himself dumb. Suppose you should eat too much, and have a fit of sickness in consequence, should you say God, or your doing wrong, made you sick? Would it not be a good plan when any thing happens to yourself to consider, whether there may not be some wrong in you which is the cause?

MR. ALCOTT. Perhaps Zacharias was made dumb, in order that he might not communicate his doubts to others. The paternal sentiment cannot be uttered, its sign is feeling; it is inward. How do feelings get into your minds?

SEVERAL. God sends them.

MR. ALCOTT. Do you take them all?

LUCY. No; we are not good enough.

AUGUSTINE. We have not room enough for all.

MR. ALCOTT. How many of you think your own spirit stands in the presence of God? (Many held up hands.) Why does it?

CHARLES. Because Conscience is always with us.

MR. ALCOTT. When you do wrong — does your spirit stand in the presence of God then?

EMMA. God sees us even then.

MR. ALCOTT. Do we see God then?

WILLIAM B. No; if we did, we should never do wrong. [16]

MR. ALCOTT. Do you think that this vision was in the mind of Zacharias, and that no visible shape appeared to his eyes?

EDWARD B. I do not believe mere imagination could make him dumb.

CHARLES. I don't see why Edward says mere Imagination.

MR. ALCOTT. He was thinking of Imagination in its common interpretation of Fancy. But Imagination is the state of mind that makes us see clearly. It is the Spirit co-working with Reason, with all the energy of the Soul.

(Anecdotes were here told to show Edward B. that a mental condition was always one link in the chain of causes, that produced an outward effect.)

EDWARD B. Yes; I understand now. And I think Zacharias did see the angel within his own spirit.

MR. ALCOTT. *(Reading)* "After those days Elisabeth conceived." What does conceive mean?

LUCY. She found out in her spirit.

MR. ALCOTT. It would not do for children to be born without their parents being prepared to take care of them. Mothers always have signs and feel disposed to keep hidden, or retired, and think about it; and it is right they should, for it is a great thing to have the care of a child. *(Pause.)* Good mothers, spiritually minded mothers, are very happy, when they find a child is going to be given them.

CHARLES. I can't conceive that there can be any mothers who are not good ones.

MR. ALCOTT. There are some mothers who are not thankful for children. They think of the care and trouble these will give them.

CHARLES. I should think a child would always be a pleasure.

MR. ALCOTT. It is to those who understand it. Mothers know as soon as God intends to give them the child, and they retire as Elizabeth did, and think of it a great deal; they make clothes for it; they think how it will look, they often hope it may look like some one they love, and by having beautiful thoughts and feelings they often make it beautiful. But I knew a mother who used to say wicked things because her child was coming. When it was born, and she heard its voice, however, she could not resist it. Afterwards the child died, but she was a better woman ever after. Sometimes God sends bad people very beautiful children, that they may be attracted by outward beauty to look deeper.

GEORGE K. It has been a very interesting conversation this morning.

MR. ALCOTT. How long have we been conversing?

LUCY. I should think about half an hour.

MR. ALCOTT. Why does time seem to be destroyed while we talk?

EMMA. Because we are not thinking of time.

LUCIA. Because we are in eternity.

MR. ALCOTT. Our subjects have but little to do with time. All who have been very much interested may rise. (*All rose smilingly.*) You seem to be deeply interested in this account of the preparation for birth, or the appearing of spirit to the external senses.[17]

CONVERSATION VI

• • •

ANNUNCIATION OF SPIRIT TO MATERNITY:

Chastity

Mr. Alcott called the attention of the children to the subject, and then read:

VISION OF MARY

And in the sixth month the angel Gabriel was sent from God unto a city of Galilee, named Nazareth, to a virgin espoused to a man whose name was Joseph, of the house of David; and the virgin's name was Mary. And the angel came in unto her and said, Hail, thou that art highly favored, the Lord is with thee: blessed art thou among women. And when she saw him, she was troubled at his saying, and cast in her mind what manner of salutation this should be. And the angel said unto her, Fear not, Mary: for thou hast found favor with God. And, behold, thou shalt conceive in thy womb, and bring forth a son, and shalt call his name JESUS. He shall be great, and shall be called the Son of the Highest: and the Lord God shall give unto him the throne of his father David: And he shall reign over the house of Jacob for ever; and of his kingdom there shall be no end.

Then said Mary unto the angel, How shall this be, seeing I know not a man? And the angel answered and said unto her, The Holy Ghost shall come upon thee, and the power of the highest shall overshadow thee; therefore also that holy thing which shall be born of thee shall be called the Son of God. And, behold, thy cousin Elisabeth, she hath also conceived a son in her old age: and this is the sixth month with her who was called barren. For with God nothing shall be impossible. And Mary said, Behold the handmaid of the Lord; be it unto me according to thy word. And the angel departed from her. (Luke 1:26-38.)

(After reading this passage, Mr. Alcott asked the usual question.)

CHARLES. I made a picture in my mind, of the angel's coming to Mary; but I cannot describe it.

LEMUEL. I do not think Gabriel ought to have told Mary until after John was born, because John came to prepare the way.

SAMUEL R. I do not know what was the use of John's coming to announce Jesus.

WELLES. Did Socrates have a forerunner?

MR. ALCOTT. Anaxagoras (you see his bust over the book-case) is thought to have prepared the way for Socrates, by teaching that God was Thought. Others had taught that God was Water or Fire or some material substance. None seem to have had the idea of spirit.

(Here Mr. Alcott said that Socrates might be called a forerunner of Plato and Jesus. All good men prepare for the good that follows. They are bound together as a band of brothers, and shake hands across centuries.)

ANDREW. In old times God spoke in dreams that came to pass. God told Mary in a dream that she was to have a son.

MR. ALCOTT. Does God speak in dreams now?

ANDREW. No; he has spoken enough in dreams in past times.

GEORGE K. And he has spoken by prophets, so that dreams are no longer necessary. Enough has been done and said to make people good if they will be.

MR. ALCOTT. Are people made good?

GEORGE K. Some of them.

MR. ALCOTT. Have enough been made good?

GEORGE K. No; for enough would be all.

FRANKLIN. The Bible is now instead of visions.

WILLIAM B. We can think more. We have more thoughts and better ones, and do not need dreams.

CHARLES. We are better acquainted with our minds than they were.

EDWARD J. Our minds are like God; so we do not need the dreams.

(Mr. Alcott here made some remarks on dreaming; and spoke of a lady, whose conduct for the next day was foretold in a dream, in all its details, the night before; and who believed the dream was sent for her good. A story was also told of a lunatic, who committed murder and arson because he dreamed a great many times, that God commanded him to make a burnt offering and sacrifice; which he interpreted to mean the neighbouring church and its minister; and how he was tried and condemned, but the execution was remitted on account of a general conviction that he was crazy, and how he lived in prison, very contentedly, the rest of his life.)

GEORGE K. God meant some harmless sacrifice and burnt offering. But that man was naughty and made it out so.

MR. ALCOTT. Was it right not to punish him?

GEORGE K. It was right not to kill him, if he was crazy; but to imprison him, where he could do no more mischief.

(The rest held up their hands).

WILLIAM B. Mr. Alcott, I think that man was deceived on account of his own sinfulness; and that no man, who is sinful, ought to be so very sure that his inward feelings are understood by him rightly. Zacharias, you know, had this self distrust, which arose from his knowing that he had sinned. He could not feel sure, even when the vision was really a true one.

MR. ALCOTT. Then you think visions are possible?

WILLIAM B. Oh yes! But only Jesus Christ could feel sure of all his visions, because he only knew that he was perfect.

(Mr. Alcott here spoke of insanity, as originating in want of temperance in the individual, or in his ancestors.)

EDWARD B. It says in the Bible, that the sins of fathers shall be visited on their children.

MR. ALCOTT. And they are visited in this manner; sin produces disease; diseases are inherited from generation to generation. You suffer from evils that were done before you were born. Your diseases were caused not by your parents, perhaps, for they may be suffering from diseases received from others. You may be doing something now which may influence the health of others after you are dead. The evils of no kind of self-indulgence end with one's self. I have known families where diseases have descended for generations. Joseph, what do you think of the reading?

JOSEPH. Mary ought to have believed the angel without asking any questions.

MR. ALCOTT. She asked in surprise, I think, not in doubt. Why was she called "highly favored"?

CHARLES. Because she was to have a holy child.

LUCIA. Because she was good.

FRANK. Because her son was to be a good man.

EMMA. Good mothers all have good children.

LEMUEL and OTHERS. No; my mother is good.

GEORGE K. She was highly favored because she loved, and her child was to love every body, and God.

MR. ALCOTT. Why was he called, "Son of the Highest"?

WILLIAM B. Because he never sinned.

MR. ALCOTT. Do the high never sin?

WILLIAM B. The high in this world do, but not the high in the spiritual world.

MR. ALCOTT. What is meant by, "the throne of his father David"?

CHARLES. Power over Spirit.

MR. ALCOTT. Such power as Napoleon's?

CHARLES. No; that was power over men's bodies. But Jesus had both.

MR. ALCOTT. Those who only aim at the material lose the spiritual. Those who aim at the spiritual attain both.

CHARLES. It does not mean a material throne.

MR. ALCOTT. What does it mean by saying, "of his kingdom shall be no end"?

CHARLES. It is eternal, immortal.

MR. ALCOTT. How do you know that the spirit is eternal, immortal?

CHARLES. Because it is invisible and belongs to God.

MR. ALCOTT. From what does it take its immortality?

FRANKLIN. From good Spirit, from God.

MR. ALCOTT. And from the Human Spirit, which is ever living, and has its Life in itself. Why was this child called the Son of God?

EDWARD J. Because he was like God. Being like God is being his son.

EMMA. The holy spirit is the son of God.

AUGUSTINE. Jesus is the Son of God.

MR. ALCOTT. Such of you as think that the spirit, the power of God, was acting when you were beginning to BE, may rise. (*Half rose; the rest said they did not understand the question.*) Such of you as think that when your fathers and mothers loved each other, and wanted a child of their own to love, God was present and gave a spirit from himself, in answer to their prayer, may rise. (*All rose.*) How should you think a mother would feel, when she knew she was to have a child?

CHARLES. I should think she would feel holy and happy.

MR. ALCOTT. Was Jesus' birth different from common births? (*A few held up hands.*) Those who think there is something like his birth in every birth, may rise. (*All the rest rose.*)

CHARLES. No angel appeared to my mother, but perhaps a thought came to her.

WELLES. I have not yet found out whether angels come in bodies or not.

MR. ALCOTT. What do you think about it?

WELLES. I have always thought that angels were spirits in heaven, but had bodies when sent down on earth.

MR. ALCOTT. Who think angels have bodies, which are as much a part of their life as ours are? (*Some held up hands.*) Was this angel an appearance to Mary's eyes?

CHARLES and SUSAN. Yes.

MR. ALCOTT. Or was it a deep thought in her mind?

THE REST. It was a thought.

ANDREW. Mary saw the angel with her spirit; for the angel came into her spirit, and her imagination gave it a shape.

FREDERIC. When I have been sick I have seen all manner of shapes that my own imagination made.

AUGUSTINE. We are all angels in bodies.

MR. ALCOTT. Do the rest think so? (*All rose.*)

LUCIA. We were all angels when we were babies.

MR. ALCOTT. Why did the angel say to Mary, "The Lord is with thee"?

GEORGE K. I don't know. The Lord is always with us.

ARNOLD. The Lord is with us when we are good.

AUGUSTINE. The Lord is with us when we are bad, or we could not live.

MR. ALCOTT. He then keeps us from destroying ourselves, as we should do if we did wrong continually. "In God we live and move and have our being." You seem to have been much interested today. I am glad these conversations please you so well. On what subject have we been talking this morning?

SEVERAL. Preparing for birth.

MR. ALCOTT. It is a subject upon which more should be said than has been. It should not be thought of, except with the purest and holiest feelings. I am glad to find that your associations regarding it are so pure and worthy.

CONVERSATION VII

* * *

INCARNATION OF SPIRIT:

Gestation

Mr. Alcott remarked on the subject of the last conversation, and began with the reading:

INTERVIEW BETWEEN MARY AND ELISABETH

And Mary arose in those days, and went into the hill country with haste, into a city of Judah; and entered into the house of Zacharias and saluted Elisabeth. And it came to pass, that, when Elisabeth heard the salutation of Mary, the babe leaped in her womb: and Elisabeth was filled with the Holy Ghost. And she spake out with a loud voice, and said, Blessed art thou among Women, and blessed is the fruit of thy womb. And whence is this to me, that the mother of my Lord should come to me? For, lo, as soon as the voice of thy salutation sounded in mine ears, the babe leaped in my womb for joy. And blessed is she that believed: for there shall be a performance of those things which were told her from the Lord.

And Mary said,

My soul doth magnify the Lord, and my spirit hath rejoiced in God my Saviour. For he hath regarded the low estate of his handmaiden. For behold, from henceforth all generations shall call me blessed. For he that is mighty hath done to me great things; And holy is his name. And his mercy is on them that fear him from generation to generation. He hath showed strength with his arm; he hath scattered the proud in the imagination of their hearts. He hath put down the mighty from their seats, and exalted them of low degree. He hath filled the hungry with good things, and the rich he hath sent empty away. He hath holpen his servant Israel, in remembrance of his mercy, as he spake to our fathers, to Abraham, and to his seed for ever. And Mary abode with her about three months, and returned to her own house. (Luke 1:39-56.)

(Mr. Alcott then asked, what does the word "Salutation" mean?)

GEORGE K. Talk.

LUCY. Greeting.

CHARLES. Can we not salute a person angrily?

SEVERAL. No; salute means a welcome.

RECORDER. The Latin word sal-u-te means in health.

MR. ALCOTT. Why did Elisabeth feel so sure of having a child, when Mary saluted her?

GEORGE K. I suppose Mary told her of her vision.

FREDERIC. Elisabeth knew by Mary's countenance.

WILLIAM B. And by her whole manner.

MR. ALCOTT. What filled Elisabeth with the Holy Ghost?

CHARLES. She was glad to have a good child; that made her full of spirit. It was called a holy spirit, because she was full of love, joy, hope, and faith.

ALEXANDER. It made her spirit holy to see, by Mary's countenance, that she was to have such a child.

MR. ALCOTT. Do you think Elisabeth's spirit was made holy by Mary's salutation being filled with so much gladness? *(All held up their hands.)* What is the expression of the countenance when a person is full of joy?

(Here Mr. Alcott asked about the expressions of joy, and all the children told how they felt at meeting friends; and Charles said that we did not know what to do when we were joyful.)

MR. ALCOTT. We feel as if something was done to us. Where does joy come from?

CHARLES. From the heart.

MR. ALCOTT. How does it come into the heart?

CHARLES. From the Spirit.

MR. ALCOTT. What is meant by the word *quicken?*

CHARLES. Enliven — you say "quickening ray."

MR. ALCOTT. Yes, and we say, "the quick and the dead." Jesus quickened men. Joy quickens the heart. When Mary's salutation sounded on Elisabeth's ear, she felt that the child promised was hers. It was quickened into being. This always takes place some time before a child is born. Why did Elisabeth speak "with a loud voice"?

LUCIA. Because she was glad.

MR. ALCOTT. Was it a rough, unpleasant voice?

LUCIA. No; it was sweet.

MR. ALCOTT. The voice has its meaning also. Why was Mary called blessed?

AUGUSTINE. Because she was going to bring forth something blessed.

JOHN B. The Son of God.

MR. ALCOTT. Were your mothers the mothers of God's children?

CHARLES. I am not God's son, but we all belong to him. I am naughty.

MR. ALCOTT. When you were born, I mean.

(Most of them rose, but Charles persisted he was not.)

SAMUEL R. I am not, now.

MR. ALCOTT. Do you never think of God as your Father? When you say the Lord's prayer, and say "our Father," do you not think of him as your Father?

CHARLES. Yes; I am my father's son, and Jesus was God's Son.

MR. ALCOTT. I know we have an earthly father; but did your earthly father make your soul?

CHARLES. No; God made my body and soul too, and gave me to my father and mother.

GEORGE K. Jesus was the only good Son.

MR. ALCOTT. Are all the bad sons the sons of earthly parents?

GEORGE K. All our goodness is the son of God, and the badness is not the son of God.

MR. ALCOTT. What does blessed mean?

LUCIA. To be happy.

CHARLES. To have a particular feeling from God.

MR. ALCOTT. What does it mean by, "Blessed is the fruit"?

FRANK. Blessed is the child.

MR. ALCOTT. Through which part of us does God bless us?

ANDREW. Through our spirits.

MR. ALCOTT. Do you ever feel blessed?

ANDREW. No.

GEORGE and EMMA. Yes; when we have done right.

CHARLES. Yes; when I think of my parents, and the good house I have to live in, and my clothes, and the good school I go to.

MR. ALCOTT. These are blessings, but go farther inward — blessedness is within you.

CHARLES. I don't think that doing right blesses us. It is our duty to do right. My conscience never blessed me, but sometimes lets me receive blessings; but they come from God afterwards.

MR. ALCOTT. Is not God always ready to bless? Does not being blessed depend on you?

CHARLES. Perhaps it does; but the blessing is something else than being prepared for it.

MR. ALCOTT. Do you carry your heart into every thing?

CHARLES. I never knew any body but Jesus whose heart went into every thing.

MR. ALCOTT. Did you never feel repose, quiet, as if you were living in God?

CHARLES. No; because I am always wanting something.

MR. ALCOTT. But were your heart in what you did, you would feel this repose, this blessedness.

(Mr. Alcott gave a paraphrase from the reading: "The babe seemed to be in my arms.")

LUCIA. That was because she was so glad to see Mary.

(Lucy, Charles, and Lemuel described the pleasure of meeting their fathers after an absence.)

MR. ALCOTT. Did something within make you run up to your father, Lemuel, when you saw him?

LEMUEL. Yes.

MR. ALCOTT. Was it a holy spirit or an unholy one?

LEMUEL. A holy spirit, full of love.

EMMA. I never can speak at such times.

(All wanted to speak on this subject, but Mr. Alcott said there was not time.)

MR. ALCOTT. What does love make?

LUCIA. Obedience.

GEORGE K. Happiness.

FRANK. Holiness.

MR. ALCOTT. Does it not make something to love? If you want love, what must you do?

CHARLES. You must begin and love.

MR. ALCOTT. Love begets love, and is not a baby love made flesh and shaped to the eyes? Love forms babies. Could bad passions make the soul of a baby?

CHARLES. Bad people have children.

MR. ALCOTT. But would not the children be better if their parents were better?

CHARLES. Yes; after they were born and could follow their example.

GEORGE K. I think that the baby's goodness has something to do with the goodness of the father and mother, and their badness makes its badness.

SAMUEL R. I don't think there are any bad babies.

MR. ALCOTT. No bad spirits; but if the spirits are surrounded with bodies diseased, do you think they have as good chance to be immediately good?

CHARLES. Oh no; I think the spirit will not have near so good a chance if it has a bad body.

MR. ALCOTT. Suppose you want to have a beautiful flower; you have the seed and you want to plant it; do you think nothing of the soil in which it is to grow? Do you not fill your flower pot with the finest, freshest soil, and put it in the sunshine?

CHARLES. Yes; and water it and tend it, and watch over it very carefully.

MR. ALCOTT. And do you think it is equally important in what soil a soul is planted?

SEVERAL. Yes.

MR. ALCOTT. The parents have much to do in regard to the body of a child. God helps, as he does about the rose seed. The Body is the Soil of the Soul. The heart, when thus full of life and joy, is said to be quickened. Mothers feel this when they know children are to be given to them. The angel of love first tells a mother that a child is coming. Sometime after she has other signs. "Blessed is she that believed, for there shall be a performance to her of those things told by the Lord." What does that mean? (*No answer.*) Faith brings out what is planted in the spirit into the external world.[18] What is, "magnifying the Lord"? (*No answer.*) Is it doing right or saying words?

SEVERAL. Doing right.

LUCY. I think when we do right we magnify our own spirits.

LUCIA. We cannot magnify God; we cannot even show all of God out in our spirits.

EMMA. It does not mean that you can magnify God himself, but every body, when they do right, makes God seem greater to themselves.

CHARLES. I think as our spirits are a part of God, when we do right we magnify God.

MR. ALCOTT. What does she mean by, "he has regarded the low estate of his handmaid"?

LUCY. It means, she thought she was not good, and God had made her better.

MR. ALCOTT. What is low estate?

ALEXANDER. Humbleness.

WILLIAM B. She had not outward riches.

LUCY. I thought low estate meant wickedness.

MR. ALCOTT. Why should "all generations call her blessed"?

CHARLES. The Catholics call her Blessed Virgin all the time, so that is fulfilled.

MR. ALCOTT. Is your mother blessed?

CHARLES. No; not to have such a son.

MR. ALCOTT. I do not ask whether the son is worthy of her, but whether she is worthy to have a son.

CHARLES. She would not be very worthy, if she was not worthy to have me.

MR. ALCOTT. All mothers might be blessed. And here, nearly two thousand years after, in Boston (very far from Judea) a company of children are repeating those words, and calling her blessed! These words are a quotation from the Hebrew prophets. It is a part of one of those prophetic poems that she quoted, because it seemed to apply to herself. And how well it does apply! Why does it seem to her that "he hath showed strength with his arm"?

WILLIAM B. Because Mary was nothing very great till she had this gift.

MR. ALCOTT. What is the "imagination of the proud"?

LUCY. The love of earthly, worldly riches.

MR. ALCOTT. How had he "filled the hungry"?

LUCIA. It was the hungry for spiritual food.

MR. ALCOTT. (Reading) "As he spake to our fathers, to Abraham." What had he said to Abraham?

LUCIA. He had said, "Count the stars; thy children shall become as numerous".

MR. ALCOTT. How long did Mary stay?

SEVERAL. Three months.

MR. ALCOTT. How do you suppose they passed their time?

MARTHA. In conversation about the angels, and about what their sons should be.

LUCIA. And about what their sons should do.

WILLIAM B. How they should take care of their children's spirits.

CHARLES. And how the Lord had blessed them.

MR. ALCOTT. Do you think it was a happy three months?

LUCIA. I should think it would have passed quickly.

LUCY. I should think Mary would have stayed longer.

GEORGE K. I shouldn't; I think she would want to go home and see about her own house.

GEORGE. I should think she would have wanted to see her husband.

MR. ALCOTT. Have any of you more to say about this visit of Mary's?

(*Some conversation ensued about her age, and it was observed that she probably was very young.*)

MR. ALCOTT. They doubtless did as all mothers should before so great an event as the birth of a spirit on the earth. In our next conversation we shall come to the birth of John the Baptist.

CONVERSATION VIII

* * *

NATIVITY OF SPIRIT:

Family Relation

Mr. Alcott began by asking what was the conversation upon the last time and then he read:

THE BIRTH AND NAMING OF JOHN THE BAPTIST

Now Elisabeth's full time came that she should be delivered: and she brought forth a son. And her neighbours and her cousins heard how the Lord had showed great mercy upon her; and they rejoiced with her. And it came to pass, that on the eighth day they came to circumcise the child; and they called him Zacharias, after the name of his father. And his mother answered and said, Not so; but he shall be called John. And they said unto her, There is none of thy kindred that is called by this name. And they made signs to his father, how he would have him called. And he asked for a writing-tablet, and wrote, saying, His name is John. And they marvelled all. And his mouth was opened immediately, and his tongue loosed, and he spake and praised God. And fear came on all that dwelt round about them: and all these sayings were noised abroad throughout all the hill country of Judea. And all they that heard them laid them up in their hearts, saying, What manner of child shall this be! And the hand of the Lord was with him. And his father Zacharias was filled with the Holy Ghost, and prophesied, saying, Blessed be the Lord God of Israel; For he hath visited and redeemed his people, And hath raised up an horn of salvation for us, In the house of his servant David; as he spake by the mouth of his holy prophets, which have been since the world began: That we should be saved from our enemies, And from the hand of all that hate us: To perform the mercy promised to our fathers, and to remember his holy convenant; the oath which he sware to our father Abraham, that he would grant unto us, that we, being delivered out of the hand of our enemies, might serve him without fear, in holiness and righteousness before him, all the days of our life. And thou, child, shalt be called the prophet of the Highest, for thou shalt go before the face of the Lord to prepare his ways; To give knowledge of salvation unto his people, by the remission of their sins, through the tender mercy of our God; Whereby the day-spring from on high hath visited us, To give light to them that sit in darkness and in the shadow of death; To guide our feet into the way of peace, And the child grew, and waxed strong in spirit, and was in the deserts till the day of his showing unto Israel. (Luke 1:57 to the end.)

MR. ALCOTT. Now what came into your minds while I was reading?

JOSIAH. The deserts seemed to me a great space covered with sand, like that in the hour-glass. The sun was shining on it, and making it sparkle. There were no trees. John was there alone.

EDWARD J. I thought the deserts meant woods, with paths here and there.

LUCY. I thought of a space covered with grass and some wild flowers, and John walking about.

CHARLES. I thought of a prairie.

ALEXANDER. I thought of a rocky country.

AUGUSTINE. I thought of a few trees scattered over the country, with bees in the trunks.

GEORGE K. I thought of a place without houses, excepting John's; and flowers, trees, and bee-hives.

MR. ALCOTT. I should like to hear all your pictures, but as I have not time, you may tell me now what interested you most?

CHARLES. The prophecy of Zacharias.

LUCIA. Elisabeth's saying the child's name must be John.

LUCY. Zacharias finding his speech again.

ANDREW. The birth of the child.

MR. ALCOTT. How was it?

ANDREW. I thought, one night, as Elisabeth was sleeping, an angel brought her a child, and made her dream she had one, and she awoke and it was lying at her side.

WILLIAM B. I think he was born like other children except that Elisabeth had visions.

MR. ALCOTT. Do any of you think your mothers had visions of you?

(Several.)

GEORGE K. I thought God sent an angel to give her a child. It cried as soon as it came and waked up its mother to give it something to eat.

LUCIA. When John was first born, his mother did not know it, for he was born in the night; but she found it by her side in the morning.

CHARLES. Elisabeth must have had some vision as well as Zacharias, or how could she know the child was theirs? Zacharias could not speak.

NATHAN. I don't see why John came in the night. All other children come in the day.

MR. ALCOTT. No; more frequently in the night. God draws a veil over these sacred events, and they ought never to be thought of except with reverence. The coming of a spirit is a great event. It is greater than death. It should free us from all wrong thoughts. And now I don't want you to speak; but to hold up your hands, if you have ever heard any disagreeable or vulgar things about birth. *(None raised hands.)* Men have been brought before Courts of Justice for saying vulgar things about the birth of Christ; and all birth is sacred as Jesus Christ's. And I have heard of children saying very profane things about it; and have heard fathers and mothers do so. I hope that none of us will ever violate the sacredness of this subject. What is meant by "delivered"?

WILLIAM B. She delivered her child to Zacharias.

OTHERS. No; God delivered the child to Elisabeth.

CHARLES. Elisabeth's thoughts made the child's soul, and when it was fairly born she was delivered from the anxiety of the thought.

MR. ALCOTT. Yes, the deliverance of the spirit is the first thing.

And I am glad to find, that you have so strong an impression of that. The physiological facts, sometimes referred to, are only a sign of the spiritual birth. You have seen the rose opening from the seed with the assistance of the atmosphere; this is the birth of the rose. It typifies the bringing forth of the spirit, by pain, and labor, and patience.[19] Edward B., it seems, has some profane notions of birth, connected with some physiological facts; but they are corrected here. Did you ever hear this line, "The throe of suffering is the birth of bliss"?

GEORGE K. Yes; it means that Love, and Joy, and Faith, lead you to have suffering which makes more happiness for you.

MR. ALCOTT. Yes; you have the thought. And a mother suffers when she has a child. When she is going to have a child, she gives up her body to God, and he works upon it, in a mysterious way, and with her aid, brings forth the Child's Spirit in a little Body of its own, and when it has come, she is blissful. But I have known some mothers who are so timid that they are not willing to bear the pain; they fight against God, and suffer much more.

CHARLES. I should think it ought to be the father, he is so much stronger.

MR. ALCOTT. He suffers because it is his part to see the suffering in order to relieve it. But it is thought, and with good reason, that if there were no wrong doing there would be no suffering attending this mysterious act. When Adam and Eve did wrong, it was said that Adam should earn bread by the sweat of his brow, and Eve have pain in bringing her children into the world. We never hear of trees groaning to put forth their leaves.

CHARLES. They have no power to do wrong.

MR. ALCOTT. True; God only gives them power to put forth, and they do it without pain. A rose has no pain in being born. (*Pause.*) You may give me some emblems of birth.

ALEXANDER. Birth is like the rain. It comes from heaven.

LEMUEL. Lives streamed from the ocean first; now smaller streams from the larger ones, and so on.

SAMUEL R. Birth is like the rising light of the sun; the setting is death.[20]

ANDREW. God's wind came upon the ocean of life, and washed up the waters a little into a channel, and that is birth. They run up farther, and that is living.

MR. ALCOTT. I should like to have all your emblems but have not time. There is no adequate sign of birth in the outward world, except the physiological facts that attend it, with which you are not acquainted. Why did they call the child John?

SEVERAL. Because the angel told them to.

RECORDER. The Hebrew word John means gift of God. They felt he was so kindly given that they called him Gift.

(Here Mr. Alcott asked if every child was not a gift of God. They assented, and then there was some conversation upon names, and their own names were traced.)

MR. ALCOTT. Why was it "noised abroad"?

SEVERAL. It was a great event to have a child born from such old parents.

MR. ALCOTT. And in the country, especially a hilly country, the people being imaginative, seem quite disposed to look beyond external things. They are apt to think singular events typify, or are a sign of, something supernatural.

CHARLES. Why in a hilly country more than any where else?

GEORGE K. Because they see more and have more imagination.

NATHAN. One can't have imagination in a city.

CHARLES. Some country fellows are very stupid.

MR. ALCOTT. That is true; but still the country affords advantages which the city does not. Should you not like to have more mountains and valleys and streams about Boston?

ANDREW. Yes; a great many more.

(Mr. Alcott spoke of the effect of the Ocean on himself, seen first, when he was twelve years old.)

MR. ALCOTT. But in that hilly country, they wondered what kind of child this would be. How had the Lord "visited his people"? Does the Lord visit his people now?

CHARLES. Yes; in little babies.

MR. ALCOTT. Every one is a visitor on the Earth from the Lord. I hope you will all be pleasant visitors. Some visitors are very unpleasant; they do not like what is given them to eat and drink; they do not like the beds they lie on. Do you think a drunkard is a pleasant visitor? Is he doing what he is sent to do?

(They all laughed.)

EMMA. I am not a very pleasant visitor, but I have a very pleasant visit.

LEMUEL. He had visited their spirits.

FRANKLIN. By sending John to tell that Jesus was coming.

MR. ALCOTT. What is it to redeem a people?

LUCIA. To make them good.

EDWARD B. To save them from sin.

MR. ALCOTT. A man who loves to eat and drink, an intemperate man, a passionate man, is a slave to the body; and when his spirit is released from his body, by renewing thoughts, that withdraw his attention from his body, he is redeemed, just as a prisoner taken out of a dungeon is said to be redeemed from captivity. How many of you are redeemed?

NATHAN. I am not quite, but almost.

MR. ALCOTT. What is it to "sit in darkness"?

CHARLES. To be wicked.

MR. ALCOTT. Tell me what the shadow of death means. Would there be any shadow without light? Which was made first, light or darkness?

CHARLES. Darkness. It seems to me that there was darkness first; I can't think otherwise.

MR. ALCOTT. Is darkness real, positive? I thought darkness was the shadow of light. What if the sun should be put out?

ANDREW. Then there would be darkness.

NATHAN. When there is darkness we would not know it if light had not been first.

MR. ALCOTT. Which of you think light came first? If light made the darkness, then if there had been no light there would have been no darkness. When the light goes out of this room does any thing come in?

CHARLES. Yes; darkness comes in.

MR. ALCOTT. Nothing comes in; and I cannot conceive of there not being light. Darkness is the absence of light to our external senses.

MR. ALCOTT. If John was the day-spring, who was the risen sun?

ALL. Jesus.

MR. ALCOTT. What is it to "wax strong in spirit"?

CHARLES. To stand fast by God.

FRANKLIN. To grow better and better.

EDWARD B. Why are Jews held in such contempt, when Jesus was born a Jew.

FRANKLIN. Because they killed Jesus, and said, "his blood be on us and our children."

MR. ALCOTT. Who think it is a wicked prejudice?

ALL. There are no right prejudices.

MR. ALCOTT. What has been the subject of this conversation?

NATHAN. Putting spirits into bodies.

MR. ALCOTT. And the nativity, or birth of spirit in the flesh.

CONVERSATION IX

* * *

MARRIAGE OF SPIRIT:

Conjugal Relation

Mr. Alcott began the conversation with the reading:

VISION OF JOSEPH

Now the birth of Jesus Christ was on this wise: When as his mother Mary was espoused to Joseph, before they came together, she was found with child of the Holy Ghost. Then Joseph her husband, being a just man, and not willing to make her a public example, was minded to put her away privily. But while he thought on these things, behold the angel of the Lord appeared unto him in a dream, saying, Joseph, thou son of David, fear not to take unto thee Mary thy wife: for that which is conceived in her is of the Holy Ghost. And she shall bring forth a son, and thou shalt call his name JESUS: for he shall save his people from their sins. Now all this was done, that it might be fulfilled which was spoken of the Lord by the prophet, saying, Behold, a virgin shall be with child, and shall bring forth a son, and they shall call his name Emmanuel, which being interpreted is, God with us. Then Joseph being raised from sleep did as the angel of the Lord had bidden him, and took unto him his wife: And he knew her not till she had brought forth her firstborn son: and he called his name JESUS. (Matt. 1:18 to the end.)

(After the reading Mr. Alcott asked what interested them most.)

JOSIAH. I thought most of Jesus' being born.

MR. ALCOTT. And what did you think being born was?

JOSIAH. It is to take up the body from the earth. The spirit comes from heaven, and takes up the naughtiness out of other people, which makes other people better. And these naughtinesses put together make a body for the child; but the spirit is the best part of it.[21]

(Here Mr. Alcott asked if there was anything to be said on Josiah's idea.)

NATHAN. I think Jesus was good at first, body and all, and he made the body better while he lived.

MR. ALCOTT. Yes; I know that some of you thought that Jesus was so good that his body went to heaven.

GEORGE K. I don't think there was any naughtiness in him, or in any babies, but when they do wrong it comes, and they repent, and are born again.

MR. ALCOTT. Does repentance make the body perfect again? Temperance would keep it good. I want to ask you about Josiah's idea, which is, that the body is made out of the naughtiness of other people.

ANDREW. I can't think that it takes the naughtiness away from other people, because it is all good at first.

MARTHA. I think just as Andrew does.

CHARLES. I don't see what Josiah means.

SAMUEL R. I don't think bodies are either bad or good.

NATHAN. It don't take the bad away from other people, but gets bad itself.

MR. ALCOTT. What is birth?

CHARLES. Putting the spirit into a body; having the body put round the spirit.

MR. ALCOTT. But where is the body taken from?

CHARLES. I don't know.

GEORGE B. I think people get bad, and when they get bad they throw away their goodness, and God takes the goodness and makes it up into little babies.

NATHAN. God makes the body and does not put any goodness into it, and then the spirit comes and makes the body better.

MR. ALCOTT. I want all of you to account for the origin of the body.

How is the body made, Charles, what does it come from?

CHARLES. I don't know any better way to say, than the old way in the Bible, that it was made out of the dust.

MR. ALCOTT. Which is as much as to say you have no opinion at all of your own.

GEORGE K. It is a spirit coming into the body. God makes the body. The spirit always was. It was not made at that time. When you do wrong and repent, you are born again.

MR. ALCOTT. I will now tell you what I think. The spirit makes the body just as the rose throws out the rose leaves. I cannot tell you how the rose leaves come out of the rose. But I think the spirit throws the body out. The body is the outside of the spirit — the spirit made visible. I don't think God made my spirit and then my body, and brought them together, but I think that God makes my soul, and my soul all the time makes my body, just as something in the rose seed makes the rose leaves.

EDWARD C. I thought I saw Jesus come down from heaven, when you read.

WILLIAM B. When mothers have children they are always good, better than at other times. Mary's vision had made her good —better than other people, and so her child was better.

LUCY. I liked the angel's appearing to Joseph and telling him not to be afraid.

SAMUEL T. It was beautiful where the angel came to Joseph in a dream.

AUGUSTINE. The birth was so peculiar, because the child was different, more holy than other children. If such a child should come again, there would be the same signs and wonders, that the father and mother might get ready to take care of it.

MR. ALCOTT. Suppose you knew all that happened before you were born, and all the interest God took in it, and all that the angels took in it; do you think you should have known any thing as wonderful as these things?

CHARLES. I don't think near so much would happen.

MR. ALCOTT. Who knows but the same wonders are going on in

every case of birth, and that we are mistaken in supposing that this account of birth belonged to Jesus alone, rather than was an emblem of all birth?

EMMA. I think the outward facts were different, because he was born in a different place and under different circumstances; but there was no other difference.

NATHAN. I don't think they all felt the same when I was born as when Jesus Christ was, because I am not as good as Jesus was.

MR. ALCOTT. All may rise, who think with Emma, that some outward circumstances were different. (All rose.)

CHARLES. I should think Mary would feel rather more, because she knew what a great son she was going to have.

MR. ALCOTT. Perhaps it was Mary's idea that she was going to have a Saviour in her son; and her faith in the thought, that brought this message to her, made him what he was, or helped to do so, together with Joseph's constancy to her.

CHARLES. I don't think it is so, because it says, Joseph was going to put off Mary.

MR. ALCOTT. But he did not put her off.

CHARLES. Because an angel came to him in a dream.

MR. ALCOTT. And he trusted in the inward thought and feeling of his dream. Suppose your parents had thought, before you were born, that you were to be a Reformer, and had kept this thought unwaveringly uppermost, and their friends had sympathized with them in this, and all circumstances had been arranged in reference to it?

CHARLES. I do not think I should have been a Messiah.

ALEXANDER. The angel came, so that Mary and Joseph might become good; so that they could teach their child, lest he should have faults.

JOHN B. I imagined the angel, but I cannot put my idea into words.

FRANK. The angel ought to have told Joseph that it would be wrong for him not to marry Mary, after he had promised to.

MR. ALCOTT. Frank is very decided; he tells what God ought to do;

he thinks God does wrong, for he does not see the spiritual fact.

EDWARD B. I thought of Joseph lying on a splendid bed in a splendid room. And the angel had on a white glistening robe, flowing round his feet, and a golden girdle round his waist, and a glittering crown and wand, and flaxen hair over his shoulders, and he told Joseph to keep his promise.

RECORDER. How could a poor carpenter in Nazareth, have a splendid room?

EDWARD B. An angel would not come into a poor looking room. It would not be appropriate.

RECORDER. Do they never visit poor men's huts?

(After some conversation, Edward seemed to think, that such outward splendors were not particularly appropriate to angels, at least, upholstery.)

MR. ALCOTT. Was this angel in Joseph's mind or out of it?

EDWARD B. There was a real angel, but different persons' imaginations would have shaped him differently. I believe there are different kinds of angels: Some are to be born as men; some are ministering angels, who had lived in bodies once; some who like Gabriel, have never had a body, and never will have one. These are called visiting angels.

EDWARD J. I wonder why the angel did not tell Joseph to marry Mary before?

MR. ALCOTT. Did he not tell him what to do, as soon as he began to inquire what he should do?

EDWARD J. I should think the father would know about the child's coming, as soon as the mother.

MR. ALCOTT. Mothers always know first.

EDWARD J. Yes; because they have most to do with the children.

(Here Mr. Alcott spoke of the Maternal Sense, and made it one with the Maternal Love that watches over infancy like a second Providence — God made visible to protect; and asked them if they felt differently towards their fathers and mothers. None thought

they loved one better than the other; but some said they felt differently. Charles, and Nathan, and others, said they felt exactly alike about them.)

MR. ALCOTT. How do you know, Charles, which you are feeling about?

CHARLES. I know which I am thinking about. I feel about them exactly alike.

GEORGE K. I thought about Joseph's kindness to Mary. I think that he always let her choose about things, what they should have for dinner, and such things; and when he had any thing, he always gave it to her, and would go anywhere to carry things when she asked him to. I think Joseph had a good room, because he was a carpenter, and could make everything; but I think an angel would be more likely to go to a poor person's house, because the poor are generally happier.

MR. ALCOTT. Do any of the rest of you think as George does, that the poor are happiest? *(All expressed the Idea that the poor were happier than the rich.)* Why?

CHARLES. Because they have not so many chances, and anxieties, and do not have to think about so many bills.

GEORGE K. The poor are not tempted so much to do wrong.

EMMA. I think the rich can be as happy as the poor.

MR. ALCOTT. Those, who think neither riches nor poverty make happiness, may stand up. *(All rose.)* What does happiness depend on?

CHARLES. On the state of mind.

MR. ALCOTT. Name the state of mind.

SAMUEL R. Conscience must be at peace.

MR. ALCOTT. Happiness depends on the state of mind first, and secondly on the use we make of it. But should you go out in the street and ask people as you meet them, thus — Man! are riches essential to happiness? Certainly, he would say. Madam! are riches essential to happiness? Why, how can you ask such a question! Boy! do you think riches essential to happiness? Oh yes! — how could I have good dinners and rich clothes, without riches? I am very glad that you, so early in life, have learnt the true view of this subject. And now I want each of you to ask yourselves this — Are my father and mother spiritual persons — are they devoted to the culture of their own and other people's spirits, as much as they should be, or do they care more than I wish about outward things? I do not wish you to tell me.

NATHAN. I am sure I don't know.

(None of the rest answered.)

CHARLES. I was interested in the angel's coming to tell Joseph that he need not fear to marry Mary.

MR. ALCOTT. Why do you think Joseph doubted about it?

CHARLES. Because he thought Mary was too holy for him, and he did not want to have the child be the son of a carpenter's wife, lest people should not think so much of him.

ANDREW. I think the reason the angel told him to marry Mary was, because she was going to have such a holy child, who would make him a better man.

LUCIA. I thought of Joseph walking in the fields, where there was grass and flowers. He was thinking about marrying Mary, and he lay down and went to sleep, and an angel came, with glistening hair and robes, and a dove on each shoulder, and told him to marry Mary.

MR. ALCOTT. Was he alone?

LUCIA. Yes; there was no other person holy enough to know any thing about it.

MR. ALCOTT. How did the angel look to you?

LUCIA. As small as an infant, and had a smile like a child, and his words sounded like music.

MR. ALCOTT. Do you generally think of angels as infants?

ALL. I do! I do!

MR. ALCOTT. One of the prophets, speaking of a great era, a renovation of things by the spirit, said it would bring God among men. And Matthew quoted these words, saying, that they were fulfilled, when Jesus was born, for he was a God among men. Is God with you?

MARTHA. I think "God with us" means that we have Spirit, and God is in our spirit.

ANDREW. God is in our conscience.

MR. ALCOTT. Does God come to every Parent when the Baby comes? *(Most rose.)* How many of you have lost the God you brought with you? Do those that sit around me now, have as much of God in them as they would have had? *(No answer.)* Is God with us when we walk out and see the ocean, and mountains, and streams? *(All assented.)* God is with us even in our passion; we take his strength to destroy ourselves; we turn God round against himself.

GEORGE K. He is spiritually with all good men. It says, in a book which I have at home —

> If I could find some cave unknown,
>   Where human feet had never trod,
> Yet there I should not be alone,
>   On every side there would be God.

FRANK. If you call Jesus "God," and God "God," I think there would be two Gods, and that is the same as worshipping statues.

AUGUSTINE. I think that Jesus and God are not two but one. If we were to say Jesus, or to say God, we should mean the same thing, only Jesus is God in a body.

JOHN B. I think the same.

GEORGE K. God is God; Jesus is Godlike.[2223]

MARTHA. I think Jesus is Godlike.

CHARLES. I think he is God.

MR. ALCOTT. Who think Jesus is Godlike? *(All rose.)* Who think Jesus is God? *(Martha, Nathan and George K. sat down.)* You, who are standing, think Jesus is Godlike and God also?

GEORGE K. I think he is *only* Godlike.

MR. ALCOTT. Is God with us? (*All held up hands.*) What is the most striking fact that proves God is with us?

EMMA. God is with us, because he speaks to us through our Conscience.

MR. ALCOTT. How many think our life is God?

AUGUSTINE. God makes our life.

MR. ALCOTT. How many think our love is God?

GEORGE K. Some of God, not all.

MR. ALCOTT. How many think our faith is God?

AUGUSTINE. The spirit is flowing over us, and what we get is God in us.

MR. ALCOTT. Is our body God in any sense?

GEORGE K. It is God's work.

MR. ALCOTT. All may rise who think there is any sense in which the body is God. (*No one rose.*) All may rise who think there is no sense in which that can be said. (*All rose.*) I think there is a sense in which the body may be called God.

CHARLES. I wish you would explain how.

MR. ALCOTT. I cannot, because you cannot look through Physiology; and the language is liable to misconstruction. George spoke very well, when he called it God's work. Our next conversation will be on the birth of Jesus, which point in his history we have now reached. We have seen what preparations God makes in order to bring a spirit into the world, and make it visible to our eyes, by clothing it in flesh.

CONVERSATION X

• • •

ADVENT OF SPIRIT:

Infancy

Mr. Alcott remarked on the taxing, and read:

THE BIRTH OF JESUS

And it came to pass in those days, that there went out a decree from Caesar Augustus, that all the world should be taxed. (And this taxing was first made when Cyrenius was governor of Syria.) And all went to be taxed, every one into his own city. And Joseph also went up from Galilee, out of the city of Nazareth, into Judaea, unto the city of David, which is called Bethlehem (because he was of the house and lineage of David): To be taxed with Mary his espoused wife, being great with child.

And so it was, that, while they were there, the days were accomplished that she should be delivered. And she brought forth her firstborn son, and wrapped him in swaddling clothes, and laid him in a manger; because there was no room for them in the inn. And there were in the same country shepherds abiding in the field, keeping watch over their flock by night.

And, lo, the angel of the Lord came upon them, and the glory of the Lord shone round about them: and they were sore afraid. And the angel said unto them, Fear not: for, behold, I bring you good tidings of great joy, which shall be to all people. For unto you is born this day in the city of David a Saviour, which is Christ the Lord. And this shall be a sign unto you; Ye shall find the babe wrapped in swaddling clothes, lying in a manger. And suddenly there was with the angel a multitude of the heavenly host, praising God, and saying, Glory to God in the highest, and on earth peace, goodwill toward men.

And it came to pass, as the angels were gone away from them into heaven, the shepherds said one to another: Let us now go even unto Bethlehem, and see this thing which is come to pass, which the Lord hath made known unto us. And they came with haste, and found Mary, and Joseph, and the babe lying in a manger. And when they had seen it, they made known abroad the saying which was told them concerning this child. And all they that heard it wondered at those things which were told them by the shepherds. (Luke 2:1-20)

(He read this twice [as they requested it a second time] and then asked for their thoughts.)[24]

JOHN D. I saw the mother standing by a manger, with a little child in it. I have seen a picture of it.

JOSEPH. I saw the angels coming to the shepherds.

FRANKLIN. I saw the picture of the whole: the people going up to be taxed all along the road; the manger and child and mother; the angels coming to the shepherds; and the angels going away.

AUGUSTINE. Gabriel, the angel of the Lord, was dressed differently from the other angels. He had stars on his robe, which was blue.

MR. ALCOTT. Why was he dressed differently?

AUGUSTINE. Because he brought a new kind of message. Blue is an emblem of faith.

MR. ALCOTT. Is not green like faith?

AUGUSTINE. No; green is more like fear. Mary was sitting on a pile of straw, and the baby, clothed in white, was in a stall. It had hazel eyes. There were cows in the other stalls.

ALEXANDER. I saw the angel coming to the shepherds. The sky was black; but there was one red spot, out of which the angels came. The first angel had a crown on. The baby was in a manger, and there were cows each side of him.

WELLES. The sky seemed to me clear blue. The first angel was the largest, and he had a crown on, and there was a long line of smaller angels, clothed in white, following. Then I saw the shepherds going and finding Jesus in a large place full of hay. He was lying high, and Joseph and Mary are standing near, and looking at him, and smiling because they are glad to have him.

JOHN B. I see the manger. The baby was dressed in white, with stars all over his dress; the stars are a sign of love. The stable was not very large, and cattle are there. There was a building close by where there were a good many people — some standing outside and trying to get in. But it is too full.

LEMUEL. There was a large house and barn; Joseph and Mary are on the hay, and the baby is in the manger. There are angels coming down just in sight afar off, and the light about them shines into the barn and wakes up the cattle. The angels are dressed in satin with diamonds.

GEORGE B. I saw the angels dressed in green.

JOSIAH. I think it was rather a high part of the barn, and a child was lying in the midst of the crowd, and there was a ray of light on its forehead, that lighted up the whole barn. And an angel was sitting on a cloud above, dressed in purple, with a sceptre and with a hat and feathers of purple, and there were other angels flying in and out, singing goodwill; and far off on a hill were shepherds, and there were little bits of angels flying round, and there was music playing, as if it were all the flutes and all the harps in the whole world playing together. The chief light was on the barn and on the hill. [25]

MR. ALCOTT. Was there light on the barn outside?

JOSIAH. Oh yes! and, Mr. Alcott, I can see the watchmen of the city sitting, and the battlements, and the travellers stopping and asking the watchmen, what all this light means.

FRANK. I don't see how there could be a cloud in a barn.

JOSIAH. Oh! the barn was as high as this room; and the cloud was as high as that stove funnel. It was a pink cloud, such as we often see at sunset.

MR. ALCOTT. Why do you think this child was laid in a barn?

JOSIAH. Oh! because he was so good, he could not be laid in a handsome bed like others!

MR. ALCOTT. Why is it not, as it was with Jesus, when all babes are born?

JOSIAH. Because he was wiser and better and gooder.

MR. ALCOTT. What if there should be just such another child born?

JOSIAH. Why, then something of the same kind would take place I suppose, though not exactly the same things.

ANDREW. I see a little baby in a barn about as large as this room; and the baby is on a hayloft in one corner, and a crowd of people are at the door. The baby has a pink and purple robe, with a ring on his finger.

MR. ALCOTT. Where did the ring come from?

ANDREW. His heavenly father put it on because he was pleased with him. The angels came in a long curve line which reached from the sky to the place where the angel stood who spoke to the shepherds, and there seemed to be more angels still behind. (*He described their dresses.*)

EDWARD J. I think the angels were dressed in sky. They had feathers and diamonds on their heads. Those angels who are singing are in a thing that keeps them all together, and have harps; and the angel of silence is there besides.[26] Jesus is dressed in sky too. Mr. Alcott, I made up some of this while I was telling it. I did not think it all when you were reading.

HALES. I like to think of the shepherds going home from seeing the child.

NATHAN. I think of the baby lying in the stall, and a lamp overhead, and a great many people looking at him and smiling, because they are glad he is come.

FREDERIC. I thought of the hill and the angels coming down; the shepherds were great stout men.

(*The rest of Frederic's picture, quite unique for its rustic simplicity and good sense was not transcribed.*)

EMMA. The reason of the light is, that goodness sheds light.

LUCIA. I think the angels were standing on a cloud; and there were three or four little baby angels. The older angels had on white garments figured with lilies and roses. The sheep were under a tree. The angels sung; but the angel of silence played on a harp and did not sing. Gabriel had a rod with a star on it, and he told them Jesus was born. As soon as Gabriel had said this, the angels began to sing to their harps. In the inn there was a very small bed, which they gave to Mary to put in the stall for the baby to lie on. It was just large enough for Jesus. Jesus had blue eyes, and a white robe, with stars on it, and the stars looked down from the sky into the window. And Mary had a plume that she was waving over him. The angels had no crowns on. I think that would have spoiled the whole, it would have been so earthly — they had wreaths of flowers.

EMMA. I think Mary was bending over Jesus and pressing the hay down, lest it should get into his eyes.

LUCIA. The angels, I think, took care of the sheep, while the shepherds went to Bethlehem. And angels were flying round the barn where Jesus was. Between the hill of the shepherds and the barn was a plain, covered with flowers, and a brook ran through it.

WILLIAM B. I thought of a road and a tavern on one side. Just behind was a very large barn; and the tavern was full, and they went into the stable and cleared one manger, and clothed the child in some old dirty rags.

(Here the children, who, during the above pictures had evinced the most lively pleasure, and occasionally had added circumstances to the various pictures [George K., for instance, giving the shepherds a dog] evinced the most lively disgust, and said, "no, no!" Some stopped their ears, and would not hear any more. Mr. Alcott said, You judge William too quickly; let me read the rest. But even after he had, they were not satisfied.)

GEORGE K. Let him have the rags if he wants them, but at least let them be clean.

WILLIAM B. (continued) And the mother was laid down and held the child up in a standing posture. The shepherds brought young lambs as presents to Jesus. When the shepherds told of Christ's birth in the city, all the bells were rung, and the people hurrahed, but not boisterously, that a king was born. In the next stall to Jesus there was an ass, and when the ass saw Jesus, he ran out of his own stall, and lay down before Jesus' stall.

MR. ALCOTT. Why should they take ragged clothes?

WILLIAM B. They were poor, and taken by surprise; besides, such clothes were emblematic of his earthly state.

MR. ALCOTT. Why were lambs brought?

WILLIAM B. They are emblems of innocence.

MR. ALCOTT. What is meant by the prostrate ass?

WILLIAM B. The ass knew the truth. You know animals have a kind of instinct.

RECORDER. Why should the ragged clothes be dirty? That seems to me very disagreeable.

WILLIAM B. Why, that has a meaning, but I cannot express it.

EDWARD B. I thought of the shepherds receiving the tidings, sitting on an eminence; and the flocks lying about on the ground, and the sky opened, and the light shone all round many miles, but not as far as Bethlehem. And an angel came down, not like the other angels that had come, but a smaller one, with a pink and white robe, and a plain gold girdle, and a gold band on his head. The other angels that came after, had no bodies, but only heads and wings — golden wings. And after they had told the shepherds, they went back and heaven closed. Then the shepherds went to Bethlehem; and angels followed, who were invisible to the people until they got into the barn, where they could be seen. And the people of the inn could not get near the barn, because there was an angelic influence that kept them away, for they were not worthy.

LUCY. I was interested in the angels' coming. They brought Jesus in a chariot. He brought with him a bible clasped with diamonds. He had diamonds on his head. Mary kissed him.

MR. ALCOTT. Do the rest think Jesus was brought by the angels?

JOSIAH. I don't know how he came.

NATHAN. Mary carried him into the barn, but I do not know where she got him.

LEMUEL. The angels could not bring his body.

FRANK. A carriage and horses from the sky brought the body. (*The rest thought angels brought him except Edward B.*)

MR. ALCOTT. Do any of you think you were delivered by angels to your mothers?

LUCIA and OTHERS. The spirit was, but not the body.

EMMA. The body was in the spirit. After angels bring the spirit, the body grows out of it, as the rose opens out of the bud.

WILLIAM B. The mother has something to do with making the body.

SEVERAL. So I should think.

MR. ALCOTT. Why did the shepherds say they had "glad tidings"?

ALEXANDER. Because he was the Saviour.

EMMA. Of our spirits.

FRANKLIN. From our sins.

EDWARD B. The Jews thought he would be a saviour from the Romans.

MR. ALCOTT. The tidings were "to all people." How?

LEMUEL. Because he was good, and goodness will stay always.

MR. ALCOTT. Does evil always stay?

ONE. No.

MR. ALCOTT. What is the effect of sin on our spirits?

EDWARD J. Hell.

MR. ALCOTT. What does that word signify?

EDWARD J. Fire and brimstone.

MR. ALCOTT. Such fire as is in our grate, or does fire signify something else?

EDWARD J. I think it is the fire that burns our spirits.

MR. ALCOTT. What is this fire?

EDWARD J. Horror.

FRANKLIN. The punishment of conscience.

GEORGE B. Anger is hell.

ALEXANDER. Revenge is hell.

LUCY E. Remorse is hell.

LUCIA. A great reproach of conscience, but not a little reproach, is hell.

CHARLES. Envy is an inward fire.

MR. ALCOTT. Those who think there is a place called hell, where there is fire like that in the grate, hold up your hands. (*Not one.*) Now those who think this word (which you have found for yourselves) is the sign of a state of mind, signify it. (*All rose.*)

JOSIAH. Hell is a valley, I think, where they breathe evil spirits and writhe.

MR. ALCOTT. An outward valley, or — ?

JOSIAH. A sign of naughtiness. Mr. Alcott, I have not been in that valley of hell for several days.

MR. ALCOTT. Well, I am glad of it. We may say then that Jesus came to save us from wrong states of mind; from breathing in evil spirits as Josiah says. Now you may tell what Jesus came to save us from?

FRANCIS. From wickedness.

MR. ALCOTT. What kind of wickedness?

CHARLES. From anger.

NATHAN. From lying.

MR. ALCOTT. Why not from eating too much, drinking too much, getting angry?

ANDREW. Keeping us from cheating, swearing.

CHARLES. In one word, from punishment.

MR. ALCOTT. Why did the angels sing "Glory to God in the highest"?

WELLES. Because Jesus was good.

ALEXANDER. And "highest" is the emblem of holy.

MR. ALCOTT. Why did they sing, "On earth peace"?

WILLIAM B. Because peace would be made in the world by what he taught.

MR. ALCOTT. Can any of you bring peace on earth and good will to men?

GEORGE K. Yes; by our example.

WELLES. I think it means peace of conscience.

EMMA. How beautiful it would be if no one ever did wrong!

WELLES. If it had not been for Adam —

MR. ALCOTT. If it had not been for Welles — and for Mr. Alcott —and for all imperfect human creatures!!

LUCIA. If there were no wicked ones there would be no state prisons.

EDWARD B. No incendiaries nor pickpockets.

JOHN B. No murders, no wars.

MR. ALCOTT. There would be "good will towards men."

AUGUSTINE. Men would be kind to one another.

EMMA. They would say "I will not do wrong."

FRANKLIN. And be generous.

MR. ALCOTT. "And Mary pondered these things in her heart."

EDWARD J. What does "ponder" mean?

MR. ALCOTT. To weigh, think about, consider what meaning is hidden.

EDWARD J. She pondered in her heart, because Jesus was her son.

MR. ALCOTT. Was there joy when you were born? (*All said yes.*) Do you think any of you will prove Saviours, even to one poor ignorant soul?

LUCY. I guess Josiah and Emma will.

MR. ALCOTT. And why not Lucy, and Welles, and every one of you? Why not joy in heaven when you were born, and angels sing? (*All smiled.*) Was there joy in heaven when you were born?

NATHAN. There was some, but not so much as when Jesus was born.

MR. ALCOTT. Who think birth is a time for joy in heaven and earth? (*All rose.*) It says, also, that there is joy in heaven when a sinner repents, and you say, George, that it is the new birth. Repentance makes us to be born over.

GEORGE K. Yes.

MR. ALCOTT. What has been the subject, to-day?

ANDREW. Spirits taking on a body.

MR. ALCOTT. Yes; the Soul's birth to the eyes. The eyes double our souls. The senses double our vision. They reveal the Soul's shape, as figured in a body of flesh. This [next] passage needs no paraphrase. What is a paraphrase?

SEVERAL. Thoughts put into words, into any person's words.

WILLIAM C. Taking other words for the same thoughts.

(Every scholar answered in like manner. All had the idea.)

MR. ALCOTT. When I paraphrase I do not put better words. The Bible itself has usually the best expression, but I sometimes use other and plainer words; and now tell me, How many of you like to have me paraphrase, and understand the sense better? *(All held up hands.)*

ONE. Every lesson is more interesting than the last!

MR. ALCOTT. I am glad that your interest continues as we proceed. The subjects become more and more interesting. In our next conversation we shall speak of the consecration in the temple at Jerusalem.

CONVERSATION XI

* * *

CONSECRATION OF SPIRIT TO SELF-RENEWAL:

Religion

Mr. Alcott began the conversation by reading a description of the Jewish Temple. He spoke of one of Raphael's Cartoons, representing the beautiful gate of the temple, (lately exhibited) and which many of the children had seen. He then read:

CONSECRATION IN THE TEMPLE

And when eight days were accomplished for the circumcising of the child, Joseph called his name JESUS, which was so named of the angel before he was conceived in the womb. And when the days of her purification according to the law of Moses were accomplished, they brought him to Jerusalem, to present him to the Lord; (As it is written in the law of the Lord, Every male that openeth the womb shall be called holy to the Lord). And to offer a sacrifice according to that which is said in the law of the Lord, A pair of turtle-doves, or two young pigeons.

And, behold, there was a man in Jerusalem, whose name was Simeon; and the same man was just and devout, waiting for the consolation of Israel; and the Holy Ghost was upon him. And it was revealed unto him by the Holy Ghost, that he should not see death, before he had seen the Lord's Christ. And he came by the Spirit into the temple: and when the parents brought in the child Jesus, to do for him after the custom of the law, then took he him up in his arms, and blessed God, and said, Lord, now lettest thou thy servant depart in peace, according to thy word: For mine eyes have seen thy salvation, which thou hast prepared before the face of all people; A light to lighten the Gentiles, and the glory of thy people Israel. And Joseph and his mother marvelled at those things which were spoken of him. And Simeon blessed them, and said unto Mary his mother, Behold, this *child* is set for the fall and rising again of many in Israel, and for a sign which shall be spoken against, (Yea, a sword shall pierce through thy own soul also,) that the thoughts of many hearts may be revealed. And there was one Anna, a prophetess, the daughter of Phanuel, of the tribe of Aser: she was of a great age, and had lived with an husband seven years from her virginity and she was a widow of about fourscore and four years, which departed not from the temple, but served God with fastings and prayers night and day. And she coming in that instant gave thanks likewise unto the Lord, and spake of him to all them that looked for redemption in Jerusalem. And when they had performed all things according to the law of the Lord, they returned into Galilee, to their own city Nazareth. (Luke 2:21-39.)

(At their request he read this lesson twice, and explained the law of Moses respecting purification and consecration of children.)

MR. ALCOTT. Now what have you in your minds?

EDWARD C. The turtle-doves, but I do not know what they were for.

JOSIAH. I had a picture of the christening.

(He described the temple with ornaments of gold; the priests' dresses; Simeon with a beard and long robe, holding the child up on one arm, and raising the other to heaven, — kneeling, and with little hair on his head.)

MR. ALCOTT. Let us not have so many of these pictures today; we had a great many last time; let us have more thoughts and fewer images.

LEMUEL. I thought the temple was as large as the state house, and there was an altar and knife laying on it, with a pearl handle and golden blade; the priest had the child and Mary and Joseph were kneeling.

MR. ALCOTT. You are thinking of the circumcision, though I did not dwell on that.

FRANK. I imagined the temple and the child standing on the altar. Joseph had on a gold striped long gown, and Mary had a silver striped gown, and a pearl on her head. The floor was covered with apples, and things to be sacrificed.

AUGUSTINE. I imagined the temple was a good deal like this temple, and had one room larger than this. The altar was mahogany, with steel on the top, to keep it from being burned. There was a knife with a golden carved handle and silver blade. The two turtle-doves were standing on the altar, waiting for the priest to offer them up. And there was a pulpit, with a minister in it, reading out of a book. Mary and Joseph were before the altar, looking happy, and thinking about what the priest was reading.

Simeon had the child and was caressing him. And they all had white caps on. There was a congregation of people sitting behind as in a common church. The sacrifice was made with sweet smelling wood.

MR. ALCOTT. Can you not refrain from these elaborate pictures? I prefer to have the thoughts which the reading suggests.

EDWARD J. I saw Joseph and Mary carry the pigeons and lay them on the altar; and the priest took a knife and killed them, and offered them. Simeon had Jesus, and was sitting down praying; and Anna the prophetess was praying.

MR. ALCOTT. Did you like to hear the reading?

EDWARD J. I like to hear everything in the Bible.

WILLIAM B. I thought of Mary going into the temple, with one hand up to her eyes, and her baby in the other. She was thinking what her child was going to be, and how she should educate it, and Joseph was thinking the same things, and the Priest was thinking what great things the child was going to do.

ALEXANDER. I only had a picture.

MR. ALCOTT. We will omit it.

EDWARD B. I cannot separate my thoughts from the picture.

MR. ALCOTT. If you think there are thoughts mingled with your picture, you may give it.

EDWARD B. The temple was four times as large as this room, and the altar was about a quarter as large. The priest had a large knife, and cut the child a little; but Jesus did not cry as other children would have done, because God gave him power to bear it. There was nobody in the temple but the parents, and Simeon. Simeon said he could now lay his head down in peace, because Jesus had come. He knew he had come to the spirits of men, while other people thought he was to come to drive out the Romans — a great warrior and conqueror.

MR. ALCOTT. Was he not a conqueror?

EDWARD B. Only over spiritual enemies.

MR. ALCOTT. What spiritual enemies?

EDWARD B. Revenge, and anger, and —

MR. ALCOTT. Impatience?

EDWARD B. Impatience is not a sin.

MR. ALCOTT. Who else think Impatience is not a sin? (*Almost all held up hands.*)

CHARLES. Patience is the opposite of impatience.

MR. ALCOTT. Who think Jesus Christ was patient always? (*All held up hands.*) What word means a state of mind above all trouble?

CHARLES. Patience.

MR. ALCOTT. Including patience — God has it. Only think of God getting in a passion!

NATHAN. God would not be God if he was in a passion.

MR. ALCOTT. Are you like God when you do?

FRANCIS. Not the least like God.

MR. ALCOTT. I must tell you the word I mean — Repose. People that have repose are less troubled about outward things. They look down on the world as God does. The greatest Souls are full of repose. But is not Impatience the beginning of anger? (*They agreed and said it was wrong, except Charles who later changed his mind.*)

CHARLES. I am only impatient because other people are, and I do not think impatience is a sin.

LUCIA. I thought when Jesus was coming to the temple, he was borne by his parents, who seemed to be like servants to him. When they carried him into the temple, Simeon spread out his arms and took him, and blessed God, and Jesus, and the parents. And the priest took a long sharp knife, and cut the child a little, but he did not cry.

MR. ALCOTT. You seem to think that Jesus began to teach patience at eight days old, by not crying when he was hurt? What is meant by the cutting?

CHARLES. It showed that it was of small consequence, whether the body was hurt or not.

EDWARD B. It was to distinguish the Jews from other nations; but it was very, very cruel, I think.

MR. ALCOTT. Was there any spiritual meaning in it?

SOME. It was to teach patience.

SAMUEL R. Jesus meant to teach us not to mind the body's pain.

CHARLES. It is of small consequence, when the body is hurt to make the spirit better.

MR. ALCOTT. Do you suppose that he was conscious at this time, and intended to set an example? (All.) And you think, Charles, that pain is of no consequence, if it makes us better. People who suffer the most are often the best. People who suffer least do not know much. Can you name any suffering that has made you better?

CHARLES. When I have been punished and my body has been hurt, as when you punish me on the hand. But when I punish you I feel worse, because I know that you have done nothing wrong, and I have nothing to feel angry about, as you have all the bodily part, and I had rather be punished some other way any time.

MR. ALCOTT. As many of the rest of you, as have felt a great deal more when they have punished me, than when punished them-selves, may rise. (All who had been so punished rose.) When one person gives himself up to be punished by another, what do you call it?

SEVERAL. Self-sacrifice.

MR. ALCOTT. And perhaps circumcision is an emblem of self-sacrifice. Simeon was told by the Holy Ghost, that this was the Saviour. Does the Holy Ghost ever tell you anything? What is the Holy Ghost?

NATHAN. I don't think it ought to be called God's Ghost, but Spirit.

MR. ALCOTT. How does the Holy Spirit work?

NATHAN. In our body.

MR. ALCOTT. How does it get into the body?

NATHAN. Through our mind.

CHARLES. It means good spirit.

MR. ALCOTT. Have any of you ever felt the Holy Ghost influencing you, and when?

NATHAN. When I obey my father and mother.

MR. ALCOTT. In what does it act?

GEORGE K. In Conscience.

THAN. In all our faculties.

CHARLES. Conscience told Simeon it was Jesus.

MR. ALCOTT. I asked if any of you had felt the influence of the Holy Spirit.

FRANK. Yes. (*Others held up hands.*)

MR. ALCOTT. I should like an instance. If you have ever felt something which illuminates, enlightens, presses you on — something you cannot resist — when everything was clearer — when it seemed as if now the whole truth was found. It did not seem yourself. (*No one gave an instance.*) What is the best name for this feeling, this illumination?

CHARLES. Is it the supernatural?

MR. ALCOTT. The supernatural is in it.

CHARLES. Is it Revelation?

MR. ALCOTT. Revelation is in it.

NATHAN. Is it belief?

MR. ALCOTT. Belief is only in the head. Did you ever hear the word Inspiration? Inspire means to breathe in. God acts from the other side in inspiring you. A great many people go outward to find God.

NATHAN. God inspires by outward things.

MR. ALCOTT. In looking at the Beautiful, without, we see signs of the inward, and God inspires us.[27]

CONVERSATION XII

* * *

ADORATION OF SPIRIT BY HALLOWED GENIUS:

Infant Holiness

Mr. Alcott read:

THE ADORATION OF THE WISE MEN

Now when Jesus was born in Bethlehem of Judaea in the days of Herod the king, behold, there came wise men from the east to Jerusalem, saying, Where is he that is born King of the Jews? For we have seen his star in the east, and are come to worship him. When Herod the king had heard these things, he was troubled, and all Jerusalem with him. And when he had gathered all the Chief Priests and Scribes of the people together, he demanded of them where Christ should be born. And they said unto him, in Bethlehem of Judaea: for thus it is written by the prophet. And thou Bethlehem, in the land of Judah, art not the least among the princes of Judah: for out of thee shall come a Governor, that shall rule my people Israel. Then Herod, when he had privily called the wise men, enquired of them diligently what time the star appeared. And he sent them to Bethlehem, and said, go and search diligently for the young child; and when ye have found him, bring me word again, that I may come and worship him also. When they had heard the king, they departed; and, lo, the star, which they saw in the east went before them, till it came and stood over where the young child was. When they saw the star, they rejoiced with exceeding great joy. And when they were come into the house, they saw the young child with Mary his mother, and fell down, and worshipped him: and when they had opened their treasures, they presented unto him gifts; gold, and frankincense, and myrrh. And being warned of God in a dream that they should not return to Herod, they departed into their own country another way. (Matt. 2:1-12.)

(He read this twice, and asked what thoughts or images it brought into their minds.)

EDWARD C. I had the shape of a star in my mind. It did not look like the other stars. It was smaller, and brighter, and more beautiful.

NATHAN. I thought about the king and the star.

MR. ALCOTT. Did the star mean anything?

EDWARD C. Yes. But I don't know what.

MR. ALCOTT. Did you like Herod, Nathan?

NATHAN. No. He was going to kill the child, and that was not right. I think the star was John, showing where Jesus was.

MR. ALCOTT. How could John get up there?

NATHAN. Why, you know he was not born yet.

MR. ALCOTT. John was born. He was six months old. Was the star the sign of John?

NATHAN. Yes.

EDWARD J. I think Zacharias did not tell Herod that Jesus was born, because he knew that Herod would destroy him if he knew it.

MR. ALCOTT. How came Zacharias there?

EDWARD J. Why, Herod called all the chief priests together, you know. Afterwards Herod called the Chaldeans.

MR. ALCOTT. Who were the Chaldeans?

EDWARD J. People who told kings their dreams.

MR. ALCOTT. Were these wise men, Chaldeans?

EDWARD J. It says so in my "Bible Stories."

MR. ALCOTT. Did you think the wise men good?

EDWARD J. Yes; and so they saw the star. Other people did not see the star; naughty people could not see it. Naughty people cannot see such stars as that; they can only see the common stars that shine in the night; only good people see such stars as this one was.

MR. ALCOTT. Are there many such stars?

EDWARD J. No. God only made one, for Jesus.

MR. ALCOTT. Did God make any star when you were born?

EDWARD J. I guess not, but I don't know; I could not see.

MR. ALCOTT. Do any of you think God made stars for you when you were born?

EDWARD J. Perhaps there was a little star made.

WELLES. Conscience is the star we have.

(All held up their hands, assenting.)

JOSIAH. I think the star was a little smaller than the sun and looked like the moon, with rays all round. It stopped over the place where Mary and Joseph were, and it was low down. The wise men came opposite to it. Jesus was lying in the manger, with white hair, like George's, and serene eyes, and slender white cheeks, and very white hands, and white clothes, with a star right here *(pointing to his forehead)* and two angels came down and took hold of his hands.

MR. ALCOTT. Did he know the angels?

JOSIAH. Oh yes. He had been accustomed to see them in heaven. And God sent down a box, and the angels opened it, and a sweet perfume of incense came out, because Jesus was good.

MR. ALCOTT. These are fancies, Josiah, to which there is no end. Do you think any such angels came when you were born?

JOSIAH. There might have been spirits all about in the room, but neither my mother nor I could see them.

MR. ALCOTT. You did not know the angels as Jesus did?

JOSIAH. No; because I never stayed in heaven. Mr. Alcott, I think there must have been a great many more signs when Jesus was born than are told. I think of a bow and arrow which came down out of heaven, without any body to hold them, and the bow shot the arrow out of itself, and the arrow flew above the clouds; which is a sign of the spirit of Jesus, which goes higher than all things.

MR. ALCOTT. That is enough, Josiah.

JOSIAH. Mr. Alcott! I have a great deal more to say; my mind is full of things, with meanings to them.

ALL. Oh do let him say all, Mr. Alcott.

MR. ALCOTT. Why did I check Josiah?

FRANCIS. Because there was not time.

CHARLES. Because he was going into outward things so much.

MR. ALCOTT. Now, John, you may speak.

JOHN B. I thought the King wanted the men to go and find Jesus, and come back and tell him; and when you read that, I guessed that he wanted to kill him. — The wise men followed the star which was in front of them, till it stopped over the manger. They knelt down and worshipped the child, and opened their bag and took out their gifts. They gave the gold to the mother for him, for he would not know about such earthly things. But he knew the wise men. The star was a diamond shape, as large as the moon, very high, and spread great light all round, and was shining down on the house. And God told the wise men not to go back.

MR. ALCOTT. Why did Herod wish to destroy Jesus?

JOHN B. Because he thought that he would want to be king. And God told Joseph, when he had just gone to bed, in a dream.

MR. ALCOTT. Did God speak by a voice or in a shape?

JOHN B. In a shape, but he told him in words.

MR. ALCOTT. Does God ever speak to you in dreams?

JOHN B. Yes.

MR. ALCOTT. And how?

JOHN B. When I go to bed, sometimes, after I have been naughty, I dream that if I die, I shall not be so good. After I have been good, and have done what mother wants me to, I dream of pleasures. When I am not good, God is sorry and I am sorry, and that gives me pain, and I wake up better.

MR. ALCOTT. How many of the rest of you think God visits you in your dreams?

(*Many held up hands.*)

EDWARD J. I never dream.

MR. ALCOTT. Was Joseph's dream different from your dreams?

(Many held up hands.)

CHARLES. It was more holy, it was to foretell so great a thing.

JOHN B. It was more true.

ALEXANDER. There was more sense in his dreams than in ours.

JOHN D. He had more faith in his dreams, because he was more spiritual.

WILLIAM B. I very seldom have any dreams, but when I do, I think very often, that I am told to do wrong things, and sometimes I do them, and then evil befalls me. And I do not see how anybody can know what dreams are really sent by God to direct them. I believe there are good dreams, but I don't see how Joseph could know. But sometimes I have thought that people around Jerusalem and thereabouts, seldom had dreams, and when they did they were those that they should mind.

MR. ALCOTT. You say you seldom dream?

WILLIAM B. I often dream of little outward things that seem to have no connexion; but I very seldom have long connected dreams. But when I have done wrong, I have dreamed that a wolf was coming to eat me up, and other frightful things. I think God punishes in this way those who do wrong, but I had rather be punished in any other way than by frightful dreams.

MR. ALCOTT. Is such punishment effectual?

WILLIAM B. I think it is.

LEMUEL. Herod was very bad. He ought not to have sent those wise men, so it was deceiving. He was a murderer. He told a lie when he said he was going to worship.

CHARLES. I thought the star represented God's eye looking on his son to protect him. Herod called the wise men privily, because he was afraid of a rebellion. If the angel had not appeared to Joseph, Herod would have destroyed Jesus.

MR. ALCOTT. Why should this star be in the East?

CHARLES. Because there the sun rises.

MR. ALCOTT. Why does the sun rise in the East. *(No answer.)*

What is sun rising an emblem of? (*After a while he added*) What is that act called, which brings forth the Spirit to the eyes?

CHARLES. Birth.

MR. ALCOTT. What is the spirit born from?

CHARLES. From Spirit, from God.

MR. ALCOTT. Then is not the East the emblem of God? And where should Wise Men come from, if not from the East? Wisdom comes from the birth-place of light and life. The star was an emblem of Holiness. Some of the light came down and stood over the place where the child was. Is not the Soul a spiritual star which glitters out at the eyes?

WILLIAM B. I think he called the wise men privily, because he wanted to make them believe that he wanted to worship; but he did not wish the Jews to think that he wanted to worship, even for a short time. I do not think God appeared in a shape or with a voice to Joseph, but that he moved his conscience with his spirit, so that Joseph felt he must go.

LUCIA. The first thought I had was about Joseph's journey into Egypt. He and Mary were on asses, and Jesus was in Joseph's arms. I then thought of the wise men journeying in another direction. Then I thought of Herod waiting for their return, and his rage when they did not come. The star was larger and shone brighter than the rest. It disappeared when Mary and Joseph were going to Egypt, for God did not want it to show Jesus to Herod.

FREDERIC. Herod was very treacherous in telling the wise men he was going to worship, when he was going to kill.

MR. ALCOTT. How do you think the wise men knew that the star was the Jewish King's?

LUCIA. God told them so.

CHARLES. There had been a rumor through the land that Jesus was to be born, and when they saw that there was a new star, they knew there was somebody born.

WILLIAM B. Simeon was a prophet, and he might have given rise to the rumor that Christ should be born when that star appeared. He seemed to know the child.

MR. ALCOTT. Do you think common stars mean anything?

(Many held up hands.)

FRANK. The stars mean other worlds.

(Mr. Alcott explained the meaning of Astronomy, and then spoke of Astrology, and what astrologers thought they found out by the stars.)

MR. ALCOTT. Astronomers find what they seek; Astrologers seek in the stars what is to be found in conscience alone.

ALEXANDER. And in bumps on the head.

(Mr. Alcott here told what the theory of Phrenology was, without saying whether he believed in it or not.)

EMMA. I think we can judge by actions best.

MR. ALCOTT. Yes; words are deceptive signs; and actions sometimes tell lies.

(He then read the quotation from the Prophet, with which the Jews answered the wise men, and asked who was that Governor?)

MR. ALCOTT. Why did the wise men rejoice when they saw Jesus?

LUCIA. They thought from the looks of the star, that Jesus was going to be very great and good.

MR. ALCOTT. Why did they give him gifts?

LUCIA. Because they wanted to distinguish him.

WILLIAM B. Because they respected him.

CHARLES. It was the custom of the East.

MR. ALCOTT. Were any presents made when you were born?

FRANKLIN. Presents are made sometimes when a child is named from a particular person.

ANOTHER. The child is a present to its mother.

MR. ALCOTT. Why did they worship him?

SEVERAL. Because he was great and pure.

MR. ALCOTT. Were you worshipped when you were born?

SEVERAL. *(Laughing)* No.

CHARLES. We were adored by our mothers.

MR. ALCOTT. If you were not worshipped, you were not thought about as you should have been. Wise men reverence the new born.

LUCIA. Yes, in one sense, they worship, because children are so pure, and innocent, and spiritual.

MR. ALCOTT. Are there any Child-Worshippers now — any Wise Men now that worship children?

EMMA. I think they worship what is spiritual and Godlike in them.

MR. ALCOTT. In all children as in Jesus?

EMMA. Yes; except that they do not give gifts. They worship by feeling.

MR. ALCOTT. We should have the same feeling when we see a pure child as when we feel God within us. What if every body worshipped children, would it not be a different world from what it is now? How could it be?

CHARLES. Why they would worship little babies.

EMMA. It would be different from what it is now.

MR. ALCOTT. And if they began worshipping little babies, and went on worshipping, and, bye and bye, the babies joined in, what would be worshipped?

SOME. Spirit.

MR. ALCOTT. If we do not worship our babies, whom we have seen, how shall we worship God whom we have not seen? Have any of you been worshipped?

FRANCIS. Only by our mothers.

MR. ALCOTT. In what sense should a babe be worshipped? How should it be?

LUCIA. By being taken care of, and thought about and loved with spiritual love.

MR. ALCOTT. Has it any love from God itself?

LUCIA. Love came with it from heaven.

MR. ALCOTT. What must be done with this love?

LUCIA. It must be made to grow out.

MR. ALCOTT. How can love be made to grow out?

LUCIA. By loving it first.

CHARLES. The face of a young child has something in it which makes its mother love it.

(Mr. Alcott here asked them if they had infant brothers and sisters, and if they should not hereafter think there was something very precious and sacred in their souls, to be worshipped — and if this would not lead them to refrain from teasing them, disappointing, thwarting, neglecting them, and leaving them to cry. They responded with much interest to all these questions.)

CHARLES. I think a mother who leaves her child to cry, is a barbarian.

MR. ALCOTT. So she is if she can help it. She should never let anything interfere with the care of her child; but keep its little body comfortable in order to bring out its mind. For the body is a small part. The spirit is to be brought out in love and confidence and faith, before the mind can be cultivated, before the child can talk. These duties are not yet well understood by mothers. But they wish to do all they can, generally. Of all persons, mothers are most faithful to their duties. And when children are neglected or injured, it is usually because mothers have other duties, from which they are not relieved by others as they should be, and as they would be, if all felt right upon this subject, and reverenced children as they ought to do.

WILLIAM C. We have a little baby at home, but I never thought of its soul.

MR. ALCOTT. So you thought it was a little body only, and that was all? You forgot its spirit.

WILLIAM C. Yes.

MR. ALCOTT. Oh, then you have never seen the child which God loves.

(He then read a paraphrase. The children expressed deep interest in this conversation.)

CONVERSATION XIII

* * *

APOSTACY OF SPIRIT:

Malignity

MR. ALCOTT. What kind of wisdom had the wise men, of whom we talked last time?

EDWARD B. The knowledge of the stars and learned books.

FREDERIC. They knew things some sly way.

MR. ALCOTT. Were they jugglers? I don't think so.

FRANKLIN. They had the power of prophecy by means of the stars which helped them some.

(Here Mr. Alcott asked, how many of them thought that by studying the stars they would learn their own fate. He described casting horoscopes, and said some people still believed in astrology, yet now people studied their babies' horoscopes in their own characters.)

CHARLES. Wisdom is knowledge of God.

LUCIA. They studied their own minds, they tried to find out good and evil.

FRANK. I think it was worldly wisdom.

RECORDER. What is that?

FRANK. Knowing how things are made.

MR. ALCOTT. What was the other kind of wisdom?

MARTHA. Spiritual.

MR. ALCOTT. Which world do you study for that kind of wisdom?

FRANCIS. The inward world.

EMMA. Because the inward world includes the outward.

MR. ALCOTT. Which makes us wisest?

FRANCIS. The spiritual.

CHARLES. Both.

MR. ALCOTT. Yes; both are desirable. The Wise Men reverenced children; and their wisdom consisted in perceiving in the infant spirit the sign of holiness; of God.

(Having enlarged a little on this, he read:)

MASSACRE OF THE INNOCENTS

And when they were departed, behold, the angel of the Lord appeareth to Joseph in a dream, saying, Arise, and take the young child and his mother, and flee into Egypt, and be thou there until I bring thee word: for Herod will seek the young child to destroy him. When he arose, he took the young child and his mother by night, and departed into Egypt: And was there until the death of Herod: that it might be fulfilled which was spoken of the Lord by the prophet, saying, Out of Egypt have I called my son. Then Herod, when he saw that he was mocked of the wise men, was exceeding wroth, and sent forth, and slew all the children that were in Bethlehem, and in all the coasts thereof, from two years old and under, according to the time which he had diligently enquired of the wise men. Then was fulfilled that which was spoken by Jeremy the prophet, saying, In Rama was there a voice heard, Lamentation, and weeping, and great mourning, Rachel weeping for her children, and would not be comforted because they are not. But when Herod was dead, behold, an angel of the Lord appeareth in a dream to Joseph in Egypt, saying, arise, and take the young child and his mother, and go into the land of Israel: for they are dead which sought the young child's life. And he arose and took the young child and his mother, and came into the land of Israel. But when he heard that Archelaus did reign in Judaea in the room of his father Herod, he was afraid to go thither: notwithstanding, being warned of God in a dream, he turned aside into the parts of

Galilee: And he came and dwelt in a city called Nazareth: that it might be fulfilled which was spoken by the prophets, He shall be called a Nazarene. (Matt. 2:13-23)

And the child grew, and waxed strong in spirit, filled with wisdom: and the grace of God was upon him. (LUKE 2. 40.)

(He then asked for their thoughts.)

GEORGE B. I don't think Herod was a good man, because he killed all the children in Bethlehem.

MR. ALCOTT. You may each of you make a picture of what I have read.

FRANK. I thought of a temple on one side, and two steeples out of it, and two stone stairs up to the top, and a row of houses on one side, and the door open of one house, and the house was empty; and on the sidewalk there was a man and child dead; all was still; the houses were empty, and the people were on the tops of the houses.

EDWARD C. I saw the children killed, and God telling Joseph to take Jesus away.

EDWARD J. I thought I saw one of the children when they were hanging him. I thought I should not like to be there. I saw a great many men and children. The children were standing up and not killed yet.

NATHAN. I saw a very great temple, and a board laid up high, and a spring of water at the end of it, and they rolled the children down the board into the spring.

JOSIAH. There was a great door to the house where Herod lived, and a great steeple; and little steeples all about; and Herod looked out of a window, at the men killing the children. The children were tied to a string, and struck on the head with an axe, by one of Herod's servants; and their mothers were looking out of the windows.

WILLIAM C. I saw a great house where Herod was, and his servants went into the houses, and asked how old the children were, and all under two years old they took and killed.

ALEXANDER. I thought Herod sent all his ruffians to kill the children with swords. He was standing at the door at first, waiting for the wise men, and was angry at their not coming back.

JOHN B. I thought of a house as large as this temple, with large iron doors, large window. Because the wise men did not come back, Herod sent out his servants to kill all the little babies. And he stood upon the steps looking. He heard some weeping. It was the mothers, and he pretended that he was weeping. Then I thought of Joseph's dream in Egypt, and the journey back from Egypt.

LUCIA. When Herod saw that the wise men did not come back, he was angry. Then he thought he should certainly kill Jesus if he killed all the children. So he sent out his men to kill them. The mothers were trying to keep their children out of the hands of the men. And I saw Egypt in my mind, when Joseph and Mary were there, and Joseph asleep. And his conscience seemed to me to tell him that Herod was dead, and he might go back. And I saw him and Mary carrying the child back; and when he heard Archelaus was reigning he went to Nazareth, because he was afraid Archelaus would be just like his father.

EDWARD J. I wish you would read the history of Palestine, Mr. Alcott.

EDWARD B. This was my picture. I thought of Herod sitting on his throne, waiting for the wise men; and he waited so long that he had to turn his face round to hide it, it was so red and angry. Soon he called the soldiers to go and kill all the children in Bethlehem; and as soon as the mothers heard of this order, they took their children in their arms, and ran about the streets, screaming. And I saw many children on the side walks dead, and their mothers tearing their hair. And I thought Herod himself seized on one child which he thought might be Jesus, and threw it out of the window, and its own mother caught it, and then a soldier seized it, and killed it.

CHARLES. I imagined Herod, just as his anger was raging, and his passionate order was given to the soldiers to kill every child. And they went out and did as he commanded; and the mothers were so frantic, that they tried to kill the soldiers themselves. I imagined there were stone steps to the houses, and both mothers and children were pitched down the stone steps and killed. And all this while, Herod was looking out at the window, and seeing the slaughter; and at last he could bear it no longer, and stopped it. But when he found Jesus was not killed, he repented of this mercy.

MR. ALCOTT. What name would suit the character of Herod?

JOSIAH. A wicked crocodile; for he sought for Jesus, by the wise men, under the pretence of worshipping him; and the crocodile deceives his prey by crying like a child. So Herod was like a crocodile.

LUCIA. A tiger-hearted murderer.

EDWARD J. A tyrant and pirate.

EMMA. Very revengeful and cruel.

EDWARD B. He was like a hyena, a very great abomination.

NATHAN. A deceiver and a thief.

MR. ALCOTT. What did he steal?

NATHAN. Children.

EMMA. I think after the children were killed, Herod was sorry, though he felt glad at first.

MR. ALCOTT. Who else think he was sorry? (*All but three held up their hands.*) What was the feeling that filled Herod? Have you any feeling within you, which, carried out, would lead to such an act?

GEORGE K. Anger.

CHARLES. Revenge-madness.

MR. ALCOTT. Not the madness of insanity.

ANDREW. Passion.

HERBERT. Envy.

MARTHA. Hatred.

EMMA. Cruelty.

MR. ALCOTT. Was Herod worse than you, when he was born? (*None thought so.*)

FREDERIC. I think it was bad enough for Herod to kill Jesus; but to kill so many children!!

SAMUEL R. I think if the wise men had come back and told Herod the truth, he would have killed Jesus and no other, and that would have been bad enough.

MR. ALCOTT. Who think Herod believed in Astrology? (*Many did.*) The stars might have influenced his imagination. Superstition makes people cruel. He feared that he should lose his throne.

CHARLES. Why did the soldiers obey him?

MR. ALCOTT. He was a despot. To disobey him would have been instant death.

GEORGE K. I should rather have died than to have done such a thing.

MR. ALCOTT. Could you expect much moral courage from them?

CHARLES. I should rather they would have destroyed men and women.

MR. ALCOTT. Yes; and soldiers rarely do hurt children. Sometimes they have done so; but the roughest soldier usually respects a mother's feelings.

(*Mr. Alcott here described a similar scene to the massacre as taking place in Boston, and their brothers and sisters the victims. He then asked some questions to find out whether the children thought they should be filled more with pity for the children, or anger for the men; and how much they would think of punishing the men, and what their feeling about punishment was. My record is too confused for me to give the details. Some conversation ensued on punishment in school, and Mr. Alcott asked who felt pleasure when they saw other boys punished.*)

SEVERAL. When they have troubled us, we do.

JOSIAH. I feel pleasure in seeing boys punished. I don't know why.

WILLIAM B. Is it the pleasure of revenge?

EDWARD J. I do not know, but I take pleasure in it.

MR. ALCOTT. Who think the feeling wrong? (*All rose.*) Have any of you felt pleasure in seeing others punished when they have troubled you?

CHARLES. I don't — because I think that if I had not been here, they would not be punished.

MR. ALCOTT. Why do you tell me of the faults of others?

CHARLES. Because I don't want them to do so to me or to anybody else.

(*Mr. Alcott cross-questioned Charles, and he said that he took no pleasure at all in seeing others punished; that as far as they were hurt, he was sorry; that however angry he might be, a boy's being punished took all his anger away.*)

SAMUEL R. I sometimes think they deserve it; but I take no pleasure in their punishment.

EMMA. No. MARTHA. I sometimes do, when they have plagued me.

MR. ALCOTT. Do you think Herod had this feeling?

SEVERAL. He did not think those babies deserved punishment.

MR. ALCOTT. No; it was selfish love of power. I think Josiah's reason was, that the dramatic effect took his eye. And that is, I suppose, the reason why people go to hangings. They feel sorry for the man, but they want to see how it is. When I was sixteen years old I walked sixteen miles with Dr. Alcott[28] to see a man hanged; and when he was thrown off I fainted away. I had no pleasure in it. — And again, at another time I went to a Prison, and saw the prisoners come up a ladder from below, where they were obliged to sleep. They came up at the point of the bayonet, and were chained and put to their work.

EMMA. I should not want to go to such a place.

MR. ALCOTT. No; I did not get over it for some time. I had no idea of what I was going to see.

CONVERSATION XIV

• • •

GENIUS OF SPIRIT:

Childhood

MR. ALCOTT. There is no account given us of the time between two years old and twelve of Jesus' life. What do you think Jesus used to do when a boy?

(Most of them expressed a difficulty in conceiving him a boy — except when talking in the Temple.)

CHARLES. I think of him in his father's carpenter's shop making crosses and tombs and such things. And I think he would try to carve out God.

RECORDER. That is the last thing, Charles, that a Jew would think of carving, as it broke the first commandment.

MR. ALCOTT. But you mean, Charles, that he would strive to express an Idea by it. Yes; it is plain Jesus had something of an Artist's mind; else his language had not been so picturesque. He was in Egypt among splendid works of art in his childhood, which perhaps helped out his imagination. Who do you think taught him to read?

FRANKLIN. He taught himself.

MARTHA. I never thought he learnt anything from books.

EMMA. I think his mother helped him learn.

MR. ALCOTT. But when he was twelve, something occurred, which I will now read.

JESUS WITH THE DOCTORS IN THE TEMPLE

Now his parents went to Jerusalem every year at the feast of the Passover. And when he was twelve years old, they went up to Jerusalem after the custom of the feast. And when they had fulfilled the days, as they returned, the child Jesus tarried behind in Jerusalem; and Joseph and his mother knew not of it. But they, supposing him to have been in the company, went a day's journey; and they sought him among their kinsfolk and acquaintance. And when they found him not, they turned back again to Jerusalem, seeking him. And it came to pass, that after three days they found him in the temple, sitting in the midst of the doctors, both hearing them, and asking them questions.

And all that heard him were astonished at his understanding and answers. And when they saw him, they were amazed: and his mother said unto him, Son, why hast thou thus dealt with us? Behold, thy father and I have sought thee sorrowing. And he said unto them, How is it that ye sought me? Wist ye not that I must be about my Father's business? And they understood not the saying which he spake unto them. And he went down with them, and came to Nazareth, and was subject unto them: but his mother kept all these sayings in her heart. And Jesus increased in wisdom and stature, and in favor with God and man. (Luke 2:41 to the end.)

(Mr. Alcott asked what interested them most?)

NATHAN. Jesus talking with the ministers.

MR. ALCOTT. What is he talking about?

NATHAN. God.

HALES. I thought about Jesus with the ministers.

JOSIAH. I thought about his parents returning and looking for him. They travel in that country on an ass's back, with a basket on the ass to ride in. Jesus and his mother were in the basket when they went up, and the people were walking all round, but Jesus was not there when they were returning.

SAMUEL T. Jesus was sitting with the doctors, he was in the pulpit.

EDWARD J. I had no thought, but I heard it all.

JOHN D. Jesus knew a great deal more than the doctors who stood round him listening.

JOSEPH. I thought Jesus ought to have told his father and mother that he was going to stay behind.

MR. ALCOTT. Well, how do you explain that he did not?

JOSEPH. Perhaps he did not know when they went.

MR. ALCOTT. What do you suppose he was doing all that time?

JOSEPH. He was talking with the ministers.

MR. ALCOTT. Should you have liked to talk with them, had you been in his place?

JOSEPH. Perhaps I should, but I don't know.

WELLES. When you were reading, I thought, that Jesus knew his father and mother had gone, but still that he thought he would stay and teach the doctors a little while.

JOHN B. I imagined Jesus going into the temple where a great many ministers were teaching people to be good. But Jesus did not see his parents go out, and they thought he was following behind, till bye and bye, when they were almost home, they looked round and found he was not there — so they went back and found him teaching people to be good, which is what God is doing all the time. This was what interested me most.

FREDERIC. I thought of Jesus arguing with the doctors. He was trying to make them think that what he was saying was true, and they were trying to make him think that what they were saying was true. But Jesus' arguments were the best.

AUGUSTINE. I thought they were trying to say something which Jesus could not answer, to try him. But he answered everyone, without any trouble.

GEORGE B. I think of him asking questions to teach the doctors.

LEMUEL. I understand the answer he gave to Mary. It was God's business.

MR. ALCOTT. What is God's business?

LEMUEL. Being good, and talking and teaching about good things.

GEORGE K. To do what he wants us — act out.

MARTHA. To set good examples.

CHARLES. Keeping free from doing wrong; and not giving up to temptation.

MR. ALCOTT. Such of you as think that you have not always been about your father's business may stand up.

(*All rose.*)

ALEXANDER. I think of him preaching to the doctors; but I really think it was wrong for him to stay there without telling his parents.

MR. ALCOTT. You mean that you do not see how it was right?

ALEXANDER. No; it seems to me it was wrong.

MR. ALCOTT. Are any more perplexed with this thought? (*Several raised their hands.*) Do you think if you understood all about it you should think it was wrong?

ALL. I suppose not.

WILLIAM B. Yet I must say I cannot understand why Jesus did not tell his parents that he was going to stay there. It does not seem to me that it was right.

RECORDER. Jesus was carried up to the temple at twelve years old, in conformity to the Jewish custom, to be enrolled among the males of the nation. It was Moses' direction that every child should be taught the Jewish history and laws. At this time it is probable that the boys were asked questions by the learned men, to see if they were properly educated. They could also ask explanations of what they did not understand in their law and history. Jesus was probably engaged in such a conversation as this. I think it was only strange that his parents should have gone without him. I should think that in any case of a son, and more especially in the case of such a son as that, the parents would have watched what passed at such a memorable era of every Jew's life. I see no failure of duty except in the parents.

WILLIAM B. That takes away all my difficulties.

MR. ALCOTT. Does it help any of the rest?

(All held up hands.)

CHARLES. He thought his heavenly father's business was of most consequence.

MR. ALCOTT. When you are perplexed in this way, I wish you would say, "I do not see how it was right for Jesus to do so and so, " for it is not pleasant to hear little boys say, "I think Jesus did wrong," — none of you think so.

WILLIAM C. I was interested in Jesus' talking with the doctors; because it was remarkable that he should say such things at twelve years old.

MR. ALCOTT. How came he to know so much?

WILLIAM C. Because he was God's son.

MR. ALCOTT. Did God teach him in a particular way, different from the way in which he teaches the rest of his children?

WILLIAM B. Yes, he taught him before he came into the world.

MR. ALCOTT. How do the rest of you think Jesus was taught by God?

JOSIAH. I think God made him think, God made him understand, before he came from heaven, and God spoke to his spirit afterwards as he does to ours, only a great deal more.

MR. ALCOTT. Did God whisper into his mind?

JOSIAH. No, God made him think.

AUGUSTINE. I think if we should be as good as Jesus God would act on us just so, and we should know as much as he. He resisted the temptations.

MR. ALCOTT. What temptations?

AUGUSTINE. The appetites and passions; if we should resist them we should know as much as he did.

JOHN B. Jesus was just the same as we are, only a great deal better.

MR. ALCOTT. How was he "just the same"?

JOHN B. Why God made him, and God made us.

MR. ALCOTT. Was it God or Jesus who made the difference between Jesus and us?

JOHN B. Jesus.

WILLIAM B. I think God made the difference, for God does not help us so much as he did Jesus.

MR. ALCOTT. Who think, that even if you do all you can, God will not help you as much? (*Many rose.*) Does God help you as much as he did Jesus.

CHARLES. I think he helps us in proportion — as much as we deserve.

MR. ALCOTT. He offers just as much, but you do not take it. All that think that if you did all you could, God would help you as he did Jesus, may rise. (*Most rose.*) What makes the difference? Is it not a choice of the Will? Do you think Jesus was a favorite?

WELLES. I do not like to say so. I think Jesus was helped that he might help others.

THE REST. So do I.

MR. ALCOTT. Now those may rise who think that if you should do as much as you can, you would be helped as much as Jesus was?

(*Several rose.*)

AUGUSTINE. Everyone would be like Jesus if everyone was as willing as God is.

JOHN B. I cannot understand why Jesus Christ was so much better than anybody else. I don't see how, or why.

MR. ALCOTT. Do other people try as much?

JOHN B. I don't see what made him try so much more.

RECORDER. That is the very question, John, which all the world are asking. It takes a life to answer it — Why is it that Jesus tried; and why do not others try; and how can all be made to try as he did.

MR. ALCOTT. It will be the effect of these conversations, to answer this question, I hope.

GEORGE K. I was most interested in his growing wiser and better every day, as is mentioned in the last verse.

MR. ALCOTT. What does "grow in wisdom and stature" mean?

GEORGE K. His mind grew, and his body grew.

MR. ALCOTT. Can you give some emblem of this?

GEORGE K. He opened out like the tree from the nut.

MR. ALCOTT. Could it be seen how he opened out?

GEORGE K. They could not see his spirit, but they could see his body grow.

MR. ALCOTT. You may give some emblems of Jesus' growth.

LUCIA. He was like the seed, which sprouts underground a good while, first. And, Mr. Alcott, I was interested about their seeking him among their acquaintance. As they were travelling home, Joseph wanted to talk with Jesus, and so he found out he was gone, and began to seek him with great anxiety.

MR. ALCOTT. What does kinsfolk mean?

LUCIA. Relations.

MR. ALCOTT. How many have heard the words "kin, akin, kindred, kind, kindly"? "Kind" was the old Saxon word for nature.

ONE. I think it is strange that Jesus was not frightened at being left so long!

EMMA. He knew God would take care of him.

CHARLES. God would take care of his own son! —

MR. ALCOTT. Do you suppose it possible for children to make remarks which would make their parents better?

FRANCIS. I don't see why they should not.

MR. ALCOTT. Suppose a child is well instructed in spiritual things, and converses on these with his parents, and makes them understand better than they did before, though they had learned these before. (One asked, how could that be?) Because the child understands his own nature; which gives him the meaning of all words and all instruction.

FRANKLIN. I like best their finding him in the temple, and his telling them what he came into the world for.

CHARLES. I thought the doctors asked him questions, not to get information out of him, but to try him; and they were taught in spite of themselves, and very much shamed.

EMMA. I was interested in Jesus' answer to Mary.

EDWARD J. So was I, and at their not understanding what he meant.

MR. ALCOTT. What did he mean?

EDWARD J. God's business.

MR. ALCOTT. What kind of questions do you think Jesus asked the doctors; what sort of a conversation was it?

GEORGE K. I think he asked whether they loved God, and loved to pray to God, and what sort of men they were.

EMMA. I think he asked questions about God in man, about Spirit.

CHARLES. I thought he asked questions to try their learning; for they thought they knew a great deal; he asked what they believed about God.

WILLIAM B. I think the doctors asked Jesus questions, not to puzzle him, but to see what he knew; and he asked them questions so as to tell them the truth when they made mistakes.

(Here Mr. Alcott said, Perhaps he was not aware that he knew more than they did. He inquired, and listened to what they said, and then answered what was in his mind simply. The children here that listen best, answer best, and some answers given here have surprised people, and they have wondered how young children should understand such things.)

EMMA. I don't think we know much.

MR. ALCOTT. No; and self-knowledge is not likely to make people vain; but knowledge of rocks and shells and such outward things often does.

EMMA. I heard that a person said, that he should think we would know too much to say such things as we do.

MR. ALCOTT. I suppose he did not understand what you meant by the things you said.

SEVERAL. I thought it was a pleasant conversation.

OTHERS. It was more of a discussion than a conversation.

MR. ALCOTT. Why were they astonished at his answers?

WILLIAM B. Because they implied so much knowledge of God and spiritual subjects.

LEMUEL. This was the best sort of knowledge.

SEVERAL. Because he was so young.

MR. ALCOTT. Did Jesus go there to teach or to be taught? I have often been taught by what very small children have said; and astonished at their answers. I think Jesus went there to be taught; but his very questions taught them. Has truth any age? Is it not always the same in young and old? Is it not immortal? Truth is old.

CHARLES. Yes; because it always was.

MR. ALCOTT. And Truth is young; it is perpetually renewing itself. All wisdom is not in grown up people. — Do you believe there are any children now, who instruct grown up people by their under-standing and their answers? *(Many thought so.)* Was it natural for Mary and Joseph to feel anxious?

ALL. Yes.

MR. ALCOTT. Was it natural for Mary to say what she did to her son?

ALL. Yes.

MR. ALCOTT. What feeling did her words express?

SEVERAL. Anxiety; a mother's love.

(Mr. Alcott remarked at large on a mother's love.)

RECORDER. Did you hear how, at the fire in Sea Street the other night, a mother rushed into her burning house for her child, through the flames, and was burnt up with it?

(All testified great interest.)

MR. ALCOTT. Do any think that was wonderful?

SEVERAL. Not wonderful. It was natural.

MR. ALCOTT. Was it not beautiful?

JOHN B. Yes, but it would have been hard-hearted if she had not.

MR. ALCOTT. Do fathers and mothers now "wist" or "know" what their children are doing, what is going on in their minds, even when they are in the cradle, smiling and moving their little hands? (*There was no answer.*) Who have a little brother or sister at home? (*Some held up hands.*) Do you know what is going on in that little babe's mind? (*None.*) How many desire to know? (*Several held up hands.*) Do you think these little infants are about their father's business? (*Several held up hands.*) How many think it is a little animal, with nothing in its mind, and with no more goodness than a little kitten's as I heard a person say once? (*Four held up hands.*) Who think its goodness is much more positive than a kitten's? (*All the rest.*) Was the infant Jesus just like any little baby you know? (*All thought so but four.*) William B. thinks babies have no goodness at first. How do they get it?

WILLIAM B. I don't know.

AUGUSTINE. God gives it.

MR. ALCOTT. Who think that the spirit within is the real child, and the body but shows where it is? (*All raised hands.*) Who think that when babies play, and smile, and love, they have begun their father's business? (*All.*) Why did not Mary understand Jesus' answer?

MARTHA. She thought of Joseph's trade.

MR. ALCOTT. Do parents generally understand what is going on in the hearts and minds of their children?

WILLIAM B. Parents very seldom understand what passes in their children's minds, especially concerning spiritual subjects and their feelings.

(*Almost all the rest rose to assent to the same opinion.*)

MR. ALCOTT. Children are often about their father's business and parents are so much interested in their own, that they do not know it. Suppose a child is reading a book which interests its mind very much, and its mother calls it off and says, go and buy me a glass of gin, would that be calling him to or from his father's business? And when fathers keep their children at work and give them no education, yet all the time they can obtain, the children devote to their own improvement — is not that "the Father's" business? Very often children are absorbed in what interests them, and their parents reprove them, and yet they may be about their "Father's business." And you should not roughly interrupt it. Now let me ask you one question more — Do you think your parents sympathize with you as much as you would like to have them? (*All rose.*) Do you think Mr. Alcott does?

CHARLES. Not so much as my father and mother; but a great deal.

(The rest raised hands in assent. Mr. Alcott read a paraphrase, and spoke of the subject of this and the next conversation.)

CONVERSATION XV

* * *

INTEGRITY OF SPIRIT:

Filial Piety

Mr. Alcott recalled the subject of the last conversation, and then read:

JESUS AT NAZARETH FOURTEEN YEARS

And he went down with them, and came to Nazareth, and was subject unto them: but his mother kept all these sayings in her heart. And Jesus increased in wisdom and stature, and in favor with God and man. (Luke 2:51, 52.)

MR. ALCOTT. These verses contain all that is said of Jesus, from the time he was twelve till he was thirty years of age. What do you suppose he was doing all these eighteen years?

ANDREW. I think he was doing good to people, making them better.

MR. ALCOTT. Was he running of errands for his mother, and helping his father and mother?

FRANCIS. No indeed.

EMMA. I think he was doing things of that kind.

CHARLES. I think that all the time he had, he devoted to reading especially the Bible, and all the money he had he saved in order to buy good books, which he read.

MR. ALCOTT. You think he cultivated his mind. Do you think he studied nature?

MARTHA. Yes; he went into the Creation, and heard the birds sing, and saw the flowers, and the streams.

MR. ALCOTT. You do not think then that his eye was dull. Did he grow over nature, or did Nature grow over him?

CHARLES and OTHERS. He grew over Nature.

MR. ALCOTT. Have you ever imagined what kind of a person the father of Jesus was?

FRANCIS. I think he had a long beard, and was rather old.

CHARLES. I think he was a plain man, and went to church, and was very decided in his manner about things; not but that he was perfectly kind, but he would set his foot down, and say things should be so and so.

ANDREW. I think he looked like the bust of Plato. (*Pointing to the corner of the room.*)

MR. ALCOTT. How does Mary represent herself to you?

MARTHA. I think she was young, and her hair fell over her neck.

EMMA. I think she was very beautiful.

MR. ALCOTT. Do you mean inward or outward beauty?

EMMA. Both.

CHARLES. I think she was an angel before she was a woman. It seems to me, as if she must have been.

ANDREW. I think she looked like an angel, and like a woman too.

SAMUEL R. I thought she was very beautiful.

CHARLES. I thought she had a great deal of maternal feeling, and that made her beautiful; and that she looked like the Circassian women, very simple, and when not engaged in cleaning up her house, Jesus was sitting by, reading to her. Her eyes were dark blue.

FRANK. I think they were light blue.

CHARLES. And her hair was black.

EMMA. I thought it was brown.

MR. ALCOTT. I always have imagined her of light complexion, with delicate features, full blue eyes and light hair; and the the son resembled the Mother.

CHARLES. I think of Jesus reading to her, and when he could not pronounce a word his mother would take a needle and point out the letters, and show him how the word was spelt.

MR. ALCOTT. Well! I never thought of Jesus as learning to read, but as a quiet, meditative Child, who observed his own Nature, and Creation.

EMMA. When he was not engaged for his parents, I think his usual occupation was to go out into the woods to walk.

MARTHA. Sometimes I think he had a book in his walks.

CHARLES. I think he had a garden, and every day he went into it and gathered flowers for his mother.

MR. ALCOTT. Yes; I have seen a very beautiful picture of Jesus in his childhood, with flowers in his hands. He liked to be influenced by Nature; he was imaginative; he had a magnificent imagination; he was poetical; he seemed to have every thing in his mind; it was a perfect mind — good Sense, just Judgment, entire Faith. He grew up like a tree in the midst of Nature. The scenery around Nazareth was very impressive. Nazareth was not a city, but a town.

EMMA. I think if I could draw, I could show exactly how the house looked in which he lived, I seem to see it so clearly.

EDWARD J. That reading does not bring anything to my mind, it is not long enough.

WILLIAM C. I think he was growing wise.

JOHN B. I think that after he went to Nazareth, he told his mother what he had been doing in the temple, and what his "Father's business" was, and she kept it all to herself.

ALEXANDER. I think the reason she did not tell anybody what he said was, because she did not want people to praise him. She did not want him to be proud, for she did not know that he could not be proud, but she knew from the angel, that he was to be great.

WILLIAM B. He wanted to do right.

MR. ALCOTT. Why did he want to do right?

EMMA. Because he loved his parents.

MR. ALCOTT. Love, love! How many of you have that love, which makes you want to obey your parents, both when they ask you, and before they ask you, as Jesus did?

(*Most held up their hands.*)

EDWARD J. I don't know exactly.

MR. ALCOTT. What word expresses yielding to instruction easily? It is a beautiful word.

EMMA. Submissive.

MR. ALCOTT. There is submission in it.

GEORGE B. Obedience.

MR. ALCOTT. It leads to obedience. I must tell you the word; it is docility.

CHARLES. I thought that word applied to animals.

MR. ALCOTT. Animals have it, but it may be applied to men. Andrew is docile; Emma is docile; Charles disputes; he has a sturdy will; he does not like to bend. The opposite of docility is obstinacy; the excess of docility is weakness. Jesus was docile, asking and receiving, ready to be taught. Who among you are docile? (*Some.*) The opposite of docility is forwardness also. Can any of you remember when you wanted to do something very much, and knew your parents did not want you to do it, but they had not said anything to you about it; and yet you gave up your want? (*Some held up hands.*) How many of you mind your parents, because you think they will punish you, and in some way make you do as they wish?

(*Some hesitated, but none acknowledged. Here Mr. Alcott repeated these questions, and asked if they felt as ready to obey as was best, and as they wished to.*)

CHARLES. Towards my parents I feel willing; I don't know as I do towards others.

MR. ALCOTT. Do you think you are docile?

CHARLES. Yes.

MR. ALCOTT. I do not. I must differ from you in this. I think you lack docility. I am not aware that any of you have ever acknowledged that you avoided doing wrong from the fear of punishment.

NATHAN. Josiah has.

MR. ALCOTT. How is it now?

EMMA. I have been influenced by it sometimes.

(Several others acknowledged.)

MR. ALCOTT. I think I was influenced by the fear of punishment when I was a boy; and I want you all to think if you do not sometimes think among other motives for obedience, that if you do wrong you may have a clap on the hand, or be punished some other way.

CHARLES. I am not afraid of being clapped on the hand.

MR. ALCOTT. I am not sure that you are not sometimes influenced by the thought of that among other things.

CHARLES. I am not!

MR. ALCOTT. I hope you will not get excited on this subject, Charles. You mean that you can bear it, and you do bear it very well; but I think it is not agreeable to you.

CHARLES. No; not agreeable; but I am not kept from wrong by fear of it.

EMMA. When I do wrong I never think of doing it till I have done it, and then I know it.

MR. ALCOTT. You do not premeditate evil. How many of you premeditate doing wrong? *(Several rose; Emma also.)* You think something may be done, which you know is wrong, yet you do it.

NATHAN. I am not kept from doing it by being clapped on the hand.

CHARLES. Nor I.

MR. ALCOTT. Those who have been punished within the last six months, may rise. *(A good many rose.)* Now those who have done wrong, whether punished or not. *(All rose but Nathan.)* Have you not done wrong for six months?

NATHAN. No.

MR. ALCOTT. Have you not been angry; nor struck anybody, nor said anything wrong; nor felt anything wrong during this time?

NATHAN. No *(to each item answering)*.

MR. ALCOTT. Well; you are an extraordinary person. No one else would say so. *(Nathan did not answer.)* Suppose Luke had written down that Jesus sometimes quarrelled with his companions, sometimes disobeyed his mother, &c.

JOHN B. I should not have believed him.

SAMUEL T. I should have torn the leaves out of my Bible.

AUGUSTINE. The apocryphal Bible tells a great many such stories.

EDWARD J. I should like to hear some of them.

MR. ALCOTT. No; we cannot waste the time. Charles, what are you interested in today?

CHARLES. Jesus' being subject to his father and mother means, that he felt their superiority in knowledge and age.

MR. ALCOTT. Did Jesus always do such things with his hands as he was asked to do by his parents? *(All thought so.)* But the mind does things as well as the hands. Did his mind do such things as his parents wished; did he, with his ready love, foresee their desires? *(They assented.)* And do you know what is going on in your mother's mind? Do you enter into her views, and ideas, and feelings so as to accommodate your conduct to her wishes? The reason there is so little obedience is, that mothers do not know what is in the children's minds, and the children do not know what is in the mothers' minds.

FRANCIS. I think my mother knows what is going on in my mind pretty often; but I do not know what is going on in hers, except sometimes.

MR. ALCOTT. Love gives one a knowledge of the inmost nature of another. Such as love know most of those they love. There is a saying which has a great deal of truth in it — "Love and do what you will;" but hate, and you must be restrained, or you will do nothing but what is wrong. Are children's minds ever superior to those of their parents? (*Some thought so.*) What is your opinion at present; do you think there are some children superior to their parents?

(*Several held up hands.*)

CHARLES. I think every little baby is holier than its father and mother.

MR. ALCOTT. But suppose the father and mother had not lost their babyhood. How many of you think you have lost your holiness? (*All rose.*) I know children who get so used to scratch one another's faces, that they do not mind it in the least. They have lost their sensibility; but at first it is not so.

MARTHA. I know a little child that always cries when her brother is hurt.

RECORDER. Josiah has a little brother that not only cries when some one is hurt, but whenever anything is broken.

EMMA. My sister is rather careless, and when she breaks anything she is very sorry.

FRANCIS. My brother likes to tread on worms.

MR. ALCOTT. And you know that one boy in this school confessed, that at first he did not like to put worms on a hook, but afterwards he made such a beast of himself that he did not care. This is cruelty; but tenderness does not like to see pain or to give it. It feels there is something holy where there is life. It respects life, even in a bug. We do not know but Herod began his cruelty in being cruel to insects.

EMMA. An infant is superior to its parents in goodness.

MR. ALCOTT. Name some of that goodness.

EMMA. An infant is more holy. It has a different kind of goodness from that of an excellent man.

LUCIA. It never knew how to do wrong. But good men did wrong when they were young.

MR. ALCOTT. How came they to begin?

LUCIA. They saw others do wrong.

MR. ALCOTT. But how did the first persons begin?

LUCIA. They were tempted by their passions?

MR. ALCOTT. Have little children any passions?

LUCIA. Yes.

MR. ALCOTT. Where do passions come from? *(There was no reply.)* Was Jesus tempted while a child? And did he eat of the tree of knowledge?

WILLIAM B. He was tempted, but he did not do the evil, and he was not tempted so often as we, because he was holy.

MR. ALCOTT. Do you see any distinction between holiness and virtue?

SOME. Yes.

MR. ALCOTT. What is virtue?

CHARLES. It is acting.

MR. ALCOTT. Virtue comes by the trial of our holiness. It is holiness brought out and represented.

CHARLES. Can we be virtuous unless we are holy?

MR. ALCOTT. Virtue is the sign of holiness; it is holiness drawn out.

MR. ALCOTT. How was Jesus employed eighteen years at Nazareth?

SEVERAL. Working in his father's shop.

MR. ALCOTT. What was his mind doing?

SEVERAL. He was thinking of what he came into the world for?

MR. ALCOTT. Each one of you may think what you came into the world for, and tell me.

> *(They did not seem to think they came into the world on any particular mission, but Mr. Alcott seemed to convince them that they must have done so, and that each one must find out for himself what it was, as Jesus probably did, by self insight, and observation of nature and life.)*

MR. ALCOTT. Now I should like to know what you came into the world for — what is your mission on earth?

SAMUEL R. To do good and be good.

MR. ALCOTT. Such of you as think that your souls came into your bodies to do what Jesus did, may rise.

(*Most rose.*)

EMMA. Different things, but of the same kind.

MR. ALCOTT. How many of you have begun to feel this, and also an interest in the goodness of every child you meet in the street? (*Emma rose.*) Could any of you give up anything you liked for the sake of making others better and happier?

FRANCIS. I could.

CHARLES. I want to get myself good first.

EMMA. Some people never do themselves or anybody else any good.

MR. ALCOTT. And so you, Charles, are engaged all the time in getting yourself good!

CHARLES. Not all the time.

MR. ALCOTT. I should say that the great end for which we came into the world, was to grow — to unfold the spiritual nature —spiritual growth. Perhaps none of you have yet felt what your great end is. I think I was thirteen years old when I began to think about my mission.

EMMA. I did not begin very early.

MR. ALCOTT. You have thought how you could use your faculties, however. Has any other one thought about it much?

FRANCIS. I have thought about it some.

CHARLES. I think I shall use my Soul in selling oil.

MR. ALCOTT. And in doing that, you may do a great deal of good. The humblest life may be a bright one. A beggar may be a glorious creature; and so may a rich man.

GEORGE B. I shall be a merchant.

MR. ALCOTT. Do you think you shall do a great deal of good, by being a merchant?

GEORGE B. I never thought about that.

MR. ALCOTT. When I was young, I first cultivated land. Then I went about the world several years. At last I thought my mind was best fitted for teaching, and here I now am, teaching in this Temple, and I hope I shall do good to many children, as well as parents, before I go to my FATHER.

CONVERSATION XVI

* * *

ORGANIZATION OF SPIRIT:

Corporeal Relations

Mr. Alcott asked how they felt disposed towards the conversation today. Two or three thought they should not be interested; and he asked why?

LEMUEL. I don't feel as if I should.

MR. ALCOTT. Well, can you not master this feeling? Try to-day.

WILLIAM C. I have the headache.

MR. ALCOTT. We have spoken sometimes of the power of spirit over body. Now see if you cannot exert your spirit so as to drive the headache away. (*He then read the Genealogy of Jesus from God.*[29]) Now tell me what this reading has brought into your minds.

SEVERAL. Nothing.

LEMUEL. It is about the generation of Christ from God.

MR. ALCOTT. What do you mean by generation?

LEMUEL. The fathers of Jesus Christ.

MR. ALCOTT. The parentage, fatherhood.

GEORGE K. Those were very hard names, yet I thought it all meant something, but I did not know what.

ANDREW. It was to show how many people lived before Jesus Christ, so as to show at what time he lived.

FRANKLIN. It was to show who his forefathers were.

MR. ALCOTT. What is a forefather?

AUGUSTINE. A grandfather, and his father. That was a list of the forefathers of Jesus, a genealogy.

MARTHA. I don't think Adam was the son of God, but I know Jesus was.

MR. ALCOTT. What do you mean by Adam's not being the son of God? Here is the assertion in the book which tells no lies.

JOSIAH. Both Adam and Jesus were the sons of God.

AUGUSTINE. In one sense, we are all the sons of God.

FRANKLIN. I think that Adam was called the son of God, because he had no earthly father, and so God made his body as well as his spirit. And God made Jesus' body, as well as spirit; for he was only supposed to be the son of Joseph.

MR. ALCOTT. Does that meet your difficulty, Martha?

MARTHA. Yes.

MR. ALCOTT. Are you the daughter of God?

MARTHA. In one sense. My spirit is.

MR. ALCOTT. But when you think of another part of yourself, do you take something else into consideration beside God?

MARTHA. My body, my parents.

MR. ALCOTT. Do you know of any word which expresses the idea of a spirit's taking on a body? I do not mean to ask you what a body's coming forth into this world all formed and perfected is; for we know that that is birth. — But there was a moment when the spirit first took flesh upon itself and began to build a body around itself. — Have you ever heard the word incarnation?

FRANKLIN. Yes, I have heard that word.

MR. ALCOTT. It means taking on flesh. It is derived from a word that means of the flesh.

GEORGE K. I always wondered where our bodies were built up. I should not think they could be built in heaven, because there is no matter there.

MR. ALCOTT. The rose is first given to us as a seed, and, by certain laws of God, it unfolds itself when it is put in the ground, and the rain and dews fall on it, and the air is absorbed into it, and the sunshine lies upon it, and many invisible particles of matter become incorporated with it. So the seed of a human being is placed in the midst of matter which nourishes it, and it grows and becomes perfected. What is the body builder?

FRANKLIN. The spirit.

MR. ALCOTT. Spirit is the body builder; Temperance is the body preserver; Self-indulgence is the body waster; Spirit acts on and through matter. Do any of you think that matter is solid, unalterable, unyielding to the agency of spirit? (*Several held up hands.*) Or is it soft, yielding, fluid, easily moved, continually affected by the spirit that stirs in it, and shapes it to our senses? (*Most held up their hands.*) Is your body what it was an hour ago in all respects? (*None.*) Is any piece of matter in the same state that it was an hour ago?

(*They instanced pieces of furniture.*)

JOSIAH. Things are not in the same places, because the earth is moving round the sun.[30]

MR. ALCOTT. And the cause of all movement is spirit. Not only the whole universe is in motion, but every thing is in a state of change within it. There are sciences, which teach how the particles of bodies are mingled together, and how these particles are of different qualities from each other, and from the compound wholes which they make; and that changes of their relative positions and proportions are constantly going on; that all things which seem to be solid are continually wasting and becoming air; and that the invisible air is at all times being absorbed into solid bodies, and becoming visible.

Spirit acts in two great laws, Renovation and Decay. Growth is Spirit, organizing bodies, or building them up. — Spirit, taking down the solid body, is death. You are now in the process of growth. Your spirits are every day appropriating to their own use, for their own manifestation, various substances, which become incorporated with your bodies, by means of these laws established by God, and which you ought to endeavour to know and obey. Bye and bye, your growth will be completed, and then the law of decay will begin to act, and the waste and dissolution will take place, which ends in death. If these laws of God were understood and observed by every spirit, there would be no pain. We should be born without giving pain, should live without pain, and should lie down and die, as if sinking into a sweet sleep. The laws of renovation and decay would each bring pleasurable sensations.

FRANKLIN. Do you think you are beginning to go down, to decay?

MR. ALCOTT. I suppose I am beginning to die.

FRANKLIN. The spirit is climbing up while the body is going down.

MR. ALCOTT. Yes, and Paul once said that He "died daily; that while the outward man (or body) decayed, the inward man (or spirit) was renewed day by day." By the laws of incarnation, Spirit is transfused through bodies, first building them up, then taking them down. When Jesus was near dying, he called his disciples, and talked of the mutability of all things outward, of the destruction of the temple, Jerusalem, of empires, and of worlds; and then he spoke of the love, and faith, and living spirit, which had nothing to do with death, and which changed in nothing save its earthly garments. This temple that we are in will decay; it is decaying. Some men first planned it, then set others to collecting materials to execute their plan, who shaped their thought at last into this large building; this temple preexisted in their spirits. But already it has mouldered some.

FRANKLIN. Is it renewing too?

MR. ALCOTT. No; for there is nothing within it, to contend, by a perpetual endeavour at renovation, against the principle of decay, as there is in the human body. The principle of renovation in a human body contends hard against the principle of decay, even when it is accelerated by self-indulgence. God contends with the drunken man, while he is accelerating decay, by his intemperance.

Do you think God flowed through all the forefathers of Jesus down to Joseph? (*Many thought so.*) Do you think his spirit flowed on through your ancestors, and down to you? (*They thought so.*) Can you say that there is any of God in you? (*Several held up hands.*) Is your spirit in him? (*Yes.*) If you are self-indulgent, do you think your spirit will remain in him, connect your body with him, and thus keep it pure, healthy, and full of innocent pleasure? (*None raised hands.*) But your spirits may fall away from him, and so your bodies become diseased, and waste away in pain? What has been our subject today?

AUGUSTINE. Genealogy.

FRANKLIN. Incarnation.

MARTHA. The supernatural in the natural.

ANDREW. Changes of body in time.

GEORGE K. Changes of matter in time.

GEORGE B. Decay and building up of matter in time.

MR. ALCOTT. Spirit working in matter; organizing fathers and children. Now all may hold up their hands who have been as much interested in this conversation as they expected to be.

ALL. A great deal more.

MR. ALCOTT. And yet our subject has been one of great difficulty. The connexion between the body and the soul is mysterious, and hard to be understood.[31]

CONVERSATION XVII

* * *

SPIRITUAL VISION:

Blessedness

MR. ALCOTT. Where did we leave John the Baptist?

JOSIAH. He was preaching in the wilderness about Jesus being superior to himself.

ANOTHER. And talking of the three baptisms.

MR. ALCOTT. What do you remember about the baptisms?

CHARLES. That fire and water were emblematic, but that the Holy Spirit was not emblematic, for it was not material.

(Mr. Alcott then read.)

THE BAPTISM OF JESUS

And it came to pass in those days, when all the people were
baptized, that Jesus came from Nazareth of Galilee, to Jordan
unto John, to be baptized of him. But John forbad him,
saying, I have need to be baptized of thee, and comest thou to
me? And Jesus answering said unto him, Suffer it to be so
now: for thus it becometh us to fulfil all righteousness. Then
he suffered him: And [he] was baptized of John in Jordan. And
Jesus, when he was baptized, went up straightway out of the
water: And straightway coming up out of the water; and
praying, lo! he saw the heavens opened unto him, and he saw
the Spirit of God descending like a dove, in a bodily shape,
like a dove, and lighting upon him: And lo! there came a
voice from heaven, saying, Thou art my beloved Son, in
whom I am well pleased. And Jesus himself began to be about
thirty years of age. (Matt. 3:13 to the end. Mark 1:9,10,11.
Luke 3:21,22, and part of 23.)

(Mr. Alcott then asked the usual question.)

AUGUSTINE. Was the spirit in the shape of a dove, or did it descend
like a dove?

MR. ALCOTT. You have the same means of judging that I have.

AUGUSTINE. I should think that the heavens opening was a sort of
vision.

JOSIAH. The sky opened, and a white dove larger than the other
doves came from heaven. God sent it, but I do not know why he
sent a dove.

GEORGE K. He sent a dove because it represents love. I think the
angel Gabriel was in the dove. It stood on Jesus. I do not know
what it means by the heavens opening. The voice came either from
the dove, or from heaven above the sky.

EMMA. The dove represents purity. I think the voice was within the
conscience of Jesus.

ELLEN. I think the dove represents love and innocence. God put love in that and sent it to Jesus, to express his innocence. God was pleased with Jesus for his answer to John.

JOHN B. I think the dove represents innocence, but I do not think as George does, that it came from above the sky, but only from the sky. It was not a common dove. God formed a spirit into a dove and sent it to Jesus, because he liked Jesus better than any body else, for he was better.

ANDREW. I think John and Jesus saw a vision; it was secret to them, and no other person saw it. It was an angel that came; but God did not want the people to see an angel, and it appeared as a dove, which was a common thing to the people. The voice was within their souls.

MR. ALCOTT. Why should it be a dove, and not a serpent?

ANDREW. Because a dove could fly, and a serpent could not. [32]

EDWARD J. A dove means goodness, innocence.

CHARLES. I think of a dove in the midst of rays of light, with an olive branch in its mouth, and on its leaves are the words, "this is my beloved son," and after that, the rays always stayed round the head of Jesus.

MR. ALCOTT. That is your fancy.

FRANKLIN. There were rays round the dove, and angels in the rays, though they could not be seen; and it was these angels in the rays that sung, "This is my beloved son."

SAMUEL R. The dove came from without, I think, and the voice from within.

MARTHA. The dove was the sign of purity and peace.

MR. ALCOTT. Did that dove ever come to you? (*No answer.*) Or any thing like it? (*No answer.*) Did your conscience never say that you had done right?

MARTHA. Oh yes; sometimes.

LUCIA. I thought, that as John baptized to show that sins were washed out, it was not appropriate for him to baptize one who was freer from sin than himself, and that was the reason he said what he did to Jesus, as if he would change places with him.

ELLEN. Was Jesus any more pure after he was baptized than before?

MR. ALCOTT. I do not often give an opinion. What do you think about that?

ELLEN. I do not think he could be purer, but he was not proud of his goodness, and thought he might be better — he was humble, the holy spirit had made him good.

MR. ALCOTT. Why did John refuse to baptize Jesus?

CHARLES. Because he thought himself unworthy to touch him. Jesus had already been baptized by the Holy Ghost and was perfect, and did not need a baptism which was only emblematic of what he already had internally. But Jesus said he wanted to give a perfect example outwardly, as well as the perfect inwardly.

FRANKLIN. Jesus was baptized, to teach the people humility.

WELLES. It was humble to be baptized with water, when he was already baptized by the Holy Ghost, and the dove descended because he had humbled himself. I seem to see Jesus come out of the water upon the grass, and a dove larger than an eagle descend upon him, and then the voice comes from heaven, and John stands in astonishment. A few people standing near saw the dove, but hardly any heard the voice.

CHARLES. Heaven means where love and truth are. I cannot express what I mean. I suppose the opening of the sky was emblematic of the opening of the spirit.

AUGUSTINE. The opening of heaven was seeing more clearly into his own state of mind.

SEVERAL. I do not understand what it means.

ELLEN. The sky hides heaven from our view.

LUCIA. We call Jesus the Son of God; could we not say Socrates was almost the Son of God?

MR. ALCOTT. Almost perhaps. But Socrates did not know as much as Jesus. And Socrates tells us that he lost his holiness, but Jesus did not. Socrates passed through the fiery baptism of repentance, and the water baptism of temperance, in order to be baptized with the Holy Ghost, which Jesus had from his birth.

LUCIA. If you do wrong once, it cannot be said that you have Perfection.

LEMUEL. A person, doing wrong but once, is a foul spring; but the foul particles may settle down, and then it will be clear again.

MANY. And they need do wrong no more.

MR. ALCOTT. That would prevent more foul matter from getting in. But what is to be done with the particles that are there?

(A long pause.)

ANDREW. You can flow away from them and leave them.

LUCIA. I think there is pure water under the mud and sand, which springs up, and softens it, and carries off the muddy particles, and leaves them somewhere, and so flows clear, and the spring is clear too.

MR. ALCOTT. What makes the water spring up and flow away? Whence comes the current?

LEMUEL. It comes from God. God is always helping.[33]

CONVERSATION XVIII

• • •

SPIRITUAL SUPREMACY:

Self-Subordination

MR. ALCOTT. We spoke last of John's preaching the baptism of repentance, purification, preparation for holiness.

LEMUEL. We talked of the emblem of an impure spring.

MR. ALCOTT. What should you think such baptism, as we now have in churches, would naturally lead to?

CHARLES. I should think it would make a person more conscientious, if he was old enough to know any thing about it.

MR. ALCOTT. Where did we leave Jesus?

SAMUEL T. Just come out of the water at Jordan.

(*Mr. Alcott read:*)

THE TEMPTATION OF JESUS

And Jesus being full of the Holy Ghost returned from Jordan: and was led by the spirit into the wilderness. Being forty days tempted of the devil. And in those days he did eat nothing. And when he had fasted forty days and forty nights, he was afterward an hungered: And when the tempter came to him, he said, If thou be the Son of God, Command that these stones be made bread. And Jesus answered him, saying, It is written, That man shall not live by bread alone, but by every word of God.

Then the devil taketh him up into the holy city, and setteth him on a pinnacle of the temple, and saith unto him, If thou be the Son of God, cast thyself down. For it is written, He shall give his angels charge over thee, to keep thee: And in their hands they shall bear thee up lest at any time thou dash thy foot against a stone. And Jesus answering said unto him, thou shalt not tempt the Lord thy God.

Again, the devil taketh him up into an exceeding high mountain, and showeth him all the kingdoms of the world, and the glory of them, and the devil said unto him, all these things will I give thee, all this power will I give thee, and the glory of them: for that is delivered unto me; and to whomsoever I will I give it. If thou wilt fall down and worship me, all shall be thine. And Jesus answered and said unto him, Get thee behind me, Satan: for it is written, Thou shalt worship the Lord thy God, and him only shalt thou serve. And when the devil had ended all the temptation, he departed from him for a season. And [he] was with the wild beasts; and the angels ministered unto him. (Matt. 4:1-11, Mark 4:12, 13, Luke 4:1-13.)

JOSEPH. I should not think Jesus would have gone into the wilderness where the devil could tempt him — I should think it was wrong to let the devil speak to him.

MR. ALCOTT. What do you mean by the devil?

JOSEPH. He is the same as you read about in Milton's Paradise; he lives in hell; he tempts people to do wrong; sometimes he tempts me, and makes me do wrong.

MR. ALCOTT. Does not Joseph make himself do wrong?

JOSEPH. Yes; but he causes me to.

MR. ALCOTT. When you tell him to go away earnestly, can you not help doing wrong?

JOSEPH. Yes; but if there were no Satan I never could do wrong.

MR. ALCOTT. Is not Joseph the Satan — have you not made a mistake in thinking the tempter was out of yourself? *(No answer.)* Should you know that your goodness was real, unless you had the power to do wrong? What do you think Satan is?

JOSEPH. A great creature.

MR. ALCOTT. Who made him?

JOSEPH. He made himself.

MR. ALCOTT. What did he make himself of?

JOSEPH. Of the stuff that is in hell.

MR. ALCOTT. Who made that stuff?

JOSEPH. God; it was good stuff till it fell down from heaven. Satan was at first a good spirit, but he took some stuff and went down to hell and made his body out of it.

MR. ALCOTT. Why did he go?

JOSEPH. He wanted something there. First God made him good, and then he saw something down in hell that he wanted.

MR. ALCOTT. What made him have such a naughty want?

JOSEPH. It put on some good shape.

MR. ALCOTT. Who made the deceiving shape that gave the naughty wants?

JOSEPH. It made itself — the place made itself.

MR. ALCOTT. I do not understand how places and things could make themselves.

(He said nothing.)

RECORDER. He seems to have an idea of the eternity of evil, founded on Milton's idea of the eternity of matter.

MR. ALCOTT. You do not make it out Joseph. But I think that your naughtiness begins in you — not in anybody else.

GEORGE B. I do not see why Jesus let the devil tempt him.

MR. ALCOTT. Jesus was led by the spirit into the wilderness.

JOSEPH. I should think the spirit would have kept the devil away.

AUGUSTINE. I suppose the spirit permitted him to tempt, to see how Jesus could overcome temptation and trial.

EDWARD J. I should think Jesus would have sent him away sooner.

MR. ALCOTT. Did he not stay long enough to find out that Jesus was the strongest?

EDWARD J. Yes.

MR. ALCOTT. Has he found that out about Edward yet?

EDWARD J. No.

ALEXANDER. God made the devil on purpose to tempt people; or, at least, when Satan had grown wicked, God used him as a tempter.

WELLES. The devil was made, so that God might see how people would act.

MR. ALCOTT. Could he not find out, without a devil?

WELLES. If there was no devil, there would be no more merit in doing right than wrong; there would be no conscience — or, at least, conscience would be of no use.

FREDERIC. I think the temptation was to show the devil that he could never get any advantage over Jesus. Jesus settled the matter with him.

MR. ALCOTT. Have you settled with the devil in this respect?

FREDERIC. No.

NATHAN. I don't see why Jesus let the devil tempt him.

MR. ALCOTT. Did Jesus have a body, that could be hungry, and want something to eat?

NATHAN. Yes.

MR. ALCOTT. Was that wrong?

NATHAN. No.

MR. ALCOTT. What wrong thing was he tempted to do?

NATHAN. To worship the devil.

MR. ALCOTT. Do you think your hungry body ever tempted you to do something wrong?

NATHAN. Yes, and I did wrong. I ate too much.

MR. ALCOTT. Was this the tempter that was in Paradise?

LEMUEL. Yes; and Jesus learnt to know good and evil by this trial.

MR. ALCOTT. What was the result of that eating in Paradise?

LEMUEL. Adam and Eve learned to know good and evil, by doing wrong instead of right.

MR. ALCOTT. Action shows the contrast.

JOHN B. Satan is a wicked spirit — but it is we who begin to do wrong.

MR. ALCOTT. Do we make the Satan within us?

JOHN B. Yes; we are Satans ourselves. He is connected somehow with our conscience.

MR. ALCOTT. Joseph, John has a different idea of Satan from you. He says we make Satans.

JOSEPH. I thought there was but one Satan who tempted.

MR. ALCOTT. Who else think that Satan is independent and lives out of the tempted souls?

JOHN B. No; he cannot, he has no body nor soul.

GEORGE K. God made one bad one to try the rest.

MR. ALCOTT. What did God make a bad one out of?

GEORGE K. Wickedness.

MR. ALCOTT. Where did he get the wickedness?

GEORGE K. He made it.

MR. ALCOTT. Goodness make wickedness?

GEORGE K. Why you know Adam and Eve did wrong and that made wickedness.

MR. ALCOTT. Oh, so Adam and Eve, after all, were the Satan makers — they made the tempter that tempted them?

SAMUEL T. All the bad things we do, make Satans.

JOSIAH. "Jesus being led by the spirit" expresses that Jesus went willingly to meditate; the devil was not a body; but that is a way to express that evil thoughts came — we call evil thoughts a devil.

MR. ALCOTT. Did Jesus expect these evil thoughts would come?

JOSIAH. No; the devil began with Adam and Eve, when they first had evil thoughts, and has increased and will increase by every body's evil thoughts, through generations and generations.[34]

MR. ALCOTT. Did he increase by Jesus Christ?

JOSIAH. No; for Jesus was good. Jesus was just like God, only he had not so much power.

JOHN D. I think God made Satan to try people.

LUCIA and EMMA. We make it ourselves, I do not know how.

CHARLES. I think evil comes from seeing others have what we want; from envy.

MR. ALCOTT. There is a remarkable difference in your answers. Some of you think God made Satan without, and others think we make him within ourselves. Those of you who think the latter, are the ones who resist evil most bravely. What was the first temptation of Jesus?

FREDERIC. He was inclined to eat bread; the inclination was the tempter.

MR. ALCOTT. Is it wrong to eat bread?

FREDERIC. It is giving way to the appetites.

EDWARD J. It would have seemed to be obeying Satan to make stones into bread.

JOSIAH. I do not see why it would be wrong for him to make stones into bread.

LEMUEL. He thought that if the devil could make him do any little thing, he would go and tell others that the Son of God obeyed him; and that would do harm.

MR. ALCOTT. What did Jesus' answer mean, "Man shall not live by bread alone"?

LUCIA. It means that the spirit is to be fed on the word of God, as the body is with bread.

MR. ALCOTT. How do you feed the spirit on the word of God?

LUCIA. When we give anything to the poor, or resist any temptation.

RECORDER. Suppose there is a chance for your spirit to feed on some of these commands of God; and your body is hungry for food, which must you choose?

LUCIA. To feed the spirit if you can do but one.

RECORDER. Suppose you were starving for instance, and could get money to buy bread, by murdering another, which should you do?

LUCIA. Starve.

RECORDER. What life would you feed in that case?

LUCIA. My spirit's life — and that was what Jesus did here.

RECORDER. Did he ever have any other occasion of making this same choice?

CHARLES. Yes; when he was crucified.

MR. ALCOTT. How many of you think you have lived on bread alone, rather than on the words of God, that give life?

(All held up hands.)

CHARLES. "Every word of God" means conscience.

MR. ALCOTT. Do you understand the second temptation?

JOSIAH. I do not see how Jesus could get up to the pinnacle of the temple. Evil thoughts could not put him there.

MR. ALCOTT. Did the devil take the body of Jesus up there?

LUCIA. Jesus must have thought of being up there.

ALEXANDER. I think the evil thought, that put him up there, was pride.

MR. ALCOTT. We must have another conversation on this subject. You have been somewhat inattentive today; and we have not finished our conversation. Temptation is a subject hard to be understood in all its bearings. It takes a life to apprehend it. Evil is ever tempting all our faculties; and few master it, holding the appetites and passions in subordination to conscience, the ruler the spirit.

CONVERSATION XIX

* * *

SPIRITUAL SUPREMACY:

Self-Control

MR. ALCOTT. Can you think today? *(All held up hands.)* What was the conversation upon last?

CHARLES. The temptations of Jesus.

MR. ALCOTT. We shall resume the subject to-day.

(Mr. Alcott re-read THE TEMPTATION OF JESUS.*)*

MR. ALCOTT. What is the meaning of the word tempt?

CHARLES. When things not your own are put in your way they tempt you.

FREDERIC. If you want to do something wrong and can scarce help it, you are tempted.

GEORGE K. If somebody encourages you in a bad want, you are tempted.

JOSEPH. If anybody urges you to do wrong, he tempts you.

EMMA. To want to do wrong is a temptation.

ELLEN. When anyone tries to persuade you that what you know to be wrong is right, you are tempted.

NATHAN. I think if anybody tells you to do anything, which you think wrong, and you do it, you are tempted.

MARTHA. Two boys may go into a confectionary, and one will persuade the other to buy something, because he hopes he will give him some.

FRANCIS. I once went into a grocer's shop with a boy, and he took some raisins out of a little barrel, went out, and the man did not see him.

MR. ALCOTT. Did you tell the man?

FRANCIS. No; I was ashamed for him.

GEORGE K. I have seen a boy tempted to do wrong by being laughed at for doing right.

MR. ALCOTT. That is the second temptation, perhaps, which comes from the love of praise, of having others like us. The other temptations mentioned were rather of the body, like the first temptation of Jesus. Do you think of any temptations coming from the mind?

FREDERIC. The mind tempts to show off.

MR. ALCOTT. How many have been tempted to do that in this school room, while conversing? (*Josiah and six others held up hands.*) When were you tempted to do so, Josiah?

JOSIAH. When I first came here, not lately.

MR. ALCOTT. Who always say things for the truth's sake, and not for display? (*All the rest rose.*) Is suffering a temptation to complain? (*They held up hands.*)

CHARLES. Slaveholders are sometimes tempted by the power they have over their slaves.

ANOTHER. Money is a temptation.

MR. ALCOTT. What subdues all these temptations?

GEORGE K. Conscience.

MR. ALCOTT. Was there ever any one in whom conscience determined that body, mind, and soul should do no wrong?

EMMA. Yes; Jesus subdued all temptations.

MR. ALCOTT. He overcame the world.

EMMA. The world means temptations.

CHARLES. The world means outward things.

MR. ALCOTT. The world means all that tempts the spirit from its own law. Do you think pure spirit can be tempted?

THE OLDER ONES. Jesus was tempted.

AUGUSTINE. We have not decided yet, whether it is Satan, or ourselves that tempts.

MR. ALCOTT. The desire, the ease of yielding, is Satan. What may the wilderness be the emblem of?

CHARLES. Solitude.

MR. ALCOTT. And the wild beasts that were there?

CHARLES. Passions and appetites.

MR. ALCOTT. It is very common to represent passions by animals; we say a person has a tiger heart.

EMMA. We say, "harmless as a dove" — "docile as a lamb."

MR. ALCOTT. Some people think that the animal creation is designed to teach us what is the tendency of the various passions. In all nations there are fables, in which the passions are played off against each other, by means of animal emblems. Jesus went into solitude, perhaps, to meditate upon the passions, and think how each one tempted the spirit.

RECORDER. And by what principle each should be regulated.

MR. ALCOTT. What does his "fasting and afterwards being an hungered" mean?

CHARLES. His mind was excited at first, so that he did not want food.

MR. ALCOTT. His mind was so peaceful, so sustained by God, that he did not need it. I never want to eat, when I am the most quietly happy. When one feels patient, he can wait for what he wants, without doing extraordinary things. Would it not have seemed impatience in Jesus to have turned the stones into bread? Would it not have seemed like distrusting God?

CHARLES. When anything seems wanting to us outwardly, we should doubt ourselves, not God.

MR. ALCOTT. What was the third temptation?

CHARLES. Bribery. The devil offered him the whole world.

MR. ALCOTT. What passion was addressed?

CHARLES. Avarice.

AUGUSTINE. I have a desire for money.

MR. ALCOTT. Was he tempted to exchange his heavenly kingdom for an earthly one?

CHARLES. To govern men's bodies, not their spirits.

MR. ALCOTT. The Genius of Jesus fitted him to be the greatest of monarchs and the richest of men.

FREDERIC. But he would not have had such real power, that would last, and increase always.

CHARLES. But if he had been a monarch he might have done a great deal of good.

MR. ALCOTT. Ah! that has been a temptation to many to get power — more power than they could use well. It is better not to go into temptation for the sake of doing good. Suppose Mr. Webster should say — I will humor people so that they shall make me President, and I will make up for doing wrong now, by governing well and doing good afterwards — would that be wise and right?

EMMA. No; because he might lose the desire to do right, if he did wrong now.

MR. ALCOTT. But suppose he says, No; I will use all my genius in illustrating what is true, and take my chance about being President — how is that?

ALL. That would be right.

MR. ALCOTT. Suppose a man does good things to be popular — does he serve the Lord?

JOHN B. No.

CHARLES. We serve the Lord when we do good for conscience' sake.

MR. ALCOTT. What did he mean by "Get thee behind me"?

EMMA. It means we must not serve for riches, or for honors.

MR. ALCOTT. But we must act according to our Idea of the Perfect, and say, get thee behind me, Appetite; get thee behind me, Passion; get thee behind me, Ambition. Perhaps this "high mountain" represented Ambition.

EMMA. My Sunday School teacher told me that there was a tradition among the Jews, that the Messiah would come from the clouds of heaven; and that the temptation of throwing himself from the pinnacle of the temple came out of that. If he had done it, he would have flattered their prejudices, and been received with honors as their Messiah.

MR. ALCOTT. Did Jesus ever do a miracle for display, or preach, to show his eloquence?

ALL. No.

MR. ALCOTT. And so Jesus was tempted in all his nature. But we must close the conversation on this passage, for the present; although we have not gone into the depths of it. There are inexhaustible meanings in it; for it represents that struggle for self-mastery, which the soul is ever making, when faithful to the Divine Law of Perfection, which conscience is proclaiming in every faculty and function of our being. Jesus subordinated the Body, Nature, and Life to this law. He overcame, and put all corporeal things under foot. And so should we strive to do. All Duty lies in striving after the Perfect.

CONVERSATION XX

* * *

SPIRITUAL REVERENCE:

Humility

MR. ALCOTT. Where did we leave John and Jesus?

SEVERAL. Jesus in the wilderness; and John at Jordan.

(Mr. Alcott pointed out the places on the map, and then read.)

TESTIMONY OF JOHN THE BAPTIST TO JESUS

And this is the record of John, when the Jews sent priests and Levites from Jerusalem to ask him, Who art thou? And he confessed, and denied not; but confessed, I am not the Christ. And they asked him, What then? Art thou Elias? And he saith, I am not. Art thou that prophet? And he answered, No. Then said they unto him, Who art thou? That we may give an answer to them that sent us. What sayest thou of thyself? He said, I am the voice of one crying in the wilderness, Make straight the way of the Lord, as said the prophet Esaias. And they which were sent were of the Pharisees. And they asked him, and said unto him, Why baptizest thou then, if thou be not that Christ, nor Elias, neither that prophet?

John answered them, saying, I baptize with water: but there standeth one among you, whom ye know not; He it is, who coming after me is preferred before me, whose shoe's latchet I am not worthy to unloose. These things were done in Bethabara beyond Jordan, where John was baptizing. (John 1:19-28.)

JOHN B. I did not understand about untying the "shoe-latchet."

JOSIAH. John wanted to express in a very strong way, how much greater Jesus was than himself.

MR. ALCOTT. What is that mode of expression called?

EDWARD J. A parable.

ELLEN. An allegory.

FRANKLIN. An emblem.

LUCIA. A figurative expression.

CHARLES. Stooping to unloose a shoe-latchet expresses feeling lowly in comparison, unworthy, humble. When he says he was not worthy to untie the shoe-latchet, he expresses a very great degree of elevation in Jesus, and great unworthiness in himself. I think John was very conscientious to deny that he was the Christ. If he had loved to get power, he would have taken advantage of their predispositon. [35]

FREDERIC. Why did not John tell them his name when they asked?

MR. ALCOTT. Was it not more important to tell them of his office? What do you suppose he meant by the "Voice of one crying," &c.?

FREDERIC. That he was a preacher of goodness.

AUGUSTINE. That he came from God.

MR. ALCOTT. Why did he not say, "I am a man crying," &c.?

FRANKLIN. He did not feel worthy to call himself a prophet.

GEORGE K. He was a preacher, and the most important part of a preacher is his voice.

WELLES. He wanted to make them think only of his preaching.

EDWARD. He was a teacher.

CHARLES. He was a herald.

MR. ALCOTT. One great man usually prepares the way for another.

CHARLES. Fulton discovered steam power, others applied it.

ELLEN. Ministers prepare the way for the Judgment Day.

MR. ALCOTT. What do you mean by Judgment Day?

ELLEN. The last day, the day when the world is to be destroyed.

MR. ALCOTT. When will that day come?

CHARLES. The day of Judgment is not any more at the end of the world than now. It is the Judgment of conscience every moment.

MR. ALCOTT. Ellen is thinking of burning worlds, open books, a Judge, an assembled universe.

LUCIA. I think the day of Judgment is when anyone dies; the conscience judges.

JOSEPH. Mr. Alcott, it does not mean any particular day; but they wanted to express how very certain and real the judgment is which goes on all the time, and so they expressed it in this way, for no words can exactly express it.

JOHN B. Whenever we do wrong it is a day of judgment to us.

MARTHA. Death is necessary for complete judgment.

EDWARD J. Death is necessary for any judgment.

AUGUSTINE. I do not think the world is to be destroyed.

(Several agreed.)

CHARLES. Some people think there is a throne of diamonds for God, and that bodies will go up.

MR. ALCOTT. Cannot you take all these outward things away from the Judgment, Ellen, and still have Judgment left?

ELLEN. Yes, but I think there are these outward things besides.

MR. ALCOTT. But to return. Why did they ask why he baptized?

GEORGE K. They seemed to think that only Elias or some prophet could baptize.

MR. ALCOTT. They perhaps understood him to say that he was no prophet. What does he mean when he says, "there is one among you whom you know not"?

WELLES. Where was Jesus?

AUGUSTINE. In the wilderness.

SOME. He was present among them there.

MR. ALCOTT. How many of think you would know a Saviour, if you saw one among you?

FRANK A. I should not know him, if he was dressed like other people.

MR. ALCOTT. Jesus was dressed like the others, and this was perhaps a good reason for their not knowing him?

CHARLES. I could tell him by his face.

WELLES. I could tell him by his actions.

MR. ALCOTT. We have had too much heat in the room today, yet some of you have been interested.

CONVERSATION XXI

* * *

CONCILIATION OF SPIRIT:

Self-Sacrifice

Mr. Alcott read:

JOHN'S TESTIMONY TO JESUS

The next day John seeth Jesus coming unto him, and saith, Behold the Lamb of God, which taketh away the sin of the world! This is he of whom I said, After me cometh a man which is preferred before me: for he was before me. And I knew him not: but that he should be made manifest to Israel, therefore am I come baptizing with water. And John bare record, saying, I saw the Spirit descending from heaven like a dove, and it abode upon him. And I knew him not: but he that sent me to baptize with water, the same said unto me, Upon whom thou shalt see the spirit descending, and remaining on him, the same is he which baptizeth with the Holy Ghost. And I saw, and bare record that this is the Son of God. (John 1.29-34.)

ANDREW. The dove came down to show John that Jesus was full of love.

MR. ALCOTT. What made the thoughts of dove and love come so near together in his mind?

ANDREW. A dove is the emblem of love. Jesus loved everybody, and everything, he never quarrelled, he was loving.

MR. ALCOTT. If you were painting a picture of this scene, should you put in the dove?

ANDREW. No; God made John imagine a dove. It was the love of Jesus in his thoughts, which his imagination shaped into a dove.

MR. ALCOTT. Suppose you had the thought of innocence in your mind, and you wanted other people to think of it with pleasure,

204 / How Like an Angel Came I Down

156 / *How Like an Angel Came I Down*

how could you represent all you felt about it in one word of an emblematic character?

ANDREW. I could think of a spring of fresh water.

ANOTHER. I should say a little lamb.

JOHN B. Jesus was called the Lamb of God because he was so innocent.

MR. ALCOTT. Where are all emblems found?

ANDREW. In Nature.

MR. ALCOTT. What is Nature?

CHARLES. An emblem of God.

MR. ALCOTT. And of the feelings of men, also.

SAMUEL T. I do not know what it means by its taking away the sins of the world.

MR. ALCOTT. Do you know how the Lamb of God could take away your naughtiness, Samuel?

SAMUEL T. No, unless it means that if you imitate Jesus Christ, it will lead you away from wickedness.

MR. ALCOTT. Well, that is a good meaning. When you began to talk of the temptation the other day, you were at first puzzled with the mountain, the pinnacle of the temple, &c.; but all was clear when you found they were emblems. Jesus Christ and his disciples talked a great deal in emblems. He used Nature to give meaning to the Soul. Do you like little lambs?

(All held up hands.)

ELLEN. They are perfect in shape.

FRANKLIN. They are emblems of innocence and humility.

ELLEN. Jesus was, really, all that a lamb is an emblem of.

MARTHA. The way a lamb teaches goodness is this; its happiness shows that its innocence is right.

MR. ALCOTT. Do you think, if there was a flock of lambs on the common, frolicking, loving one another, never quarrelling, and that were you to see them every day, you should learn not to quarrel, but be made better by having them so near you? *(Several raised hands.*) Would the lambs grow better by seeing and imitating you at play?

EDWARD. A lamb does not know what wrong is.

ANDREW. A lamb is the emblem of mildness.

MR. ALCOTT. Have you seen a butcher with his knife going to kill a lamb? It looks up to the butcher with a gentle, submissive, trusting look, and seems to say, what kind thing are you going to do to me, my good master? I am sure I shall like whatever you do. And then it lies without a struggle, and lets him put his knife in. It is surprised, perhaps, at the pain, but it thinks some good is coming in the end; it looks so very confiding and patient, as if it said, Well, I will bear it as well as I can, for I am sure you must be going to do me good. What is the lamb, all this time, an emblem of?

CHARLES. Submission.

ALEXANDER. Patience.

FRANKLIN. Forbearance.

FREDERIC. Trust.

EMMA. Self-Sacrifice.

MR. ALCOTT. And was not Jesus submissive, patient, forbearing, trustful, and self-sacrificing? Did he not give up his body with resignation and a noble fortitude? What other self-sacrifice is there, besides this of the body?

CHARLES. The feelings.

MR. ALCOTT. Are we often obliged to sacrifice our feelings?

SEVERAL. Yes, every day.

MR. ALCOTT. Have any of you sacrificed your dearest wishes to the good of others?

(*A few raised their hands.*)

RECORDER. Did any of you ever make a sacrifice, which you were sure no human being but yourself could know?

EMMA. Once.

MR. ALCOTT. Do you think that you ever made a sacrifice purely for its own sake?

JOSIAH. I do not think that I ever did. But, Mr. Alcott, why was Jesus called the lamb, rather than the dove?

MR. ALCOTT. The Jews used lambs in sacrifice.

EMMA. And Jesus was going to do what the lambs represented in the worship.

MR. ALCOTT. What act takes away sin?

CHARLES. Repentance.

MR. ALCOTT. The act I mean includes repentance, and also the reformation which flows from repentance. John preached repentance, but Jesus preached something more.

FRANKLIN. Self-Sacrifice.

MR. ALCOTT. Do you know why John said "I knew him not"?

JOSIAH. He did not know that he was the Messiah. The word Christ means anointed, you know. Kings used to be anointed in those days. Christ's anointment was the goodness and spirit God gave him, so that he might rule over other spirits.

MR. ALCOTT. How could John's baptizing make him known to the Jews, "manifest him in Israel"?

GEORGE K. Because they could know by the dove.

MR. ALCOTT. How should you be able to know Christ, if he were to come now?

EMMA. By being good.

MR. ALCOTT. John's mission was to call to repentance and purification; and this repentance and purification were necessary preparations for apprehending Christ. Goodness gives wisdom. You thought at our last conversation that there were some persons now, who preached the doctrine of John. Do you think there are any persons at the present time, who have an influence like Jesus Christ's, who baptized with the Holy Ghost? (*Several held up hands.*) Do you suppose that this repentance and purification of John's time, was like repentance and purification now-a-days? (*They all held up their hands.*) Do you think these emblems could be applied to what passes within your selves; can it be said of you that the baptism of repentance has been in your soul, and the dove has descended upon it? (*They hesitate.*)

Can you say to yourself, I have repented of doing wrong; I have turned away from my sins; I have gone down into the deep waters of baptism and washed away my sins; I have felt a spirit of holiness, gentleness, sweetness, come upon me, and seem to call me child, and tell me to hear and obey?

EMMA. I have felt so, somewhat.

ELLEN. I never felt so sorry as I ought.

(Some of them signified that they had not experienced these thoughts.)

MR. ALCOTT. Those may rise who think they have seen persons who seemed to have gone through all this. *(All rose but three or four.)* John, having seen Jesus baptized and visited by the dove, said "And I saw and bare record that he was the Son of God."

SEVERAL. He was God without the body.

MR. ALCOTT. Take away the body and would he be God? *(Many rose.)* Do any of you think that if the body were taken away, still there would be some difference?

LUCIA and JOSIAH. He had not quite so much power as God.

MR. ALCOTT. Do any of you think, that if your bodies were taken away, you should be God? *(No answer.)* Do any of you think that if a baby's body was taken away, its soul would be God?

EMMA. A part of God.

AUGUSTINE. We are all parts of God.

RECORDER. *(Aside)* What are you pursuing with these questions? You seem to wish them to come to the idea that purity of spirit is identity with God?

MR. ALCOTT. I am ascertaining their views of the difference between the absolute and derived, of God in man, and the Idea of Absolute Being typified in derivative. There is a sense in which God and man are One. *(To children)* If all the good there ever was in men were put together, would it be part of God?

FRANKLIN. It would be part of God.

MR. ALCOTT. In what sense was Jesus the Son of God?

FRANKLIN. There was no bad in him.

(More questions ensued, and the idea of identity of being, between Jesus and God was expressed by the larger number. Lucia, George K., and Josiah preserved the idea of difference of identity, but moral union.)

MR. ALCOTT. In these conversations I have asked you many questions, in order to find your views about them. Have you formed any notion regarding my opinions of the subjects talked about, from the questions asked you? Do you know what I think? All may rise who do. *(All rose.)* Who think that I believe Jesus was at first like ourselves in all respects? *(Lucia, Josiah, and George K.)* Who think that I regard him as God in a body? *(All the rest except Charles.)*

CHARLES. I cannot tell what you think; you sometimes talk on one side, and sometimes on the other. What do you think?

MR. ALCOTT. I prefer not to reply to such questions, because I do not wish to influence your opinions by mine. I teach what every pure person believes. Reflect upon these subjects, and come to your own conclusions. You will remember that when we began these conversations, we said we were going to study Spirit. And first we talked about Spirit in God; then, of Spirit in a new born Infant, brought by Angels, worshipped by Wise Men, taken care of by good Parents; then we talked of Spirit in the Temple conversing, though yet in a Child, with Learned Men, and astonishing them; then, of Spirit going to an humble Home and living in retirement obeying Parents and Laws; then of Spirit baptized and called Son by God; then of Spirit tempted and victorious; then of Spirit recognised as the Lamb of God, and Teacher of Men; and in our next conversation we shall speak of Spirit making disciples. — Do you think these conversations are of any use to you?

CHARLES. Yes; they teach us a great deal.

MR. ALCOTT. What do they teach you?

GEORGE K. To know ourselves.

MR. ALCOTT. And this is the most important knowledge. He who shall know himself shall know God, and his Fellow Men, and Nature, for all these are Imaged in his Soul. We have been studying a perfect Spirit manifesting itself in a Body like ours, and yet without sinning. The use of these conversations is to give us an Idea of this Perfect Man, this God in Flesh, and inspire us to strive to be like him.

CONVERSATION XXII

• • •

INSPIRATION OF THE AFFECTIONS:

Faith

MR. ALCOTT. Do you think that you feel the influence of these conversations when you are at home and elsewhere, and that it makes you behave better than what you would do, if we did not have them? (*Many raised their hands.*) Do you think that you all understand them fully?

NATHAN. I understand a good deal.

(*The rest raised their hands.*)

(*There was a pause.*)

(*Mr. Alcott then read:*)

FIRST DISCIPLES OF JESUS

Again, the next day after, John stood, and two of his disciples; and looking upon Jesus as he walked, he saith Behold the Lamb of God! And the two disciples heard him speak, and they followed Jesus. Then Jesus turned, and saw them following, and saith unto them, What seek ye? They said unto him, Rabbi (which is to say, being interpreted, Master) where dwellest thou? He said unto them, Come and see. They came and saw where he dwelt, and abode with him that day; for it was about the tenth hour. One of the two which heard John speak, and followed him, was Andrew, Simon Peter's brother. He first findeth his own brother

Simon, and saith unto him, We have found the Messias, which is, being interpreted, the Christ. And he brought him to Jesus. And when Jesus beheld him, he said, Thou art Simon the Son of Jona: thou shalt be called Cephas, which is by interpretation, A stone.

The day following Jesus would go forth into Galilee, and findeth Philip, and saith unto him, Follow me. Now Philip was of Bethsaida, the city of Andrew and Peter. Philip findeth Nathanael, and saith unto him, We have found him, of whom Moses in the law, and the prophets, did write, Jesus of Nazareth, the son of Joseph. And Nathanael said unto him, Can there any good thing come out of Nazareth? Philip saith unto him, Come and see. Jesus saw Nathanael coming to him, and saith of him, Behold an Israelite indeed, in whom is no guile! Nathanael said unto him, Whence knowest thou me? Jesus answered and said unto him, Before that Philip called thee, when thou was under the fig-tree, I saw thee. Nathanael answered and saith unto him, Rabbi, thou art the Son of God; thou art the King of Israel. Jesus answered and said unto him, Because I said unto thee, I saw thee under the fig-tree, believest thou? Thou shalt see greater things than these. And he saith unto him, Verily, verily, I say unto you, Hereafter ye shall see heaven open, and the angels of God ascending and descending upon the Son of man. (John 1:35, to the end.)

AUGUSTINE. They followed him because they thought "Lamb of God" must mean Christ.

GEORGE K. I think they did not mean that he should turn and speak to them; they wanted to see him do some miracles.

LEMUEL. So do I.

MR. ALCOTT. Why did they want to know where he dwelt?

CHARLES. They wanted to observe his habits, to see how he acted, so as to do so too. They wanted to hear him talk, so as to think as he did.

MR. ALCOTT. He said "Come and see."

CHARLES. That was a plain answer.

FREDERIC. They must live with him, to get the knowledge they could get in no other way, so they "abode with him that day."

ELLEN. He wanted to encourage them to be his disciples.

MR. ALCOTT. What feeling made him say, "Come and see"?

SEVERAL. Hospitality. Gentlemanliness. Politeness. Kindness. Affection.

(Mr. Alcott remarked on the true meaning of the word gentleman.)

MR. ALCOTT. What do you think they talked of that day?

SEVERAL. They talked about religion; about Spirit. They asked where he came from; what he would do.

MR. ALCOTT. How were the manners of Jesus?

SEVERAL. Gentle. Graceful. Cheerful. Sweet. Full of bright smiles.

MR. ALCOTT. What manners do you think Christianity, that is, the thoughts and feelings that were in Jesus Christ, would give every one? Do you think that if a child grew up as gentle as Jesus, as respectful to the old, as tender to every companion, without ill temper, indolence, or want of feeling, he would be graceful and polite? So they passed the time delightfully. Do you think that you ever had any such time?

SEVERAL. Yes; these Conversations on Jesus Christ.

OTHERS. In good ministers' talk.

OTHERS. In sermons.

ONE. Some sermons are dry.

MR. ALCOTT. Who have delightful ideas and feelings about ministers? *(Almost all held up hands.)* How many take great pleasure in hearing sermons? *(A few.)*

EMMA. Dr. Channing is so easy to understand.

SUSAN and OTHERS. I never understand anything.

FRANCIS. I can understand Mr. Barnard.

SEVERAL. I never understand all that any minister says.

MR. ALCOTT. Why did Andrew go and find Peter?

EMMA. Because he loved him, and wanted him to hear, too.

MR. ALCOTT. Do you think Andrew was a good brother?

SEVERAL. Yes. Kind. Generous. Affectionate.

CHARLES. He had faith that Jesus was Christ.

MR. ALCOTT. What does Christ mean?

CHARLES. Messiah.

GEORGE K. Saviour.

MR. ALCOTT. What does Saviour mean?

CHARLES. One who saves you from sin.

MR. ALCOTT. JESUS (*the Hebrew word*) means, he saves; EMMAN-UEL means, God present; CHRIST means, annointed with oil; MESSIAH means, a Messenger sent. Why did Jesus call Simon a Stone?

AUGUSTINE and ANDREW. Stone represents Faith.

GEORGE B. Courage.

LEMUEL. Courage to suffer.

NATHAN and LUCIA. Because he was strong.

FREDERIC. No; it was because he was hard-hearted and would deny Jesus.

EMMA. Peter seemed often to speak without thinking, but this is no emblem of that.

CHARLES. Peter always spoke true to his feelings.

MR. ALCOTT. Why did Jesus call Philip?

GEORGE K. To instruct him.

MR. ALCOTT. What did Philip mean by what he said to Nathanael?

CHARLES. He wanted Nathanael to have the same advantages of instruction.

MR. ALCOTT. What was meant by "an Israelite indeed"?

SEVERAL. Honest. Unpretending. Not hypocritical.

MR. ALCOTT. Have any of you guile, that is, cunning, pretension, prejudice, deceptive habits? (*Several held up hands.*) Have any of you guile in yourselves, pretence, deception?

EMMA. Very likely I have guile, but I do not know it if I have.

MR. ALCOTT. Who have guile in themselves? (*All rose but Emma.*) What does beguiled mean?

SEVERAL. Deceived. Led away.

MR. ALCOTT. What was the greatest thing which Jesus did?

EDWARD J. and OTHERS. Raising Lazarus.

EMMA. I cannot tell what was greatest.

CHARLES and JOHN B. The Crucifixion; because it had so much self-sacrifice.

AUGUSTINE. The Transfiguration, for that showed he could make their thoughts open, so they could see heaven.

LEMUEL. The Crucifixion, because he bore it so.

FRANKLIN. And was so patient with the insults.

EMMA. And he had such patience with his disciples, who went to sleep that night when he asked them to pray for him.

MR. ALCOTT. Those who think that these virtues are greater, more wonderful, require a higher power than raising the dead, may rise. (*All rose.*) What does it mean by the angels of God "ascending and descending upon the Son of man"?

CHARLES. The inward Spirit opens, and good thoughts go out and come in to the Soul.

MR. ALCOTT. Do the rest think Charles is right?

WELLES. I think he meant something besides.

(*All the rest agreed with Charles.*)

MR. ALCOTT. Why is Jesus called "the Son of man"?

AUGUSTINE. Because God is the only real Man; common men are not perfect men. Jesus was the only Perfect Man because he was God.

CHARLES. He was called "Son of man" because he was the child of earthly parents.

LEMUEL. Because his body was the Son of man; but his spirit was the Son of God.

WELLES. I don't know why he should be called the Son of man more than anybody else.

MR. ALCOTT. The "Son of man" may mean his Humanity, and the "Son of God" his Divinity. He was surely the Son of man; and some deem him so perfect that they make him God, as Augustine has said.

CONVERSATION XXIII

* * *

SPIRITUAL REFINEMENT:

Chastity

MR. ALCOTT. Where did we leave Jesus?

SEVERAL. In Galilee, with John, and Andrew, and Peter.

MR. ALCOTT. Do you remember the last words?

GEORGE K. "Hereafter ye shall see heaven open, and the angels of God ascending and descending upon the Son of man."

FREDERIC. And we said, that meant good thoughts entering in and proceeding from the Spirit of man.

(*Mr. Alcott then read:*)

MARRIAGE FESTIVAL, AT CANA, IN GALILEE

And the third day there was a marriage in Cana of Galilee; and the mother of Jesus was there. And both Jesus was called, and his disciples, to the marriage. And when they wanted wine, the mother of Jesus saith unto him, They have no wine. Jesus saith unto her, Woman, what have I to do with thee? Mine hour is not yet come. His mother saith unto the servants, Whatsoever he saith unto you, do it.

And there were set there six water-pots of stone, after the manner of the purifying of the Jews, containing two or three firkins apiece. Jesus saith unto them, Fill the water-pots with water. And they filled them up to the brim. And he saith unto them, Draw out now, and bear unto the Governor of the feast. And they bare it. When the ruler of the feast had tasted the water that was made wine, and knew not whence it was (but the servants which drew the water knew), the governor of the feast called the bridegroom, And saith unto him, Every man at the beginning doth set forth good wine; and when men have well drunk, then that which is worse; but thou hast kept the good wine until now.

This beginning of miracles did Jesus in Cana of Galilee, and manifested forth his glory; and his disciples believed on him. (John 2:1-12.)

(Mr. Alcott then asked the usual question.)

JOSIAH. The changing of the water into wine interested me most. If we had faith, and were as good as Jesus, we could change water into wine.

MR. ALCOTT. Do all think so?

(Most held up hands.)

NATHAN. I like the water changing into wine. He had more spirit than we have, but I don't see how he did it.

EDWARD J. I liked his mother telling him there was no wine.

MARTHA. I was most interested in his answer. I thought it meant that his time to do the miracle would come. I was rather surprised that his mother told him they had no wine. It seemed as if she believed he could make some, and yet he had worked no miracles before.

GEORGE K. I thought, when he said, "My hour is not yet come," that he meant his hour to die was not yet come, so he would do this miracle.

ANDREW. I cannot express my thoughts about his turning water into wine.

JOHN B. And I cannot express my thought about his saying, "Woman, what have I to do with thee?" and yet I think I know what it means.

MR. ALCOTT. Do you often have thoughts which you cannot express?

JOHN and ANDREW. Yes.

AUGUSTINE. I had some thoughts I could not express about the angels of God ascending and descending upon the Son of man.

FRANKLIN. I thought in this place, that Mary had faith that Jesus would do the miracle, and his answer meant that he would, bye and bye. It is plain she expected it, from what she said to the servants.

FREDERIC. I think as George said.

LEMUEL. I thought "mine hour is not yet come," meant the hour to do the miracle.

GEORGE B. I saw the stone watering pots in the court.

ALEXANDER. I do not think we could turn water into wine, even if we were as good as Jesus.

SAMUEL R. I think his answer meant, that there was no need of making the wine quite yet.

MR. ALCOTT. Was it such wine as we have in our decanters?

SAMUEL R. No; it tasted like wine, but it was like water. It would not intoxicate.

GEORGE K. I think it was a mysterious medicinal wine.

LEMUEL. I think they were made to think it was wine.

MR. ALCOTT. Was the miracle worked in their minds or upon the water?

(*Half thought one way, half the other.*)

EMMA. I think his mother telling him there was no wine, shows her faith in him.

LUCIA. I have nothing to say, but I was interested.

MR. ALCOTT. I like to have you say freely, that you have nothing to say, when you have nothing. But now can you tell me what is the significance of this? (*None answered.*) What does marriage mean?

GEORGE K. Deep love.

CHARLES. Union of Spirit.

MR. ALCOTT. Do you think that you see all the meaning of this miracle? (*All.*) When you were talking of the Temptation, you were somewhat puzzled, as you are now, for you were thinking altogether of outward things. The mountain, the pinnacle of the temple, troubled you. Can you not turn your thoughts inward, as you did then, and ask yourselves, what these things may be emblems of?

CHARLES. Water is an emblem of purity.

MR. ALCOTT. And wine? *(There was no answer.)* And the change?

LEMUEL. Of growing better; making good better.

ONE. The bride was purity.

MR. ALCOTT. Charles said marriage was spiritual union. Can you work up these emblems into something?

NATHAN. The water meant purity, the wine goodness.

MR. ALCOTT. And did Christ's presence sanctify the union?

> *(Mr. Alcott again read the passage, paraphrasing the fourth verse, — "Woman, my thoughts are not like yours; you are thinking of making wine; I am thinking what wine signifies.")*

MR. ALCOTT. What does this whole story signify? *(No answer.)* Which do you think was the greatest miracle, to change water into wine, or to open the minds of men into the real meaning of marriage? *(No answer.)* Where do miracles begin? *(No answer.)* Do they begin in the Spirit, and flow out into things, or begin in things?

SEVERAL. In the Spirit.

MR. ALCOTT. Where is the cause of miracles?

SEVERAL. In the Spirit.

MR. ALCOTT. Where is the Life that causes a seed to spring out and seek the light?

LUCIA. In God.

MR. ALCOTT. Where is God?

LUCIA. In the seed.

MR. ALCOTT. How is spiritual "glory" shown forth?

LUCIA. By being good.

MR. ALCOTT. Give me some fact of Nature, by which spiritual glory is shown forth.

AUGUSTINE. In the oak coming out of the acorn.

ANDREW. In the rose coming out of the bud, for there is power.

FRANKLIN. Dr. Channing shows forth spiritual glory in his thoughts and feelings, when he preaches and tries to make people good.

EMMA. God shows forth glory in Nature, and in the Soul of man.

SAMUEL T. A little baby shows forth spiritual glory.

MARTHA. A dove shows forth God's glory.

ALEXANDER. An elephant shows forth patience and nobleness.

GEORGE K. A lion shows forth the power of God.

OTHERS. The sun. The moon. The stars, &c.

MR. ALCOTT. The glory is not of things themselves; but things shadow forth the glory of God. Does any outward thing show it forth completely? Lions, flowers, stars? (*They signified dissent while he remained in the Outward creation.*) In Human Nature?

ALL. Yes; in Jesus Christ.

MR. ALCOTT. Do you think that Jesus showed forth all the glory of God; that nothing at all was withheld? (*Some said yes, some no.*) Now tell me, do you think the change of water into wine was actually made in the outward world? (*All held up hands but Francis and Franklin.*) Was that all the miracle?

(*All said no, but Alexander and Augustine.*)

AUGUSTINE. I think he had no other meaning than to show that he was willing to supply their needs.

MR. ALCOTT. Had Jesus never performed any other miracle, should you have regarded this as something very great?

(*Most held up hands.*)

WELLES. If he had not done any other miracle, I should have thought that Jesus brought the wine himself.

FRANKLIN. I think the miracle was emblematic.

MR. ALCOTT. Do others think so? And of what?

JOHN B. It was emblematic of power.

FRANKLIN. I think it was emblematic of purity, united to greater purity — to faith and love.

EMMA. And that is marriage.

MR. ALCOTT. Is marriage an emblem?

EMMA. Yes; it is an emblem of two spirits united in purity and love.

SAMUEL R. I think the whole story is an emblem of changing good into better.

GEORGE K. I think water was pure, and wine was purer, and it signified that they must purify their spirits.

MARTHA. The wine was purer than the water.

AUGUSTINE. Wine is not so pure as water — water represents truth.

ANDREW. I think the wine was the Spirit of Jesus.

WELLES. Water represents purity, but wine means more things, love, faith, &c.

MR. ALCOTT. Did you ever hear the word Chastity? That word represents something more than purity, for it implies self-restraint. This story may represent deep love, as one of you said at the beginning of the Conversation, and when deep love is restrained by principles, it is chastity.

RECORDER. I think you have led the children into an allegorical interpretation of this passage, when their own minds did not tend towards it. In no conversation has it been so difficult to keep them to the subject, nor have you suggested so much. I cannot help being gratified at this myself; because I do not believe the Evangelist had any idea of setting forth anything but the kind sanction of Jesus to the innocent festivities which celebrate marriage.

MR. ALCOTT. It is remarkable, that this is the only instance in which I have premeditated one of these Conversations. I studied this passage beforehand, and in no instance have we succeeded so ill. It is better to give the subject up to the children, and let them lead us where they will. The course pursued in this, is in violation of the plan proposed at the beginning of the Conversations, and confirms the naturalness of that plan, by the want of success which has attended this effort. I think this worthy of remark.

CONVERSATION XXIV

* * *

INSTINCTIVE INSPIRATION:

Enthusiasm

Mr. Alcott read:

PURIFICATION OF THE TEMPLE

And the Jews' passover was at hand, and Jesus went up to Jerusalem, and found in the temple those that sold oxen and sheep and doves, and the changers of money sitting: And when he had made a scourge of small cords, he drove them all out of the temple, and the sheep, and the oxen; and poured out the changers' money, and overthrew the tables; And said unto them that sold doves, Take these things hence; make not my Father's house an house of merchandise. And his disciples remembered that it was written, The zeal of thine house hath eaten me up. (John 2:13-17.)

(Mr. Alcott explained the origin of the Feast, the courts of the Temple, &c, and asked the usual question.)

JOSIAH. Jesus meant to show them that they were wicked in making any place to worship God in, a place for anything else. I can see Jesus going into the temple, and the little tables of shops, and the sheep lying about. Jesus was smiling when he went in; but when he sees this he looks pretty cross.

MR. ALCOTT. What feeling has he in his mind?

JOSIAH. I have had it sometimes — he feels that they ought not to do so.

EMMA. It was indignation.

MR. ALCOTT. What is the difference between anger and indignation?

EMMA. Anger wants to hurt, to injure; but indignation only feels the wrong, and wants to have others feel so too.

MR. ALCOTT. Is the outward expression alike?

EMMA. No; when indignant one looks resolute.

ELLEN. I think it was a sorrowful look in Jesus.

EMMA. Yes; there is sorrow in indignation.

FREDERIC. He felt displeasure; there was no anger, nor peevishness, nor fretfulness. He seemed rather impatient, but not worrisome; he wanted to get them away quick.

FRANKLIN. I have thought he cried a little.

ANDREW. His feeling was sorrowfulness for their using the temple of God as a shop.

LEMUEL. He looks red at the men who are selling in the temple.

MR. ALCOTT. Is anger right?

LEMUEL. No; but indignation is, when it does not go too far.

FREDERIC. When it does not come to blows. But he did not use the whip.

MR. ALCOTT. Who else think he did not use the whip? (*The majority thought he did not.*) What was the whip for?

SEVERAL. It was an emblem of warning.

OTHERS. Of indignation. Of chastisement.

MR. ALCOTT. What made them all go out, if he did not use the whip?

JOSIAH. He took the whip to drive the cattle out.

MR. ALCOTT. What made the people go out?

JOSIAH. Because they were afraid he would whip them. And yet it seems as if it was a kind of deception to have frightened them so. My mind is not clear about it. He must have known that he would have frightened them with his whip, and yet he could not have intended for one moment to whip them.

EMMA. They went out because he told them to go, and they were ashamed of themselves on account of something in his manner.

AUGUSTINE. I think he held up his whip, in a warning, emblematic way, and looked at each, till one by one they went out.

JOHN B. I think he whipped, but very calmly, without passion, so as to make them think.

GEORGE K. They went out because they feared his miraculous power.

MR. ALCOTT. Was there in this act anything hasty, violent, or any want of self-control?

AUGUSTINE. He never lost his self-control in his life.

MR. ALCOTT. Some people have thought that Jesus was hasty in doing this; others have thought it was a necessary severity, by which he showed them, in a manner they could understand, that they had done what was unworthy. What do you think?

EMMA. I think it would have been better not to have used the whip.

AUGUSTINE. I think Jesus knew best.

MR. ALCOTT. The whole scene may be considered as a dramatic exhibition of indignant enthusiasm. I think the use of the whip was only as an emblem; the scourge was probably made very deliberately before their eyes, and the action probably attracted the attention of all. Prophets among the Jews were in the habit of doing emblematic things. The multitude thought him a prophet, and they watched his doings, and were convicted in their consciences, and went out of themselves. Then he overturned the money-changers' tables. Jesus was earnest in the purification of the Body and the Church. He could not bear to see the Temple desecrated to the ends of trade. Against idolatry of gold he set himself on all occasions.

CONVERSATION XXV

* * *

IMMORTALITY OF SPIRIT:

Resurrection

MR. ALCOTT. What was Jesus doing, and where was he, when we left him?

ELLEN. Driving the people out of the temple at Jerusalem; and we concluded he did it with gentleness.

AUGUSTINE. And that he used the whip only to drive out the cattle.

MR. ALCOTT. Yes; that was Josiah's thought, and it seemed to please you. I have mentioned it to others since, and one person said that it was surprising that it had never been thought of before. *(He then read.)*

JESUS IN THE TEMPLE

Then answered the Jews and said unto him, What sign showest thou unto us, seeing that thou doest these things? Jesus answered and said unto them, Destroy this temple, and in three days I will raise it up. Then said the Jews, Forty and six years was this temple in building, and wilt thou rear it up in three days? But he spake of the temple of his body. When therefore he was risen from the dead, his disciples remembered that he had said this unto them; and they believed the scripture and the word which Jesus had said. (John 2:18-22.)

MR. ALCOTT. Why did he say "this temple"?

LEMUEL. Because the Body is the Temple of the Spirit.

FRANKLIN. Because he happened to be in the temple.

MARTHA. The temple is the place where people should go to worship God.

SAMUEL T. The body is a temple over the spirit.

ANDREW. The body is the temple. The spirit worships — not the body.

MR. ALCOTT. The Jews did not know of inward worship; but of outward worship. They had no idea of any other temple than one of mortar and stone, or of wood. "Forty and six years was this temple in building," said they.

FRANKLIN. After this body has decayed, it will take some new form, such as of a little baby.

SAMUEL R. The flesh decays; it becomes some other person, or remains dust.

ANDREW. If they destroyed his body, it would afterwards help to make some other body.

FREDERIC. I think those words of Jesus mean, that the spirit will be raised up to heaven, after the body is decayed, and the dust might perhaps make some other body.

WELLES. I think it meant that his spirit would go into this body and raise it up.

JOSIAH. Mr. Alcott, will you tell me where the spirit of Jesus was, while his body was hanging on the cross?

MR. ALCOTT. Where was your spirit before it came into your body?

JOSIAH. It was with God; but still, I do not see where his was at that time. He was going to build up his body again in three days; but if his spirit had been in his body then, it would have made it alive.

MR. ALCOTT. Could it not return to God, and after three days, reenter his body?

JOSIAH. I don't understand how it could.

AUGUSTINE. When Jesus rose from the dead, he only seemed to be a Body to his disciples. No one else saw him or could see him.

MR. ALCOTT. Do any of you think as Augustine does, that there was no real flesh at the Resurrection? (*No answer.*) There are some who think that if his body did not come out of the grave, Christianity is not proved. They think that the resurrction of the body from the grave is as important to the truth of Christianity as the resurrection of the Soul from the Body. Do you think the body of Jesus rose from the grave?

(Several rose.)

MARTHA and FREDERIC. I do not understand the account of the resurrection, if his body did not rise.

MR. ALCOTT. Do you think it is of small importance that his body should rise?

(All the rest rose.)

RECORDER. Did not the Evangelist mean to teach that the body of Jesus rose and left the tomb empty?

MR. ALCOTT. Yes; I think that the Evangelist so viewed it. Who think the flesh ascended? *(George B. rose.)*

FREDERIC. I think the body rose from the grave.

ELLEN. I do not think any flesh ascended, or even rose.

MR. ALCOTT. Why do painters paint a body in the resurrection and ascension?

ELLEN. Because they could not paint a Spirit.

CHARLES. I think the memory of the disciples would be so strong in Jesus, that after he was killed, his spirit would watch over the body which he had left, and they would be so afflicted, that he would take a body again, and show himself to them.

MR. ALCOTT. Did he intend to take the same body?

CHARLES. He would be there spiritually; and the memory of the disciples would be so strong that he would appear to them.

MR. ALCOTT. Do others think that it was through the strength of memory and imagination, the disciples saw him?

FRANKLIN. I think both the resurrection and ascension were in the memory and imagination of the disciples; but then they were real facts, even more real than those which the eyes perceive.

MR. ALCOTT. Which perceives the most real things, Memory, Imagination or the Senses?

(Their opinions were divided.)

MR. ALCOTT. What becomes of the body after death?

NATHAN. It becomes a part of the earth.

MR. ALCOTT. Does that grow?

NATHAN. Yes; it grows up in grass; and then the cows eat it; and then we drink the milk of the cow.

MR. ALCOTT. It is demonstrated by physiology that the matter of the human body is changed every few years; and some persons think that they can perceive as often a renewal of ideas. What builds up the body?

FRANKLIN. The spirit.

MR. ALCOTT. And when the spirit leaves the body?

FREDERIC. The body decays.

MR. ALCOTT. And perhaps becomes a rock, or a tree, or an animal. Matter is like a great sea; and the moving of matter — its universal changes — is produced by a living Spirit which pervades it. This living Spirit was what Jesus called the Father. What is meant by rising from the dead? What is it to be dead? Is death, in spirits, or in bodies?

SEVERAL. In bodies — in matter.

MR. ALCOTT. And Spirit never dies. It is immortal. It endows Nature and the Body with life. Now all those may rise who think that Jesus meant by these words, that the body which was nailed to the cross, was to come forth from the grave in three days.

(Several rose. The rest thought that he spoke of the resurrection of the Spirit from the Body.)

CONVERSATION XXVI

• • •

ANALYSIS OF THE HUMAN SPIRIT:

Human Nature

Mr. Alcott read the lesson for the day:

WISDOM OF JESUS

Now, when he was in Jerusalem at the Passover, in the feast day, many believed in his name, when they saw the miracles which he did. But Jesus did not commit himself unto them, because he knew all men, and needed not that any should testify of man: for he knew what was in man. (John 2:23-25.)

EDWARD J. The feast at Jerusalem was because God did so much for the Jews, carrying them through the Red Sea.

ELLEN. The feast was the passover. That made me think of the plagues in Egypt, and I thought, too, of the feast at Jerusalem, and of the Jews sitting or rather reposing at their tables, eating such things as we do on communion day.

MR. ALCOTT. How did Jesus know "what was in man"?

JOSIAH. He was good, and he got what he knew from God, just as I do.

MR. ALCOTT. Does God give you all the knowledge you try after?

JOSIAH. Yes; and he gave me one thing I did not try after, and that is my Spirit, and he put it in my body. My body could not go to God and try after a spirit.

MR. ALCOTT. Can your spirit carry your body to God?

JOSIAH. No; my body cannot even be carried to God. Only spirit can go to God.

AUGUSTINE. I think Jesus knew what was in man because he made men and always sees into them, and is the only real man himself.

MR. ALCOTT. Is man God?

AUGUSTINE. No; but God is the only real man.

SAMUEL R. I think as Augustine does, that Jesus made man, and so he knew what was in him; but I cannot know, for I did not make him.

MR. ALCOTT. Who made Jesus Christ?

SAMUEL R. No one made his Spirit.

FRANKLIN. Jesus always was.

LEMUEL. God tells something, if we try to get truth.

MR. ALCOTT. Yes; Jesus says, "If any one would know of the Doctrine let him do the Will of God."

WELLES. Jesus did not need the testimony of man, because virtue testifies itself. Conscience is its own testifier.

GEORGE K. He knew what was in man because he was good.

MR. ALCOTT. Do people know other people, according as they are good themselves?

GEORGE K. Yes.

MR. ALCOTT. Where did Jesus get his knowledge?

MARTHA. He went into his own Soul.

SAMUEL R. I thought Jesus found out what was in man because he was so good. People who are not good do not know what is in other people.

JOHN B. Jesus knew what was in man, because God told him.

MR. ALCOTT. In a different way from what he tells you?

JOHN B. No; but Jesus was better, and God told him more.

MR. ALCOTT. Does God's telling depend on you or on God?

JOHN B. God tells us all we ought to know always.

MR. ALCOTT. Then if you were as willing and eager to be taught by God as Jesus was, could you know as much? Is the knowledge ready for you?

JOHN B. Yes; but God gave Jesus more power than he gave me.

MR. ALCOTT. Whether he tried or not?

JOHN B. No; it does depend on trying.

MR. ALCOTT. May we say that there is a Christ in the depths of our Spirit[36] which may be brought out, if we will try as Jesus did. Do you think so? (*All rose but Frederic, Welles, and Augustine.*)

ANDREW. Jesus did "not commit himself" to the bad; for he would only tell his power to those who could understand it.

MR. ALCOTT. Could bad men see his miracles?

ANDREW. No; only the spirit's eyes can see a miracle.

MR. ALCOTT. Is the outward world committed to a blind man?

FREDERIC. No; because he has no eyes.

MR. ALCOTT. Is there not such a thing as being blind to the spiritual world?

FREDERIC. Yes; and it is not committed to some.

MR. ALCOTT. Would bad men think Jesus was bad?

ANDREW. Yes; because of their own badness.

MR. ALCOTT. Now, what does your Spirit subsist on?

ELLEN. On Christ's Spirit.

FRANKLIN. On Holiness.

CHARLES. On Good or Evil.

MR. ALCOTT. On what does Good and Evil subsist?

ELLEN. Good subsists on Christ; Evil on the opposite Spirit.

CHARLES. I don't think Evil is a real existence; but is the lessening of Good. It is the going away from Good which is called Evil; there is no being to evil.

WELLES. Good comes from God. It is God acting in a man.

ANDREW. Good is God in one sense; but when we say, it tastes good, we do not mean God. Material good is not God, but we mean, it is a good to the body.

MR. ALCOTT. And so there must be some of God in it. And is not this true; is not God Goodness, and as much of Goodness as we get, is God? Man has Good within him. God is absolute goodness. Now can you tell me what your spirit lives upon?

SEVERAL. On Goodness.

MR. ALCOTT. Did Goodness have any beginning or end?

ANDREW. No; it is Eternal, Immortal.

MR. ALCOTT. And when you do a good act, or have a good feeling, do you revive anything immortal, undying in you? (*All rose.*) But sometimes we find it, and lose it again afterwards. What Faculty takes hold of Goodness and revives the Immortal within you?

SEVERAL. The Spiritual Faculty. Conscience.

MR. ALCOTT. When we bring Conscience out and make it act; when Conscience has acted out the Spirit's thoughts and feelings, what do we call it?

CHARLES. Reason.

MR. ALCOTT. I think it something more than Reason.

SEVERAL. Faith. Love. Affection. Religion.

MR. ALCOTT. How much is there spiritual in Instinct?

CHARLES. A natural want.

MR. ALCOTT. What comes after this want? (*Several answers were given, among which were Love, Hope, and Faith.*) Well what comes next?

FRANKLIN. We imagine what it is.

MR. ALCOTT. And having shaped the spiritual life in the Imagination, what comes next?

CHARLES. Reason, which finds the why.

MR. ALCOTT. What is reason after?

CHARLES. Truth.

MR. ALCOTT. What represents Truth?

CHARLES. Imagination.

MR. ALCOTT. What is Imagination after?

CHARLES. Truth.

MR. ALCOTT. Something more. What is the spiritual faculty, Conscience, after?

CHARLES. Good.

MR. ALCOTT. And the Imagination unites them; and there is something which the Imagination finds that represents the union.

(Charles did not answer.) What do you think of that cast? *(Pointing to Chantry's cast of Lady Louisa Russell.)*

CHARLES. It is beautiful; the Imagination finds beauty.

MR. ALCOTT. What, then, have we found in man?

CHARLES. Goodness, Truth, Beauty.

MR. ALCOTT. Are these of us, or of God?

CHARLES. Of God.

MR. ALCOTT. We may have the true, the beautiful, and the good, within us; but can we have Truth, Beauty, and Goodness?

CHARLES. No; these are God.

MR. ALCOTT. The elements of human nature are,

   I. THE SENSE OF THE GOOD.
   II. THE SENTIMENT OF THE BEAUTIFUL.
   III. THE IDEA OF THE TRUE.

What is that word which comprehends all the productions of the IMAGINATION? *(No answer.)* Is it not ART? And what one word comprehends all the productions of the REASON? Is it not PHILOSOPHY? And what does the spiritual faculty, CONSCIENCE, produce?

SEVERAL. RELIGION.

MR. ALCOTT. If Jesus Christ knew what was in man, he knew all man could do and be — that he could lay hold on IMMORTALITY by his Spiritual Faculty, on TRUTH by his Rational Faculty, on BEAUTY by his Imaginative Faculty. Have you all these elements?

ALL. Yes.

MR. ALCOTT. Who think the Spiritual Faculty in them is behind all the others? *(All rose.)* Who think its slumber is Evil? *(All.)* Who think their Imaginative Faculty is not cultivated enough; that they do not shape thoughts of truth and feeling into forms of truth and art? *(Most thought so.)*

NATHAN. I have too much Imagination.

WELLES. I don't know how it is with me.

MR. ALCOTT. Do you see clearly, all that you ought to do and think?

WELLES and NATHAN. No.

MR. ALCOTT. Then you have not Imagination enough. Imagination is the representative or shaping faculty of the Soul. Now tell me, whether you have the power of putting all your sense of what is good, your notion of what is true, your feeling of what is beautiful, into words, actions, or forms? (*No one answered.*) Do you think this power of Imagination wants cultivation in you? (*All rose.*) Do you think that your Reasoning faculty is cultivated enough — that you always know *why*, and have facts to bring through your Imagination? (*None answered.*) Can you reason without Imagination?

LEMUEL. Yes.

MR. ALCOTT. What would you have to reason on, if you had no Imagination; what represents thoughts and things?

LEMUEL. Imagination.

MR. ALCOTT. How then could you reason without Imagination?

GEORGE B. You could reason on fancies.

MR. ALCOTT. Fancy is Imagination's errand boy, who goes to gather flowers; and Reason has an errand boy too; it is Understanding, who goes off by the Senses. And what is the errand boy of Conscience?

LUCIA. It has none.

MR. ALCOTT. What if Fancy should carry to Imagination what belongs to Reason; and Understanding should bring to Reason what belongs to Imagination? It is very important that these errand boys should mind their own masters. Some keep Fancy at work gathering flowers; and some keep Understanding at work gathering outward facts. There sits the Spirit on her throne, with Reason on her right hand, and Imagination on her left.

CHARLES. That is it!

MR. ALCOTT. And a little way off, before Imagination, is Fancy bending with the flowers which she has gathered, and which she brings to Imagination to name, for Fancy does not know their names. And, on the other side, Understanding brings her gatherings to Reason to name. But sometimes the Fancy and Understanding bring so many things, that the Reason and Imagination have no time to do their appointed work. But when they do, they name the things and hand them over to Conscience.

LEMUEL. Where is Conscience?

MR. ALCOTT. Conscience is the voice of the Spirit itself, and Conscience offers up what it accepts, to the Divinity. Our Conversation has been long today, and we have run over great and deep subjects. We have been seeking to find out the Wisdom and Knowledge of Jesus,

Knowledge of God is THEOLOGY,
Knowledge of Nature is PHYSIOLOGY,
Knowledge of Man is PSYCHOLOGY,
These all are enfolded in the SOUL OF MAN. Life tempts them forth from the Soul.

CONVERSATION XXVII

* * *

RENOVATION OF SPIRIT:

Regeneration

MR. ALCOTT. What did we have last?

CHARLES. An allegory on the faculties.

MR. ALCOTT. What faculty is most active in you — each?

WILLIAM C., LUCIA, FREDERIC, and JOHN B. Imagination.

WELLES. Reason.

CHARLES. Reason and Conscience are on my left side, Imagination is on the right.[37]

ANDREW. Imagination and Conscience. Once Imagination began first, now Conscience does.

MR. ALCOTT. Have you no Understanding; do you not wish to know about outward things?

ANDREW. Yes; but I cannot, for my Imagination interrupts me.

JOSEPH. I first look for what is good, and then for what is true.

MR. ALCOTT. A perfect man uses all these faculties.

CHARLES. When he is dead, he may be called Sleeping Beauty.

MR. ALCOTT. No; rather Risen Beauty. Who embodied the Good, the True, and the Beautiful?

(All rose, but did not speak. Mr. Alcott then read:)

INTERVIEW BETWEEN JESUS AND NICODEMUS

There was a man of the Pharisees, named Nicodemus, ruler of the Jews: The same came to Jesus by night, and said unto him, Rabbi, we know that thou art a teacher come from God: for no man can do these miracles that thou doest, except God be with him. Jesus answered and said unto him, Verily, verily, I say unto thee, Except a man be born again, he cannot see the kingdom of God. Nicodemus saith unto him, How can a man be born when he is old? Can he enter the second time unto his mother's womb, and be born? Jesus answered, Verily, verily, I say unto thee, Except a man be born of water and *of* the Spirit, he cannot enter into the kingdom of God. That which is born of the flesh is flesh; and that which is born of the Spirit is spirit. Marvel not that I said unto thee, Ye must be born again. The wind bloweth where it listeth, and thou hearest the sound thereof, but canst not tell whence it cometh, and whither it goeth: so is everyone that is born of the Spirit.

Nicodemus answered and said unto him, How can these things be? Jesus answered and said unto him, Art thou a master of Israel, and knowest not these things? Verily, verily, I say unto thee, We speak that we do know, and testify that we have seen; and ye receive not our witness. If I have told you earthly things, and ye believe not, how shall ye believe, if I tell you *of* heavenly things? And no man hath ascended up to heaven, but he that came down from heaven, *even* the Son of man which is in heaven. And as Moses lifted up the serpent in the wilderness, even so must the Son of man be lifted up: That whosoever believeth in him should not perish, but have eternal life. For God so loved the world, that he gave his only begotten Son, that whosoever believeth in him should not perish, but have everlasting life. For God sent not his Son into the world to condemn the world; but that the world through him might be saved. He that believeth on him is not condemned; but he that believeth not is condemned already, because he hath not believed in the name of the only begotten Son of God. And this is the condemnation, that light is come into the world, and men loved darkness rather than light, because their deeds were evil. For every one that doeth evil hateth the light, neither cometh to the light, lest his deeds should be reproved. But he that doeth truth cometh to the light, that his deeds may be made manifest, that they are wrought in God. (John 3:1-21.)

(Mr. Alcott asked what interested them most.)

JOSEPH. Jesus' saying he must be born again. That means that when the body dies the spirit is born again. The spirit is born first when the body is born; and then it is born again when the body dies.

AUGUSTINE. Nicodemus coming at night. He did so because he did not wish the people to know that he inclined to believe on Jesus, lest they should take him out of office. It would have been better in him to go by day.

CHARLES. Why, I thought to get up after he was gone to bed, showed great interest in Jesus — but perhaps Augustine's thought is right about his motive. I imagined Nicodemus in bed, thinking about Jesus, and at last getting up to go and be instructed.

SAMUEL T. I was interested about the serpent's biting.

JOSIAH. Jesus likened this world to a wilderness, and his being in it, to the serpent's being lifted up.

ANDREW. It was a sign of faith for the people to look at the serpent; but their faith cured the bites.

MR. ALCOTT. So faith can cure the serpent bites.

ANDREW. Very deep faith could.

MR. ALCOTT. Can you tell of anything else of this kind that faith does?

ANDREW. Why, in our Saviour's times, some came to life because they believed in Jesus.

MR. ALCOTT. Is there no such faith now?

ANDREW. No.

MR. ALCOTT. If you were sick, could you exercise this faith?

ANDREW. Yes.

MR. ALCOTT. Should you not want to have a physician?

ANDREW. I always do have one.

MR. ALCOTT. And the physician helps the cure.

ANDREW. God does more than the physician.

EDWARD C. Being born again interested me.

MR. ALCOTT. Have you been, or do you want to be?

EDWARD C. No.

MR. ALCOTT. Being born again means being made better in spirit.

EDWARD C. I should like to be better, but I do not want to have my body born again.

JOHN B. I think Nicodemus was interested by the miracles of Jesus, and wanted to know whether he could believe in the rest.

MR. ALCOTT. Did Jesus explain his miracles to him?

JOHN B. He talked about spiritual birth with him.

SAMUEL R. Being born again, I think, means that at death the spirit goes back to heaven. It was born before the body at first, and goes back to its first state.

MR. ALCOTT. What is the use of the Spirit's entering the body, and suffering, if we return to what we were before?

(*Samuel hesitated.*)

WELLES. It has learned to resist temptation.

MR. ALCOTT. Suppose that temptation is not resisted, and wrong is done?

WELLES. We can then form resolutions.

MR. ALCOTT. What feeling makes us form resolutions of amendment?

GEORGE B. Repentance.

MR. ALCOTT. Then what do we learn from life?

AUGUSTINE. To know more — self-knowledge.

MR. ALCOTT. What is self-knowledge?

AUGUSTINE. Knowledge of Spirit.

MR. ALCOTT. Of the Spirit's — what?

CHARLES. The Spirit's Faculties.

MR. ALCOTT. Which is Self-Consciousness? Certain knowledge, "lifts us up." A little baby is good; but being tempted by outward things, it becomes acquainted with both the outward and inward world, and thus acts out its spirit.

ELLEN. I thought being born again meant to have a new heart.

MR. ALCOTT. What is having a new heart?

ELLEN. To have all your sins forgiven.

MR. ALCOTT. How is that done?

ELLEN. By praying earnestly, with the spirit; that is, to mean and feel what we say.

MR. ALCOTT. Is feeling, all of prayer?

GEORGE K. You must think right, too.

CHARLES. And act right, and be right.

MR. ALCOTT. Some of you think, perhaps, that prayer consists in saying over some words, whether you know what the words mean or not. Is it not true striving to do right that makes prayer? (All assented.) Is it right then — a prayer — to sit at dinner and eat more than you need? (All said no.) Is it prayer to fall into a passion?

GEORGE K. That is a prayer to the dragon.

MR. ALCOTT. What is a new heart?

ELLEN. It means to want to act right; to be pure like a baby. It says "again," because once we were pure and holy.

MR. ALCOTT. And are not those demons, who go and whisper wrong feelings and thoughts into the souls of these holy ones? (All held up hands.) What shape did those demons take who went and whispered evil into the ears of your little brothers and sisters? Was it the shape of Charles, or Lemuel, or William? (All exclaimed, no.)

Did you ever strike a little brother or sister? (*Several held up hands.*) Were you not then such demons? Did you ever fret a babe — hurt its feelings — be selfish to it — set it an example of disobedience, or any other wrong thing? (*Some confessed to all these things.*) Little babies lose their babyhood — their pure and holy life, in a great measure, because those around them do not meet their holiness with love and generosity, and teach them about outward things, and bear patiently the mistakes which these little ones make with their heads, not hearts, while they are learning the outward world, and things of time. Take care that you do not help to destroy their holiness. Jesus said, "Whosoever shall cause one of these little ones to offend, it were better for him that a mill-stone were hanged about his neck, and he were cast into the depths of the sea." Who kept his babyhood?

SEVERAL. Christ.

CHARLES. God is babyhood.

MR. ALCOTT. There is truth in that, I believe; and yet it is language so liable to be misunderstood, that it had better not be used. (*There was no answer.*) We shall resume this subject at our next Conversation.

CONVERSATION XXVIII

• • •

SPIRITUAL UNION:

Faith and Love

Mr. Alcott read:

JOHN'S LAST TESTIMONY TO JESUS

After these things came Jesus and his disciples into the land of Judaea; and there he tarried with them, and baptized. And John also was baptizing in Aenon near to Salim, because there was much water there: and they came, and were baptized. For John was not yet cast into prison. Then there arose a question between some of John's disciples and the Jews about purifying. And they came unto John, and said unto him, Rabbi, he that was with thee beyond Jordan, to whom thou barest witness, behold, the same baptizeth, and all men come to him.

John answered and said, A man can receive nothing, except it be given him from heaven. Ye yourselves bear me witness, that I said, I am not the Christ, but that I am sent before him. He that hath the bride is the bridegroom: but the friend of the bridegroom, which standeth and heareth him, rejoiceth greatly because of the bridegroom's voice: this my joy therefore is fulfilled. He must increase, but I must decrease. He that cometh from above is above all: he that is of the earth is earthly, and speaketh of the earth: he that cometh from heaven is above all. And what he hath seen and heard, that he testifieth; and no man receiveth his testimony. He that hath received his testimony, hath set to his seal that God is true. For he whom God hath sent speaketh the words of God: for God giveth not the Spirit by measure unto him. The Father loveth the Son, and hath given all things into his hand. He that believeth on the Son hath everlasting life: and he that believeth not the Son shall not see life; but the wrath of God abideth on him. (John 3:22-36.)

(He then asked what most interested them.)

LUCIA. I liked the last verse, "He that believeth on the Son hath everlasting life," &c.

JOHN B. I liked this, "A man can receive nothing except it be given him from heaven." Goodness comes from heaven.

MR. ALCOTT. Why do not some people get it?

JOHN B. They don't want it. — But it comes when you do want it and try for it.

ATHAN. "He that believeth not on the Son shall not see life." I suppose that means, shall not have spiritual life; but only outward life.

JOHN B. So I think; the spirit will not go to heaven, will not be good, unless it believes.

MR. ALCOTT. Do any of you think that we cannot go to heaven till we die?

(Almost all.)

ELLEN. We cannot go till our bodies die.

NATHAN. Heaven is in our thoughts —

MR. ALCOTT. And feelings; where do thoughts and feelings come from?

NATHAN. From God.

MR. ALCOTT. Through what part of us?

NATHAN. Our Spirit.

MR. ALCOTT. Is heaven in our Spirits?

(Several.)

AUGUSTINE. We cannot go to heaven wholly till we die.

MR. ALCOTT. No one is wholly in heaven but God. Can we go to heaven at all without dying?

WELLES and ELLEN. No.

ANDREW. If we are in heaven now, I don't see how we can be said to be going to heaven.

CHARLES. Can we not go either to heaven or the other place till we die?

ELLEN. No; We must prepare for our other life while on earth.

MR. ALCOTT. Is there any connexion, Ellen, between doing right, and ascending out of this world? *(She was silent.)* You seem to think that we die; our bodies are laid in the earth; our spirit ascends up, in some shape; appears before God, who sits on a throne, somewhere?

ELLEN. Yes.

JOSIAH. Heaven is partly in the Spirit of my body, partly in God.

WILLIAM C. Heaven is where great and good people are.

AUGUSTINE. Heaven is in our spirits — in God. It is in no

particular palace. It is not above the sky. It is not material. It is wherever people are good.

CHARLES. Heaven is everywhere — Eternity. It stops when there is anything bad. It means peace and love. High and white are emblems of it.

ANDREW. Heaven is like a cloud, and God and Jesus and the angels sit on it.

MR. ALCOTT. Where is it?

ANDREW. Everywhere. Every person that is good, God looks at and takes care of.

FREDERIC. Wherever there is good.

SAMUEL R. But in no place.

FRANKLIN. Heaven is the Spirit's truth and goodness. It is in everybody; but mostly in the good.

GEORGE K. I generally imagine it very high and bright, with gold pavements, but it is not earthly gold. It is both a place and state of mind.

EDWARD J. I used to think it was a room with a pair of stairs up to it.

NATHAN. I thought it was a large sea and a ladder went up to it, and angels carried men up.

MR. ALCOTT. Which do you think would be the best heaven, a heaven made up of things, or one made of thoughts, feelings, and love.

ALL. The last, the last.

JOSIAH. (referring to the text.) Christ was the bride, and John the bridegroom's friend.

GEORGE K. No; Christ was the bridegroom and John the bride.

MR. ALCOTT. "He that hath received the testimony" — testimony to what?

CHARLES. To the Supernatural.

MR. ALCOTT. How many of your spirits testify to the Supernatural? (Several.) Do people, do the boys whom you see receive your testimony to the Supernatural; or do they say pish! and pshaw!

when you speak of your deeper feelings? (*Several rose.*) Does anything within you speak the words of God?

SEVERAL. Yes; the Spirit.

MR. ALCOTT. Can you measure — can your Reason measure the Spirit that is within you; can you gauge or weigh it? (*None held up hands.*) Does Father and Son mean God and Jesus?

CHARLES. No; it means God and any Man. [38, 39]

CONVERSATION XXIX

* * *

SPIRITUAL INTREPIDITY:

Courage and Pusillanimity

MR. ALCOTT. Imagine Jesus in Judaea, while I read.

IMPRISONMENT OF JOHN THE BAPTIST

But Herod the tetrarch, being reproved by him for Herodias his brother Philip's wife, and for all the evils which Herod had done, had sent forth and laid hold upon John, and bound him in prison for Herodias' sake, his brother Philip's wife: for he had married her. For John had said unto Herod, It is not lawful for thee to have thy brother's wife. Therefore Herodias had a quarrel against him, and would have killed him; but she could not: For Herod feared John, knowing that he was a just man and an holy, and observed him; and when he heard him, he did many things, and heard him gladly. And when he would have put him to death, he feared the multitude, because they counted him as a prophet. Now after that John was put in prison, Jesus came into Galilee preaching the gospel of the kingdom of God. (Matt. 14:5, Mark 6: 17-21, Luke 3:19.)

MR. ALCOTT. What interests you?

ELLEN. I was interested in the words "Herod feared John."

EDWARD J. Herod feared the multitude.

MR. ALCOTT. Do any of you fear the multitude and on that account refrain from doing unjust things?

(Some hands were held up.)

EDWARD C. It was wrong for Herod to lay hold of John, and bind him, and put him in prison.

MR. ALCOTT. Had John any fear of saying what he thought right, at any time?

ALL. No; never.

MR. ALCOTT. What makes a man stand up for the right all alone?

ALL. Courage — true courage.

MR. ALCOTT. Do you do it?

(No answer.)

CHARLES. I like John's open-heartedness; his telling his own opinion; his going straight forward.

MR. ALCOTT. Are you always able to do that?

CHARLES. Not always. Only Jesus Christ did it always.

MR. ALCOTT. When your father, or mother, or Mr. Alcott reproves you, do you fall into a passion — would you like to put your reprover in prison? All may answer that question.

(There were many confessions here.)

LUCY. I thought Herod put John into prison, to get him out of the way, so that he might not hear his reproof. But he did not like to kill him. *(Lucy had been absent for awhile.)*

SUSAN. Herod feared John, because he thought him so much better than himself.

MR. ALCOTT. Do you fear people who are better than yourself? Should you like to do a naughty thing before your father?

SUSAN. No; he would punish me.

GEORGE K. I liked John for telling Herod he did wrong. It is wrong to hurt a good person; and so Herod was unjust. But John was right.

MR. ALCOTT. Was John's right action an easy one to do? What was John's feeling?

GEORGE K. Courage — moral courage.

MR. ALCOTT. Did you ever have any of this?

GEORGE K. I don't remember any instance; but I think I have the feeling.

AUGUSTINE. When Herod wanted to put John to death, he feared that the multitude would hurt himself — would hurt his body and take away his power. For they believed in John. When a king thinks differently from his people, he must conceal what he thinks; or he should believe as they do.

MR. ALCOTT. Was Herod afraid of Conscience as well as of the multitude and John? Or had he drowned Conscience in his appetites and passions? For Herod was given to appetite, and was passionate. These things almost always go together. Great love of bodily indulgence produces selfishness; and selfishness produces hatred, and such passions. How many of you live in your flesh in your appetites and passions — in your bellies? (*A few held up hands.*) Who live in their angry passions, rather? (*The girls, and a few others.*)

NATHAN. Eating too much makes you angry.

MR. ALCOTT. Herod's appetites and passions are connected in this story.

EDWARD J. I like good things to eat; but I do not think I eat too much.

MR. ALCOTT. That is not living in appetite. It is right to enjoy eating — indulgence is wrong.

CONVERSATION XXX
* * *
SPIRITUAL PURITY:
Holiness

Mr. Alcott read:

CONVERSATION OF JESUS
WITH THE WOMAN OF SAMARIA

When therefore the Lord knew how the Pharisees had heard that Jesus made and baptized more disciples than John (Though Jesus himself baptized not, but his disciples), He left Judaea, and departed again into Galilee. And he must needs go through Samaria. Then cometh he to a city of Samaria, which is called Sychar, near to the parcel of ground that Jacob gave to his son Joseph. Now Jacob's well was there. Jesus therefore, being wearied with his journey, sat thus on the well: and it was about the sixth hour. There cometh a woman of Samaria to draw water: Jesus saith unto her, give me to drink. (For his disciples were gone away unto the city to buy meat.)

Then saith the woman of Samaria unto him, How is it that thou, being a Jew, askest drink of me, which am a woman of Samaria? For the Jews have no dealings with the Samaritans. Jesus answered and said unto her, If thou knewest the gift of God, and who it is that saith to thee, Give me to drink; thou wouldest have asked of him, and he would have given thee living water. The woman saith unto him, Sir, thou hast nothing to draw with, and the well is deep: from whence then hast thou that living water? Art thou greater than our father Jacob, which gave us the well, and drank thereof himself, and his children, and his cattle? Jesus answered and said unto her, Whosoever drinketh of this water shall thirst again: But whosoever drinketh of the water that I shall give him shall never thirst; but the water that I shall give him shall be in him a well of water springing up into everlasting life. The woman saith unto him, Sir, give me this water, that I thirst not, neither come hither to draw. (John 4:1-15.)

MR. ALCOTT. What interested you most?

JOSEPH. The living water. It means spiritual water.

MR. ALCOTT. What do you mean by spiritual water?

JOSEPH. I cannot express it — it is truth.

MR. ALCOTT. What is the use of common water?

JOSEPH. It cleanses.

JOSIAH. It makes you better. Jesus meant to tell her he would give her truth.

MR. ALCOTT. Did the woman understand that Jesus meant truth by water?

FRANKLIN. No; she thought of water for the body.

EDWARD J. You know she asked him what he was going to draw with; and that shows she thought it was some common stream that he spoke of.

MR. ALCOTT. What part of her nature did she use in this conversation?

EDWARD J. Her outward eyes.

MR. ALCOTT. Do you ever use your outward eyes when you should use inward faculties; and misunderstand, like this woman, who was not spiritual?

EDWARD J. Yes.

CHARLES. He told her that if she knew who it was that was speaking to her, she would also know what he meant.

MR. ALCOTT. How would she know?

CHARLES. Because if she knew his nature she would know that he spoke in emblems.

MR. ALCOTT. Is it possible for an unspiritual person to understand emblems?

CHARLES. Not without their being explained.

SAMUEL R. This woman did not understand.

MR. ALCOTT. She was one of those material people who ask the eyes to settle everything.

NATHAN. Spiritual water will never go away.

W. AUGUSTUS. He meant he could make her better. She did not understand, but I don't think it was wrong; for she had never been taught about figures of speech.

MR. ALCOTT. Is it necessary to be taught about these?

W. AUGUSTUS. Yes; when one has gone down into the passions.

MR. ALCOTT. How does that happen in a man?

W. AUGUSTUS. When he was a baby he was good; but was tempted and could not resist.

MR. ALCOTT. Could not?

W. AUGUSTUS. Would not.

MR. ALCOTT. And so it becomes necessary to lift him up out of a dry place, and refresh him with living water? In the country there are living springs, the water springs up and is never dry. Have you a living Spring?

W. AUGUSTUS. In my spirit.

MR. ALCOTT. Has it dried up at all? How has it?

W. AUGUSTUS. By passions.

MR. ALCOTT. You have seen a stagnant pool; a bad effluvia rises from it; a green substance collects on the surface; disagreeable reptiles gather round it. Why is this?

W. AUGUSTUS. Because no living water comes to it.

MR. ALCOTT. What is such a place an emblem of?

W. AUGUSTUS. A self-indulgent, bad person.

EDWARD J. Beautiful flowers sometimes grow about stagnant waters.

MR. ALCOTT. That is true; and bad people do good and beautiful things sometimes. Some of the spirit given them at first is not yet quenched. Have your spirits impurity in them? (*No one answered.*) Living water flows to purify from all evils, unless you love them.

LEMUEL. Spiritual water means every thing that is good for the spirit.

MR. ALCOTT. Name some spiritual waters.

LEMUEL. Love, Faith, Generosity, Hope, Truth.

MR. ALCOTT. Do you always drink that last water?

LEMUEL. No. (*Blushing.*)

EDWARD J. Joy is spiritual water.

JOHN. And Holiness.

JOSIAH. Knowledge of God.

GEORGE B. Obedience.

EDWARD J. I heard my sister read an allegory yesterday. (*He spoke of Miss M's allegory of Faith and Hope.*)

JOHN B. When Jesus said, I would give thee living waters, the woman thought he meant water for the body; but he meant purity.

MR. ALCOTT. What part of your nature drinks spiritual water?

JOHN B. Conscience.

MR. ALCOTT. Suppose you don't mind Conscience?

JOHN B. Then the waters will spoil, and no more pure water comes.

MR. ALCOTT. Name some spoilt waters.

JOHN B. and OTHERS. Impatience, Unkindness, Passion, Ingratitude, Anger, Selfishness, Crossness, Laziness, Ill-humour, Falsehood, Theft.

MR. ALCOTT. Do you generally think that other people must make you good or bad?

SEVERAL. Impure waters flow in to make us bad.

MR. ALCOTT. No; the waters become impure by standing still — by your not trying. And what must you do to purify yourself, if you have become impure?

FRANKLIN. You must feel remorse —

MR. ALCOTT. Which leads to repentance. But what guards the fountain from outward evil?

FRANKLIN. Resolution.

MR. ALCOTT. WILL. I will. To will.

ANDREW. (*Reads*) "And the water that I shall give thee shall be a well of water, springing up into everlasting life." The water is Spirit; spirit makes goodness; goodness lasts always.

EDWARD C. I was interested in Jesus' being weary, and sitting by the well.

MR. ALCOTT. What produces weariness?

JOSIAH. Jesus' weariness was of the body. There is a weariness of mind when it has strayed away into wickedness.

JOHN D. All the waters in me are spoiled.[40]

MR. ALCOTT. Now can you tell what has been the subject of the Conversation? Do not say, a woman, or Jesus, or a well, or water.

EMMA. The subject has been the purity and impurity of the Spirit.

GEORGE. Purifying the Spirit.

FRANKLIN. And the eternity of Spirit.

MR. ALCOTT. What word expresses the eternity of spirit in the Soul of man? (No answer.) Is it not Immortality?

(All said yes.)[41]

CONVERSATION XXXI
* * *
SPIRITUAL WORSHIP:
Prayer and Praise

Mr. Alcott read the remainder of the Scripture from the preceding Conversation:

CONVERSATION OF JESUS
WITH THE WOMAN OF SAMARIA

Jesus saith unto her, Go, call thy husband and come hither. The woman answered and said, I have no husband. Jesus said unto her, thou hast well said, I have no husband: For thou hast had five husbands; and he whom thou now hast is not thy husband: in that saidst thou truly. The woman saith unto him, Sir, I perceive that thou art a prophet. Our fathers worshipped in this mountain; and ye say, that in Jerusalem is the place where men ought to worship.

Jesus saith unto her, Woman, believe me, the hour cometh, when ye shall neither in this mountain, nor yet at Jerusalem, worship the Father. Ye worship ye know not what: we know what we worship: for salvation is of the Jews. But the hour cometh, and now is, when the true worshippers shall worship the father in spirit and in truth: for the Father seeketh such to worship him. God is a Spirit: and they that worship him must worship him in spirit and in truth.

The woman saith unto him, I know that Messias cometh, which is called Christ: when he is come, he will tell us all things. Jesus saith unto her, I that speak unto thee am he. And upon this came his disciples, and marvelled that he talked with the woman: yet no man said, What seekest thou? or, Why talkest thou with her?

The woman then left her waterpot, and went her way into the city, and saith to the men, Come, see a man, which told me all things that ever I did: is not this the Christ? Then they went out of the city, and came unto him. (John 4:16-30.)

(Before Mr. Alcott had time to ask the usual question, Samuel T. spoke.)

SAMUEL T. I was most interested in this verse: "He that drinks of this water shall thirst again, but he that drinks of the water that I shall give him, shall never thirst." He means by this, that those who heard what he taught, and did it, should live always, should never die, their spirits should never die.

MR. ALCOTT. Can a spirit die at any rate?

SAMUEL T. For a spirit to die is to leave off being good.

EDWARD J. I was interested in the words, "For the water I shall give him will be in him a well of water." I think it means, that when people are good and getting better, it is like water springing up always. They have more and more goodness.

ELLEN. I was most interested in these words, "Ye worship ye know not what." The Samaritans worshipped idols, and there was no meaning to that.

MR. ALCOTT. What do you mean by their worshipping idols?

ELLEN. They cared about things more than God.

MR. ALCOTT. What kind of false worship do you think Jesus was thinking about, when he said, "Woman, the hour is coming and now is, when neither in this mountain — "?

ELLEN. Oh! She thought the place of worship was more important than the worship itself.

MR. ALCOTT. Well! How did Jesus answer that thought?

ELLEN. He told her what she ought to worship, which was more important than where.

MR. ALCOTT. Some of you perhaps have made this mistake, and thought that we only worshipped God in churches and on Sundays. How is it — who has thought so? (*Several held up hands, smiling.*) Who knew that we could worship God anywhere? (*Others held up hands.*) What other worship is there beside that in the Church?

EDWARD J. The worship in our hearts.

JOSIAH. I was most interested in this verse, "God is a Spirit, and they that worship him must worship him in spirit and in truth." It means that to feel our prayers is more important than to say the words.

LEMUEL. And when we pray and pray sincerely.

MR. ALCOTT. What is praying sincerely?

LEMUEL. Praying the truth.

MR. ALCOTT. What is to be done in praying the truth? When you think of prayer, do you think of a position of the body — of words?

LEMUEL. (*Earnestly*) I think of something else, but I cannot express it.

MR. ALCOTT. Josiah is holding up his hand; can he express it?

JOSIAH. (*Burst out*) To pray, Mr. Alcott, is to be good, really; you know it is better to be bad before people, and to be good to God alone, because then we are good for goodness' sake, and not to be seen, and not for people's sake. Well, so it is with prayer. There must be nothing outward about prayer; but we must have some words, sometimes; sometimes we need not. If we don't feel the prayer, it is worse than never to say a word of prayer. It is wrong not to pray, but it is more wrong to speak prayer and not pray. We had better do nothing about it, Mr. Alcott! We must say words in a prayer, and we must feel the words we say, and we must do what belongs to the words.

MR. ALCOTT. Oh! There must be doing, must there?

JOSIAH. Oh! yes, Mr. Alcott! Doing is the most important part. We must ask God for help, and at the same time try to do the thing we are to be helped about. If a boy should be good all day, and have no temptation, it would not be very much; there would be no improvement; but if he had temptation, he could pray and feel the prayer, and try to overcome it, and would overcome it; and then there would be a real prayer and a real improvement. That would be something. Temptation is always necessary to a real prayer, I think. I don't believe there is ever any real prayer before there is a temptation; because we may think and feel and say our prayer; but there cannot be any doing, without there is something to be done.

MR. ALCOTT. Well, Josiah that will do now. Now will you let someone else speak?

JOSIAH. Oh, Mr. Alcott, I have not half done.

EDWARD J. Mr. Alcott, what is the use of responding in church?

MR. ALCOTT. Cannot you tell?

EDWARD J. No; I never knew.

JOSIAH. Oh! Mr. Alcott!

MR. ALCOTT. Well, Josiah, do you know?

JOSIAH. Why, Edward! Is it not just like a mother's telling her child the words? The child wants to pray; it don't know how to express its real thoughts, as we often say to Mr. Alcott here; and the mother says words, and the child repeats after her the words.

EDWARD J. Yes; but I don't see what good it does.

JOSIAH. What! If the mother says the words, and the child repeats them and feels them — really wants the things that are prayed for — can't you see that it does some good?

EDWARD J. It teaches the word-prayer — it is not the real prayer.

JOSIAH. Yet it may be the real prayer, and the real prayer must have some words. But, Mr. Alcott, I think it would be a great deal better, if, at church, everybody prayed for themselves. I don't see why one person should pray for all the rest. Why could not the minister pray for himself, and the people pray for themselves; and why should not all communicate their thoughts? Why should only one speak? Why should not all be the preachers? Everybody could say something; at least, everybody could say their own prayers, for they know what they want. Every person knows the temptations they have, and people are tempted to do different things. Mr. Alcott! I think Sunday ought to come oftener.

MR. ALCOTT. Our hearts can make all time Sunday.

JOSIAH. Why then nothing could be done! There must be week-days, I know — some week-days; I said, Sunday oftener.

MR. ALCOTT. But you wanted the prayers to be doing prayers. Now some of the rest may tell me, how you could pray doing prayers.

GEORGE K. Place is of no consequence. I think prayer is in our hearts. Christian prayed in the cave of Giant Despair. We can pray anywhere, because we can have faith anywhere.

MR. ALCOTT. Faith, then, is necessary?

GEORGE K. Yes; for it is faith that makes the prayer.

MR. ALCOTT. Suppose an instance of prayer in yourself.

GEORGE K. I can pray going to bed or getting up.

MR. ALCOTT. You are thinking of time — place — words.

GEORGE K. And feelings and thoughts.

MR. ALCOTT. And action?

GEORGE K. Yes; action comes after.

JOHN B. When we have been doing wrong and are sorry, we pray to God to take away the evil.

MR. ALCOTT. What evil, the punishment?

JOHN B. No; we want the forgiveness.

MR. ALCOTT. What is for-give-ness, is it anything given?

LEMUEL. Goodness, Holiness.

JOHN B. And the evil is taken away.

MR. ALCOTT. Is there any action in all this?

JOHN B. Why yes! There is thought and feeling.

MR. ALCOTT. But it takes the body also to act; what do the hands do?

JOHN B. There is no prayer in the hands!

MR. ALCOTT. You have taken something that belongs to another; you pray to be forgiven; you wish not to do so again; you are sorry. Is there any thing to do?

JOHN B. If you injure anybody, and can repair it, you must, and you will, if you have prayed sincerely; but that is not the prayer.

MR. ALCOTT. Would the prayer be complete without it?

JOHN B. No.

ANDREW. Prayer is in the Spirit.

MR. ALCOTT. Does the body help the Spirit?

ANDREW. It don't help the prayer.

MR. ALCOTT. Don't the lips move?

ANDREW. But have the lips anything to do with the prayer?

MR. ALCOTT. Yes; they may. The whole nature may act together; the body pray; and I want you to tell an instance of a prayer in which are thoughts, feelings, action; which involves the whole nature, body and all. There may be prayer in the palms of our hands.

ANDREW. Why, if I had hurt anybody, and was sorry and prayed to be forgiven, I suppose I should look round for some medicine and try to make it well.

(*Mr. Alcott here spoke of the connexion of the mind with the body, in order to make his meaning clearer.*)

SAMUEL R. If I had a bad habit and should ask God for help to break it; and then should try so as really to break it — that would be prayer.

CHARLES. Suppose I saw a poor beggar boy hurt, or sick, and all bleeding; and I had very nice clothes, and was afraid to soil them, or from any such cause should pass him by, and bye and bye I should look back and see another boy helping him, and should be really sorry and pray to be forgiven — that would be a real prayer; but if I had done the kindness at the time of it, that would have been a deeper prayer.

AUGUSTINE. When anybody has done wrong, and does not repent for a good while, but at last repents and prays to be forgiven, it may be too late to do anything about it; yet that might be a real prayer.

MR. ALCOTT. Imagine a real doing prayer in your life.

LUCIA. Suppose, as I was going home from school, some friend of mine should get angry with me, and throw a stone at me; I could pray not to be tempted to do the same, to throw a stone at her, and would not.

MR. ALCOTT. And would the not doing anything in that case be a prayer and an action? Keeping your body still would be the body's part of it.

LUCIA. Yes.

ELLEN. I heard a woman say, once, that she could pray best when she was at work; that when she was scouring the floor she could ask God to cleanse her mind.

MR. ALCOTT. I will now vary my question. Is there any prayer in Patience?

ALL. A great deal.

MR. ALCOTT. In Impatience?

ALL. No; not any.

MR. ALCOTT. In Doubt?

GEORGE K. No; but in Faith.

MR. ALCOTT. In Laziness?

ALL. (But Josiah) No; no kind of prayer.

JOSIAH. I should think that Laziness was the prayer of the body, Mr. Alcott.[42]

MR. ALCOTT. Yes; it seems so. The body tries to be still more body;

it tries to get down into the clay; it tries to sink; but the spirit is always trying to lift it up and make it do something.

EDWARD J. Lazy people sometimes have passions that make them act.

MR. ALCOTT. Yes; they act downwards. Is there any prayer in disobedience?

ALL. No.

MR. ALCOTT. Is there any in submission? In forbearing when injured? In suffering for a good object? In self-sacrifice?

ALL. (*Eagerly to each question.*) Yes. Yes. Yes. Yes.

(*Mr. Alcott here made some very interesting remarks on loving God with all our heart, soul, mind, &c., and the Idea of Devotion it expressed. Josiah wanted to speak constantly, but Mr. Alcott checked him, that the others might have opportunity, though the latter wished to yield to Josiah.*)

JOSIAH. (*Burst out*) Mr. Alcott! You know Mrs. Barbauld says in her hymns, Every thing is prayer; every action is prayer; all nature prays; the bird prays in singing; the tree prays in growing; men pray; men can pray more; we feel; we have more — more than nature; we can know and do right; Conscience prays; all our powers pray; action prays. Once we said here, that there was a "Christ in the bottom of our Spirits"[43] when we try to be good; then we pray in Christ; and that is the the whole.[44]

MR. ALCOTT. Yes, Josiah, that is the whole. That is Universal Prayer — the adoration of the Universe to its Author!

CHARLES. I was most interested in this verse — "The day is coming, and now is, when men shall worship the Father," & c. I think this means that people are about to learn what to worship, and where.

MR. ALCOTT. Have you learned this today?

CHARLES. Yes; I have learnt some new things, I believe.

MR. ALCOTT. What are you to worship?

CHARLES. Goodness.

MR. ALCOTT. Where is it?

CHARLES. Within.

MR. ALCOTT. Within what?

CHARLES. Conscience, or God.

MR. ALCOTT. Are you to worship Conscience?

CHARLES. Yes.

MR. ALCOTT. Is it anywhere but in yourself?

CHARLES. Yes; it is in Nature.

MR. ALCOTT. Is it in other people?

CHARLES. Yes; there is more or less of it in other people, unless they have taken it out.

MR. ALCOTT. Can it be entirely taken out?

CHARLES. Goodness always lingers in Conscience.

MR. ALCOTT. Is Conscience anywhere but in Human nature?

CHARLES. It is in the Supernatural.

MR. ALCOTT. You said at first that there was something in outward Nature, which we should worship.

CHARLES. No; I don't think we should worship anything but the Invisible.

MR. ALCOTT. What is the Invisible?

CHARLES. It is the Supernatural.

JOHN B. It is the Inward — the Spiritual. But I don't see why we should not worship the sun a little as well —

MR. ALCOTT. As well as the Sunmaker? But there are sun-worshippers.

JOHN B. Yes; a little; for the sun gives us light and heat.

MR. ALCOTT. What is the difference between your feeling when you think of the sun, or the ocean (He described some grand scenes.) — and when you think of Conscience acting in such cases as —(He gave some striking instances of moral power.) — Is there not a difference? (They raised their hands.) What is the name of the feeling with which you look at Nature?

SEVERAL. Admiration.

MR. ALCOTT. But when Conscience governs our weak body, is it not a Supernatural Force? Do you not feel the awe of the inferior before a superior nature? And is not that worship? The sun cannot produce it.

JOSIAH. Spirit worships Spirit. Clay worships Clay.

MR. ALCOTT. Wait a moment, Josiah. I wish to talk with the others; let me ask them this question — Do you feel that Conscience is stronger than the mountain, deeper and more powerful than the ocean? Can you say to yourself, I can remove this mountain?

JOSIAH. (*Burst out*) Yes, Mr. Alcott! I do not mean that with my body I can lift up a mountain — with my hand; but I can feel; and I know that my Conscience is greater than the mountain, for it can feel and do; and the mountain cannot. There is the mountain, there! It was made, and that is all. But my Conscience can grow. It is the same kind of Spirit as made the mountain be, in the first place. I do not know what it may be and do. The Body is a mountain, and the Spirit says, be moved, and it is moved into another place. Mr. Alcott, we think too much about Clay. We should think of Spirit. I think we should love Spirit, not Clay. I should think a mother now would love her baby's spirit; and suppose it should die, that is only the Spirit bursting away out of the Body. It is alive; it is perfectly happy; I really do not know why people mourn when their friends die. I should think it would be matter of rejoicing. For instance, now, if we should go out into the street and find a box, an old dusty box, and should put into it some very fine pearls, and bye and bye the box should grow old and break, why, we should not even think about the box; but if the pearls were safe, we should think of them and nothing else. So it is with the Soul and Body. I cannot see why people mourn for bodies.

MR. ALCOTT. Yes, Josiah; that is all true, and we are glad to hear it. Shall some one else now speak beside you?

JOSIAH. Oh, Mr. Alcott! Then I will stay in at recess and talk.

MR. ALCOTT. When a little infant opens its eyes upon this world, and sees things out of itself, and has the feeling of admiration, is there in that feeling the beginning of worship?

JOSIAH. No, Mr. Alcott; a little baby does not worship. It opens its eyes on the outward world, and sees things, and perhaps wonders what they are; but it don't know anything about them or itself. It don't know the uses of anything; there is no worship in it.

MR. ALCOTT. But in this feeling of wonder and admiration which it has, is there not the beginning of worship that will at last find its object?

JOSIAH. No; there is not even the beginning of worship. It must have some temptation, I think, before it can know the thing to worship.

MR. ALCOTT. But is there not a feeling that comes up from within, to answer to the things that come to the eyes and ears?

JOSIAH. But feeling is not worship, Mr. Alcott.

MR. ALCOTT. Can there be worship without feeling?

JOSIAH. No; but there can be feeling without worship. For instance, if I prick my hand with a pin, I feel, to be sure, but I do not worship.

MR. ALCOTT. That is bodily feeling. But what I mean is, that the little infant finds its power to worship in the feeling which is first only admiration of what is without.

JOSIAH. No, no; I know what surprise is, and I know what admiration is; and perhaps the little creature feels that. But she does not know enough to know that she has Conscience, or that there is temptation. My little sister feels, and she knows some things; but she does not worship.[45]

MR. ALCOTT. Now I wish you all to think. What have we been talking about today?

CHARLES. Spiritual Worship.

MR. ALCOTT. And what have we concluded it to be?

CHARLES. The Worship of Conscience in our Spirit.[46]

CONVERSATION XXXII

* * *

QUICKENING AGENCY OF SPIRIT:

Reanimation

MR. ALCOTT. Jesus was going to Galilee, you know, when he stopped at the well near Sychar. He went on to Cana, where he had made the water into wine. Here the circumstance is mentioned, which I shall now read.

HEALING OF THE NOBLEMAN'S SON AT CANA

Now after two days he departed thence, and went into Galilee. For Jesus himself testified, that a prophet hath no honor in his own country. Then, when he was come into Galilee, the Galilaeans received him, having seen all the things that he did at Jerusalem at the feast: for they also went unto the feast. So Jesus came again into Cana of Galilee, where he made the water wine. And there was a certain nobleman, whose son was sick at Capernaum. When he heard that Jesus was come out of Judaea into Galilee, he went unto him, and besought him that he would come down, and heal his son: for he was at the point of death. Then said Jesus unto him, Except ye see signs and wonders, ye will not believe. The nobleman saith unto him, Sir, come down ere my child die. Jesus saith unto him, Go thy way; thy son liveth. And the man believed the word that Jesus had spoken unto him, and he went his way. And as he was now going down, his servants met him, and told him, saying, Thy son liveth. Then inquired he of them the hour when he began to amend. And they said unto him, Yesterday at the seventh hour the fever left him. So the father knew that it was at the same hour, in the which Jesus said unto him, Thy son liveth: and himself believed, and his whole house. This is again the second miracle that Jesus did, when he was come out of Judaea into Galilee. (John 4:43-54.)

SEVERAL. I was interested in the words, "Thy son lives."

GEORGE B. I thought of the words "Except ye see signs and wonders, ye will not believe." They liked material actions, such as making the sick well.

JOHN B. He thought the nobleman would not believe without some sign to his outward eyes.

MR. ALCOTT. Can we depend on such signs as these?

JOHN B. Not so much as on spiritual miracles, such as giving up your body to make people better. To turn the water into wine is a material miracle. People like material miracles best generally — but they are not so real as the spiritual ones. All their use is to be signs of spiritual miracles.

MR. ALCOTT. Which kind do you like best?

JOHN B. Spiritual; for I can understand spiritual things better than I can material things — and sometimes material miracles deceive us, because we do not know what they are signs of, but to know the spiritual things makes me understand the material.

MR. ALCOTT. Who else understands spiritual things best? (*Many held up hands.*) Who understand material things best? (*Several held up hands.*) Can you see any connexion between the faith and the curing? What acted on the child?

WELLES. The word that Jesus said; and he said the word because of the man's faith.

MR. ALCOTT. What sort of word was it that was spoken?

WELLES. I have a thought which I cannot express.

GEORGE K. Jesus would not have cured the child, unless he had seen that the nobleman had faith.

ANDREW. So I think, but I cannot explain it.

GEORGE K. The way it cured the child was, that God heard the prayer, and cured the child for Jesus' sake.

ANDREW. But Jesus was God.

MR. ALCOTT. Do you wish to leave the subject here?

GEORGE and ANDREW. I should like to carry it deeper, but I cannot.

CHARLES. I think that Jesus prayed inwardly to God to let him cure the child, and God answered him, and he said the word, and it was said in such an impressive manner, that the nobleman remembered every thing, time and all. There was something Supernatural about the manner, and the nobleman felt it, and felt who it was that was speaking.

MR. ALCOTT. Could you explain the faith and cure without the Supernatural?

CHARLES. No; it would not be so Godlike.

MR. ALCOTT. What faculty sits in judgment when you do not feel the Supernatural?

CHARLES. The Reason.

JOHN B. Jesus could do it because he had faith in God.

MARTHA. The man had so much hope, that when he saw Jesus he had faith. I thought Jesus looked very meek and willing, and showed it by speaking in kind tones.

MR. ALCOTT. Have you ever had so much confidence in something spiritual, as to believe against external appearances?

MARTHA. Yes; but I had rather not tell.

JOHN B. I thought Jesus had robes on, and looked pleased, and spoke in a soft voice. The nobleman's voice was not like his, but rough, and he looked rough.

MR. ALCOTT. What makes softness in the voice?

JOHN B. Because of pleasantness in the spirit.

CHARLES. I thought Jesus had on a white robe that fell round his feet, and his hair hung all round his head; and at first there was a look of sorrow and pity for the poor boy's sickness. Then a smile lighted up his face, when he saw the nobleman's faith. The nobleman looked worn down with watching and anxiety; and when the smile of hope, and faith, and joy first gleamed up, his face did not seem fit for a smile, but the smile soon went all over him, like the coming forth of a sun — a spiritual sun — and the smile itself seemed to refresh him.

EMMA. I had a thought, but when Charles began to speak my thought went away. I think the voice of Jesus sounded like music.

MR. ALCOTT. Did it have hope or fear in it?

EMMA. Hope.

MR. ALCOTT. Do you think hopeful people have the most musical voices?

EMMA. I never observed; but I should think they would have.

SAMUEL R. I think Jesus was God in a Body; so he did not have faith in God, but in himself.

LUCY. Jesus made the boy live, because the nobleman did not want the signs and wonders. It was better to believe without signs and wonders.

MR. ALCOTT. Were any of you ever near dying?

GEORGE K. Yes; but I did not know it myself.

LUCY. I was very sick lately, and I was crazy.

MR. ALCOTT. Where was your Mind then?

LUCY. It was insensible within me. When it came back to me, I felt as if I was waking up.

MR. ALCOTT. How did you feel in your Spirit?

LUCY. I felt gratitude.

MR. ALCOTT. Do you suppose that feeling made you get well any sooner?

LUCY. I don't know. Perhaps it did.

ELLEN. I thought Jesus looked pleasant, kind, and happy; the nobleman looked scornful. Jesus wanted to know if he had faith.

JOSIAH. I thought there were rays of glory round Jesus' head —spiritual rays.

MR. ALCOTT. Could they be seen?

JOSIAH. No; painters only draw then in pictures to distinguish him.

MR. ALCOTT. Of all the people, whom you have known, who best deserve crowns of rays?

JOSIAH. Little babies — I know well enough what a little baby is.

MR. ALCOTT. Well, what is it?

JOSIAH. Oh, a beautiful little thing, with pretty little body, and hands, and feet.

MR. ALCOTT. And is what comes to the eye emblematic of the Spirit within?

ELLEN. If babies are so good, what does the Bible mean where it says we "go astray from the womb speaking lies"?

MR. ALCOTT. What do you think it means?

ELLEN. That the nature is bad.

MR. ALCOTT. Some people think it is so, and others think that it is the example of those grown up, which makes children speak lies early in life. The fact remains; we differ as the explanation. Do you think that you have anything in you, which, if spoken to, as the nobleman's faith was, could cure a sick brother or sister? (*Several held up hands.*) What is it?

SEVERAL. Faith.

CHARLES. Physiological Faith I should call it.

MR. ALCOTT. You mean a Faith that acts on the body. A complete knowledge of Physiology would show to us the nerves, by which the Soul acts directly on the body, and makes it move, and causes changes in it. We have a good deal of this power now, though we do not understand it so as to use it very extensively. Suppose you should look very cross or sad to a sick brother; or speak as if you were in despair; would he be likely to get better by looking at you?

SEVERAL. No; indeed.

MR. ALCOTT. But suppose you looked very cheerful and bright, and very kindly. Would that have a good effect? (*They assented.*) Does faith cure the body without other means?

SEVERAL. Faith in the doctor's medicine cures.

OTHERS. No; faith in God cures.

MR. ALCOTT. Suppose, when you took the medicine, you should feel that it would never do you the least good, would the medicine be so likely to act well? (*None held up hands.*) Can you help the medicine with your state of mind? (*All held up hands.*)

SAMUEL R. I have heard it said that people are always cross when they are getting well; and that it is a good sign.

MR. ALCOTT. How many of you think that, if a physician understood the Soul as well as the Body and Medicine, he would be more likely to cure than if he only understood the latter? *(All held up hands.)* Was there ever such a physician?

ALL. Jesus Christ.

MR. ALCOTT. Yes; Jesus was a Physiologist and Psychologist too.

CHARLES. I wish there was a School for learning Physiology and Psychology.

MR. ALCOTT. We attempt to study both in this School. Our subject this morning has been psychological, and now we must prepare for the lesson in Physiology. That comes after recess.[4748]

CONVERSATION XXXIII

• • •

SUPREMACY OF SPIRITUAL FORCE:

Awe

MR. ALCOTT. Jesus was at Cana the last time we read of him, and received a visit from a nobleman of Capernaum. Today we find him at Nazareth.

(Mr. Alcott read:)

FIRST PREACHING OF JESUS AT NAZARETH

And he came to Nazareth, where he had been brought up: and, as his custom was, he went into the synagogue on the sabbath day, and stood up for to read. And there was delivered unto him the book of the prophet Esaias. And when he had opened the book, he found the place where it was written, the Spirit of the Lord is upon me, because he hath anointed me to preach the Gospel to the poor. He hath sent me to heal the broken-hearted, to preach deliverance to the captives, and recovering of sight to the blind, to set at liberty them that are bruised, to preach the acceptable year of the

Lord. And he closed the book, and he gave it again to the minister, and sat down. And the eyes of all them that were in the synagogue were fastened on him. And he began to say unto them, This day is this scripture fulfilled in your ears.

And all bare him witness, and wondered at the gracious words which proceeded out of his mouth. And they said, Is not this Joseph's son? And he said unto them, Ye will surely say unto me this proverb, Physician, heal thyself: whatsoever we have heard done in Capernaum, do also here in thy country. And he said, Verily I say unto you, No prophet is accepted in his own country. But I tell you of a truth, many widows were in Israel in the days of Elias, when the heaven was shut up three years and six months, when great famine was throughout all the land; But unto none of them was Elias sent, save unto Sarepta, a city of Sidon, unto a woman that was a widow. And many lepers were in Israel in the time of Eliseus the prophet; and none of them was cleansed, saving Naaman the Syrian. And all they in the synagogue, when they heard these things, were filled with wrath, and rose up, and thrust him out of the city, and led him unto the brow of the hill whereon their city was built, that they might cast him down headlong. But he passing through the midst of them went his way. (Luke 4:16-30.)

EMMA. I think there was something miraculous in the escape of Jesus.

ELLEN. He would not have escaped, if he had deserved to be cast down.

MR. ALCOTT. What preserved him?

ELLEN. The spirit that was in him; they were awed by his looks.

JOHN B. God was in him.

AUGUSTINE. He did not escape because he deserved to. He deserved not to be crucified.

ELLEN. He escaped then, because it could not have done good to others to have him killed then; as it did when he was crucified.

MR. ALCOTT. What was that in him which produced the awe, of which Ellen spoke?

SEVERAL. *(At once)* Conscience. Truth. Indignation.

CHARLES. The Supernatural.

FRANKLIN. I think it was because they saw him go along without the least fear. This surprised them so, that they were motionless, until he was gone; and I think they were all left standing in amazement.

ANDREW. As he did not seem afraid of them, they thought it would be of no use to throw him down the hill. They feared he would do something to them.

SAMUEL R. His not being afraid made them afraid.

CHARLES. It seemed to me that they carried him to the very verge, before he looked at them. Then, I thought, he turned and looked, and they were so struck, that they stood motionless, with their hands up all ready to strike.

GEORGE K. I think their hands fell when Jesus turned upon them.

MR. ALCOTT. Did you ever have any person look at you, as if they saw everything in you? *(Several held up hands.)* What if you should try this method of "looking", when you are struck or injured by boys in the street?

CHARLES. Suppose a look does not do?

MR. ALCOTT. It will be time then to try some other means. Try this first.

MR. ALCOTT. Can you tell when you have seen a similar effect produced?

CHARLES. Yes; I have seen it among boys. When some boys were once abusing a little boy, they stopped short as I saw them; there seemed no reason but his looking at them. And once I was going to drown a puppy, and he looked up at me so that I could not.

EMMA. Once you looked at me when I was whispering, and I could not look at you.

JOHN B. I have felt that when I was playing in school, very often.

SAMUEL R. I once wanted a dog to do something, he did not want to; and I was going to beat him, and he looked at me so that I could not.

MR. ALCOTT. There is a creature — very feeble — who lives in your house, but in whose feebleness there is a power —

SEVERAL. Little Babies.

MR. ALCOTT. Have any of you ever been awed by a Child's face?

HERBERT. I have.

LUCY. So have I. I have tried to take a baby, and it did not want to be taken, and I did not want to, then.

MR. ALCOTT. Did any of you ever take a little baby, and swing and toss it round, without observing how it looked, or feeling any awe? How many take away things from children, without caring how they feel or look?

SAMUEL R. Yes; sometimes I have wanted to take away something from my little sister, and could not, because she looked so innocent.

MR. ALCOTT. How many think there is something Supernatural in a Babe? (*Several held up hands.*) How many of you think there was a good deal of this look in Jesus, that helped him escape? (*Many held up hands.*) Was that a miracle?

EMMA. Yes.

ELLEN. I do not think it was a miracle. It was natural that he should look so, and that they should feel it.

MR. ALCOTT. Is a miracle unnatural?

ELLEN. It has not a natural cause.

MR. ALCOTT. Could there be anything natural without the Supernatural? Supernatural means "above nature"; and does not the power above nature show itself in nature, and cause those acts which you call miraculous?

(*No answer.*)

JOHN B. I liked the passage that Jesus read. "Preaching the gospel to the poor" means, that he would teach them how to get their living. "Healing the broken-hearted" means, to comfort them when their brothers and sisters die. I don't understand about "preaching deliverance." "Recovering sight to the blind" means, curing spiritual blindness, and curing outward eyes too; so that the outward eyes may see the emblems of spiritual things. I don't understand the rest.

GEORGE K. I think "the Spirit of the Lord" is God. "The poor" means poor in money, and the preaching is to make them good and go to meeting. To "preach deliverance to captives" is, to preach in prisons, that if they would repent God would not punish them. To "recover sight to the blind" is, to clear out the Spirit's eye as well as the Body's. To "bind up the bruised" is to heal them.

MARTHA. I think to "preach to the poor" is, to preach to the poor in spirit, to those who have not goodness in their spirit; and to "heal the brokenhearted" is, to comfort the sorrowing for friends.

MR. ALCOTT. What else causes sorrow but loss of friends?

FRANKLIN. The wickedness of our friends.

CHARLES. Those would be comforted by explaining the uses of the punishments.

MR. ALCOTT. Would you like the world better, if there was no punishment and no suffering?

SEVERAL. Once I thought so.

MR. ALCOTT. Do you see any good in suffering or in punishment now? Who makes you suffer?

CHARLES. Ourselves.

LUCY. The "Spirit's annointing him" means, that God had made him good, to make those who were poor in goodness — rich.

MR. ALCOTT. Then there is another kind of poverty than of riches. Which is the worst kind of poverty?

LUCY. Poverty of kindness.

MR. ALCOTT. Do you suppose there are any very poor people, who are rich in spirit?

LUCY. Yes; the broken-hearted means being sorry for wrong-doing; and he gives them repentance to bind them up. The captives means those who are bound by their wickedness.

MR. ALCOTT. Gve me an instance of such a captive.

LUCY. A little girl, who has done wrong and is not sorry, is "captivated" by her sin; and being blind means that they cannot see goodness.

MR. ALCOTT. Did they lose their sight all at once?

LUCY. No; not all at once; but they do wickedly, and then forget the difference between right and wrong.

MR. ALCOTT. Do we begin by knowing right and wrong?

LUCY. Yes.

MR. ALCOTT. Have you lost any of your spiritual sight?

LUCY. I suppose I have since I was a baby.

WELLES and NATHAN. I did not know anything when I was a baby. There is no right or wrong in a baby.

LUCY. "The bruised" means those who are a little wicked, but want to be good; and Jesus will show them how.

MR. ALCOTT. Was the Spirit of the Lord ever upon you?

JOHN B. When I have been doing right it has helped me, and when I have been helping others.

MR. ALCOTT. Do you ever deliver the captive — those captured by bad habits — even yourselves? (*None.*) Are any of you blind? (*Several.*) Do you begin to recover sight? (*All held up hands.*) How many spend all the year acceptably to the Lord? (*None.*)

ELLEN. I want to know what Josiah thinks.

JOSIAH. I have no thoughts.

MR. ALCOTT. Suppose a person is greater, better than people around him, how will they treat him?

AUGUSTINE. He must make them understand him.

MR. ALCOTT. Suppose they are interested in other things?

AUGUSTINE. He must talk to them and convince them, not all at once, nor everyone. Those people thought a carpenter was not so high as others. But there is no reason why a carpenter's son should not be as great as any other man.

LEMUEL. Because they are poor! Some people think their riches include goodness.

MR. ALCOTT. How many of you think that, if you were to go into another town or school, and begin to talk as you do here on spiritual subjects, you should be understood; or would it be disagreeable?

LEMUEL. The schoolmaster would not let you stay.

GEORGE K. He would be glad, if he was a spiritual man, for then he would teach so himself. But I guess he would not be a spiritual man if he did not have spiritual scholars.

MR. ALCOTT. Most schoolmasters mean to be spiritual.

LEMUEL. I know one who is not spiritual.

CONVERSATION XXXIV
• • •
INSPIRATION OF GENIUS:
Divine Eloquence

(Mr. Alcott read:)

POWER OF THE PREACHING OF JESUS

And Jesus came down to Capernaum, a city of Galilee, and taught them on the Sabbath days. And they were astonished at his doctrine: for his word was with power. (Luke 4:31,32)

(Mr. Alcott then asked what thoughts they awakened?)

SUSAN. They could not understand his words, because they were so great.

MR. ALCOTT. Were the words hard words, or was the meaning great?

SUSAN. The meaning was great — inward.

ANDREW. They were not used to hear about Spirit; they were in the habit of talking about bodies, and they were surprised at the new words.

MR. ALCOTT. Did Jesus make new words?

ANDREW. No; but they were not in the habit of using such words, or thinking of such things; they did not believe there was Spirit, because they could not see it.

MR. ALCOTT. Is there anything mysterious in Spirit?

ANDREW. No; not in itself.

MR. ALCOTT. How did Jesus look, do you think, when he spoke?

ANDREW. Like a minister, only not so sober.

MR. ALCOTT. Why do ministers look sober?

ANDREW. Oh, they think they must look sober. Jesus was not sober. He did not laugh loud, but he smiled.

(*Here Mr. Alcott read a description of the person of Jesus.*)[49]

MR. ALCOTT. Do you think ministers put on a sober look?

ANDREW. Yes; I think they do. I have always thought so.

AUGUSTINE. They don't feel as they look.

(*Almost all raised their hands.*)

MR. ALCOTT. Have you not seen ministers who looked as if they put nothing on?

EMMA. I don't know anyone who puts on a face!

ELLEN. Nor I.

(*Others raised their hands.*)

WELLES. Ministers ought to look soberer than others.

ANDREW. They ought to feel so, but not look so.

AUGUSTINE. If they feel more sober, they must look so.

SEVERAL. Yes; they should look as they feel.

JOHN B. They ought to be soberer than others in the pulpit. Sometimes they may get into a frolic at home. They ought not to do that in the pulpit.

ANDREW. They ought not to be frolicsome in the pulpit, but I don't think they ought to seem better than they are.

MR. ALCOTT. What is it to be sober — what is the true sober?

ANDREW. Jesus was the true sober. He was sober when he was crucified.

MR. ALCOTT. Does it take away enjoyment to be sober?

ANDREW. No; not all enjoyment. Cheerful is sober. Soberness is in the Spirit.

JOSIAH. I don't think at all as Andrew does. I don't think Jesus was very sober, only when he did wonderful things, as when he raised Lazarus.

WELLES. I think Jesus was not sober, but serious.

MR. ALCOTT. What is the difference? Is there any?

JOSIAH. Oh yes; a great deal. There is sorrow in seriousness, and there is not in soberness. Jesus was serious in his crucifixion.

LEMUEL. Soberness is the outward; seriousness is the most inward.

WELLES. I think seriousness is some outward as well as inward.

GEORGE K. I think soberness belongs to the face more.

EMMA. I think soberness has something to do with the behaviour.

MR. ALCOTT. Is there a sober boy here?

ALL. Samuel R. is sober.

ANDREW. Lemuel is sober, except when he is on the Common.

JOHN D. I think Andrew is sober.

MR. ALCOTT. Does anyone here lack soberness?

MARTHA and ELLEN. Charles does.

OTHERS. William C. John D. Samuel T.

MR. ALCOTT. Are any of the girls sober?

ALL. Emma is.

MR. ALCOTT. Are your teachers sober? (All responded yes.) Are they too sober? (Nathan and Josiah thought so.) Who think I should make you better if I were more sober? (All but three held up hands.) Now think, but you need not say — are your fathers and mothers just about sober enough to make you good? Then ask yourselves these questions — Am I sober enough? Am I serious enough? What is meant by "His word was with power"?

JOSIAH. It means that, when Jesus prayed to God and asked him to let him have power, God gave it to him. When he said "Lazarus come forth, " his word was with power, and Lazarus came.

MR. ALCOTT. When you pray, does power come?

JOSIAH. Yes; from my Spirit.

MR. ALCOTT. But must you try?

JOSIAH. Oh yes; try within. Jesus prayed within when he said "Lazarus come forth."

MR. ALCOTT. Should you say to a little baby that was lying dead, "come forth," would it come?

JOSIAH. No; because I am not good enough.

MR. ALCOTT. Can any person do it?

JOSIAH. I don't believe anybody ever tried; perhaps they could. The Spirit must try, and that will set the mind going, and the mind will set the heart going, and the heart will set the body going. You must be full of Spirit.

MR. ALCOTT. Are any of you full?

AUGUSTINE. When I was a little baby I was full.

THE OTHERS. We all were.

MR. ALCOTT. How did you empty yourselves of Spirit?

JOHN B. and OTHERS. By doing wrong; and we can get it back by repenting.

JOSIAH. We must spend a great deal of time in the first place in prayer — and then try, when we have temptation, to withstand it.

MR. ALCOTT. What is a powerful word? What is a word full of power? What is the reason some persons' words are fuller of power than others'?

ANDREW. Some have more spirit; they have used their spirit more, and God has given them more.

MR. ALCOTT. How is Spirit weakened?

ANDREW. By doing wrong.

MR. ALCOTT. By indulgence. How many of you think that intemperance — excess of any kind — anger — weakens your minds? (*All held up their hands.*) Do any of you think there can be intemperance in doing right? (*They all laughed.*) Jesus spoke with power. Does anyone here speak with power? Is there anyone whose words always command attention?

HERBERT. Yes; Samuel R.'s

JOHN B. and OTHERS. Josiah's do.

SUSAN and OTHERS. Emma's.

LUCIA. Emma's and Josiah's.

EMMA. I think all sometimes speak with power; they command my attention.

NATHAN. I think my own words are with power.

MR. ALCOTT. You have talked here a year and a half. Have you ever said all you thought?

LUCY. I guess Emma has not.

AUGUSTINE. I always do.

(*Several others held up their hands.*)

MR. ALCOTT. What has been the subject?

AUGUSTINE. Supernatural power over wickedness.

MR. ALCOTT. What do you mean by supernatural power?

WELLES. Power over the natural — above the outward.

JOSIAH. Words have both natural and supernatural power.

MR. ALCOTT. What is the difference?

JOSIAH. Supernatural words have something to do with spirit. Natural words only express outward things.

MR. ALCOTT. Have you felt the supernatural power of words?

SEVERAL. I have.

CONVERSATION XXXV

* * *

SPIRITUAL INFLUENCE:

Example

THE MIRACULOUS DRAUGHT OF FISHES

And Jesus walking by the sea of Galilee, saw two brethren, Simon called Peter, and Andrew his brother, casting a net into the sea: for they were fishers. (Matt. 4:18.)

And Jesus said unto them, Come ye after me, and I will make you to become fishers of men. And straightway they forsook their nets, and followed him. And when he had gone a little farther thence, he saw James the son of Zebedee, and John his brother, who also were in the ship mending their nets. And straightway he called them: and they left their father Zebedee in the ship with the hired servants, and went after him. (Mark 1:17-20.)

And it came to pass, that, as the people pressed upon him to hear the word of God, he stood by the lake of Gennesaret, And saw two ships standing by the lake: but the fishermen were gone out of them, and were washing their nets. And he entered into one of the ships, which was Simon's, and prayed him that he would thrust out a little from the land. And he sat down, and taught the people out of the ship. Now when he had left speaking, he said unto Simon, Launch out into the deep, and let down your nets for a draught. And Simon answering said unto him, Master, we have toiled all the night, and have taken nothing: nevertheless at thy word I will let down the net. And when they had this done, they inclosed a great multitude of fishes: and their net brake. And they beckoned unto their partners, which were in the other ship, that they should come and help them. And they came and filled both the ships, so that they began to sink. When Simon Peter saw it, he fell down at Jesus' knees, saying, Depart from me; for I am a sinful man, O Lord. For he was astonished, and all that were with him, at the draught of the fishes which they had taken: And so was also James, and John, the sons of

Zebedee, which were partners with Simon. And Jesus said unto Simon, Fear not; from henceforth thou shalt catch men. And when they had brought their ships to land, they forsook all, and followed him. (Luke 5:1-11.)

ELLEN. I wish you would ask all the scholars round, what it means by to "catch men."

MR. ALCOTT. Well; what does it mean?

GEORGE K. I think it means that they would preach, and catch men's spirits.

ELLEN. The net was their words.

LUCY. The net was the preaching which would catch the people who believed.

MR. ALCOTT. Are there any such fishermen now-a-days?

LUCY. No — yes; ministers.

CHARLES. I think he meant they should toil hard after his death, preaching the Gospel; until all men should be caught in the net. All are not caught yet.

JOHN B. I think as Charles does. I did not think so till Charles spoke.

AUGUSTINE. It means the disciples should be good, and talk like him, and bring the bad people back to goodness.

MR. ALCOTT. How many of you ever sought to catch one of your friends to make him better?

LUCY. I have tried to teach my little brother Frank not to do something wrong, when he was going to do so.

CHARLES. Some boys have taught me something.

MR. ALCOTT. Can you remember the time when you left off catching outward fishes, and tried to do right — to catch spiritual things?

LUCY. Since I have been in this school.

LUCIA. That is the time when I began.

MR. ALCOTT. What are outward fish?

JOHN D. Trout.

OTHERS. Appetites, pleasures, &c.

MR. ALCOTT. When did you leave off fishing for outward pleasures, and think of Spirit.

GEORGE K. At the beginning of this year.

SAMUEL R. I used to fish for other things a great deal before I came here.

CHARLES. I have not left off yet, though I have begun many times.

JOSIAH. I never caught a fish in my whole life.

MR. ALCOTT. You need not understand by these questions of mine, that I disapprove of all fishing. Fish are caught for food, perhaps were intended for food; these men caught them for the food of the people who bought them. Who think that Simon and Zebedee's children caught fish for sport?

ALL. No; but to sell.

MR. ALCOTT. What is a net an emblem of?

JOHN B. When we get angry we are caught in a net.

WELLES. The net in this place was Preaching.

(Many hands were raised in assent.)

MR. ALCOTT. Is there an invisible something which seems to be always spread, and includes all events and men? *(No answer.)* What do we call that which works all the changes around us? *(He specified.)*

LUCIA. Providence.

MR. ALCOTT. And is a net an emblem of Providence? *(Many held up hands.)* Did any of you picture this scene as I read?

JOSIAH. Yes; I saw a great multitude of people standing — more than would fill all this temple in all the rooms. And they were asking Jesus to teach them. And Jesus did teach them a little while on the shore, before he went into the ship. And Simon went off from land only a little way. And, Mr. Alcott, I don't see why Jesus wanted him to row off from the land at all — why it was not enough to get into the boat.

MR. ALCOTT. Would not the people see and hear him better, if the boat was out a little way on the lake?

JOSIAH. Oh yes; and after he had preached a great while, he told Simon to row out into the middle of the pond; and Simon looked, in my mind, as if he expected him to do some miracle. But, Mr. Alcott, I don't see how one draught of fishes could fill two ships, if the net was ever so full.

MR. ALCOTT. The boats were smaller than our ships; and perhaps the nets were let down more than once.

JOSIAH. Yes; and then I saw the partners in the other ship dividing the fishes equally; and they sailed along a little before they began to sink.

CHARLES. I thought the multitude absolutely pushed him off the land, they crowded down so from behind. And the boats were new and painted with very bright colors. And Simon sat in one end of the boat mending his nets, and looking very tired. And then Jesus preached; and he told Peter to row out, so that the people might all see him; for the land was sloping. And the bright colors of the boat attracted the fishes, and so they filled both boats. I have often attracted fish by throwing bright colors on the water — and there were many more fishes than they caught.

MR. ALCOTT. Fish often swim in shoals. Can you explain Peter's wish that Jesus should depart from him?

CHARLES. He wanted to be alone, to go into his own mind, and consider what all this could mean.

LUCIA. He felt the superiority of Jesus.

MR. ALCOTT. Did you ever so feel this superiority of any person, as to wish him or yourself away?

MARTHA, CHARLES, EMMA. I have felt so.

MR. ALCOTT. What was the feeling in Peter's mind?

AUGUSTINE. A feeling of unworthiness, because he was only a fisherman.

MR. ALCOTT. What does "sinful" mean; wickedness?

AUGUSTINE. No; it means he was not much known.

(Many agreed.)

WELLES. He felt that he was not worthy of such favors.

MR. ALCOTT. What has been our subject today?

EDWARD C. The draught of fishes.

MR. ALCOTT. I don't want the outward fact, but the principle, that is our subject.

GEORGE K. Supernatural power.

JOHN B. I never can express what the subject of the conversation has been.

MR. ALCOTT. And for that very reason I wish to have you try.

WELLES. The subject has been faith.

CONVERSATION XXXVI

* * *

SENSUALITY OF SPIRIT:

Self-Indulgence

Mr. Alcott read the lesson for the day:

CASTING OUT OF THE UNCLEAN SPIRITS
AT CAPERNAUM

And they went into Capernaum; and straightway on the Sabbath day he entered into the synagogue, and taught. And they were astonished at his doctrine; for he taught them as one that had authority, and not as the Scribes. And in the synagogue there was a man which had a spirit of an unclean devil, and cried out with a loud voice, Saying, Let us alone; what have we to do with thee, *thou* Jesus of Nazareth? Art thou come to destroy us? I know thee who thou art; the Holy One of God. And Jesus rebuked him, saying, Hold thy peace, and come out of him. And when the unclean spirit had thrown him in the midst, and had torn him, and cried with a

loud voice, he came out of him, and hurt him not. And they
were all amazed, insomuch that they questioned, and spake
among themselves, saying, What a word is this? What thing
is this? What new doctrine is this? For with authority, and
power he commandeth the unclean spirits, and they do obey
him, and they come out. And immediately the fame of him
went out, and spread abroad throughout all the region, into
every place of the country round about Galilee. (Mark
1:21-29, Luke 4:33-38.)

*(He then pointed out the slight discrepancies of the separate
accounts of the Evangelists, and illustrated the subject by supposing
the children to see something happen on the Common and to come
into the schoolroom and tell him about it. He asked if all their
stories would be in the same words, or just alike as to the facts,
although they should mean to tell the truth? He then re-read Luke's
account, emphasizing the word "us" very strongly, and asked for
the thought that first arose.)*

AUGUSTINE. I thought when he said "us", that the man meant
himself and the evil spirit.

GEORGE K. I thought he meant himself and all the people who were
there with him.

MARTHA. I thought he meant the several unclean spirits within
him.

MR. ALCOTT. I should like to have each tell me his idea of an
unclean spirit.

GEORGE B. Unclean spirits are appetites, and demons are passions.

NATHAN. Demons mean wickedness.

JOHN D. Demons are bad thoughts and feelings.

LEMUEL. Unclean spirits are filthy words, and demons are passions
— anger.

*(These ideas were repeated by George K., Andrew, William,
Augustus, and Alfred [a new scholar].)*

MARTHA. Unclean spirits are falsehoods.

234 / *How Like an Angel Came I Down*

MR. ALCOTT. Did you ever think unclean spirits were creatures?

(Many held up their hands and said, pig, toad, serpent, monkey, hog, viper, &c. Mr. Alcott checked them whenever there seemed to be an answer to cause laughter, and urged them seriously and honestly to tell their real image and not invent one.)[50]

MARTHA. I always thought of a man with some kind of creature's head.

WELLES. I thought of a man, large and fat as anything, looking horribly, with very large eyes, as large as half my hand, and looking as if they wanted to shed blood. I thought of him in a dark place; sometimes I thought of a dull iron lamp hung up.

LUCIA. I always thought of a man very dirty and very fat.

AUGUSTINE. I used to think of unclean spirits as pigs with men's heads, and demons as tigers with men's heads.

EMMA. I always imagined a demon to be a man with a scowling brow. I never imagined an unclean spirit.

JOSIAH. I imagine a very dark man with a small lamp a great way off. I advance and see a very tall man with a serpent's head and horns growing out of his head, and he holds the small lamp.

CORINNA. *[a new scholar]*. I think of a snake with his head cut off, and a man's head put in its stead.

NATHAN. I think of a man so fat he cannot stand up, and he wants to kill.

FRANKLIN. I used to think of a stubby short man, very fat, with a forked tail, dressed in skeletons, and with a crown of vipers and serpents, and horns. I used to have this image, but I don't have it now.

MR. ALCOTT. Well, these have been your fancies hitherto. Now you may tell me, all of you, what you think about an unclean spirit now?

ALL. It is an appetite.

MR. ALCOTT. Have you ever unclean spirits in you?

ALL. *(But Emma)* Yes.

EMMA. I don't think I have an unclean spirit at all; but sometimes something like a demon, when I get angry.

MR. ALCOTT. Now let us leave the unclean spirits and think how the demons are brought.

SEVERAL. By anger.

MR. ALCOTT. How is anger brought into the spirit — what did your hand, your thought, your body do, when you became angry?

ANDREW. Sometimes somebody is angry with you, and then you are made angry, and that is a demon.

MR. ALCOTT. Can you think of some scene on the Common illustrating this?

LEMUEL. Why, one boy runs against another accidentally, then the last boy strikes him; then that makes the boy angry because he did not mean to hurt him at first; and now he really does hurt him, and so it goes on.

(Others expressed the idea that it was example which made the baby have an evil spirit.)

MR. ALCOTT. Do you remember — do you know a time, when any evil spirit came into one of you?

WELLES. *(Blushing)* I know, but I don't wish to tell.

MR. ALCOTT. How many think they are liable to be mastered by the unclean spirit of gluttony? *(None.)* Or of sleep? *(None.)* Or want of sleep, for there may be intemperance that way? *(None.)* Or by not wishing to wash themselves often enough?

GEORGE K. A little.

MR. ALCOTT. Or by loving to eat fat gravies? *(A general expression of disgust all round.)* Or candy? *(None raised hands; but Ellen, who sat near The Recorder, seemed not pleased with candy's being anathematized.)* Do you feel as the man who spoke to Jesus, "Let us alone; what have we to do with thee? Art thou come to destroy us?" Do you feel as if you wanted to be let alone?

ALL. No.

MR. ALCOTT. He loved his indulgencies — do you love your indulgencies?

ANDREW. No.

(*All the others seemed equally desirous of vindicating themselves, and were more willing to confess to demons than to unclean spirits.*)

WELLES. I got my unclean spirit, partly at home, and partly at a school I went to.

MR. ALCOTT. Does Mr. Alcott know what it is?

WELLES. (*Blushing*) Yes; I believe he does.

MR. ALCOTT. Does it seem to you that he often talks all round it, and that it soon must go out?

WELLES. Yes; I hope so.

AUGUSTINE. I don't see why this man calls Jesus, whom he don't like, the Holy One of God.

MR. ALCOTT. Do not bad people know that others are good?

FRANKLIN. His Conscience made him acknowledge that Jesus was good. It ruled the evil spirit in him.

AUGUSTINE. But the evil spirit thought himself as good, and all that were different from him bad.

MR. ALCOTT. All the people were astonished, and asked how he obtained this power over evil spirits. Is it strange that Jesus should have such power over the appetites and passions? Do you think there is anything in you, which has this power (such as Jesus showed) of mastering the unclean spirits within the Soul?

SEVERAL. Yes; Conscience.

MR. ALCOTT. Do any of you think that you have such power over the unclean spirits within you? (*None answered.*) But if you have such power, why are not all the demons cast out or changed into angels, and all the unclean spirits made pure?

FRANCIS. We want to keep them.

MR. ALCOTT. Well, now, how are you to master your evil spirit?

FRANKLIN. By making a resolution first, then by trying.

MR. ALCOTT. Where does the trying begin?

FRANKLIN. In the Spirit.

MR. ALCOTT. By what faculty of the spirit — can any of you tell?

ALFRED. By the mind.

JOSIAH. Everything must be set to work, the mind, and soul, and heart.

MR. ALCOTT. What is the heart?

JOSIAH. The Soul.

MR. ALCOTT. What is the soul?

JOSIAH. Why, all those words mean the same One, doing different things.

MR. ALCOTT. Does the heart work over feelings or thoughts?

FRANKLIN. The heart works over the feelings, the mind over the thoughts, the soul over all, and the body.

MR. ALCOTT. And the Spirit?

FRANKLIN. Is over all.

MR. ALCOTT. Suppose the feelings are not taken care of, but the thoughts are?

FRANKLIN. I don't see how there can be thoughts without feelings.

MR. ALCOTT. Does not all our nature work together to elevate?

LEMUEL. All, but the body.

MR. ALCOTT. Why not the body?

LEMUEL. Because that always goes downward to the earth out of which it came.

MR. ALCOTT. How many think that after this they shall think of evil spirits — when they go to dinner — or by markets, or by candy shops?

(*Ellen betrayed uneasiness at this reflection on candy shops. A lady present said to her, aside — "You love the spirits dressed in candy." — She smiled — "And would say Let us alone, why art thou come to destroy us?" — She smiled consciously.*)

MR. ALCOTT. And when you go to the vessel of pure water in the morning to wash yourself?

LEMUEL. Water is not pure, it has living creatures in it.

MR. ALCOTT. It seems pure however. What alone is pure?

SEVERAL. The Spirit.

SOME ADDED. Of God.

RECORDER. My sense of justice is wounded by these children going off with the idea that each individual demoniac or possessed person (which expressions, I think, are in these records precisely equivalent to a deranged person) is wicked.

MR. ALCOTT. Whatever was the fact with the individuals, who may have inherited their tendencies or diseases, and so be personally innocent, yet the remote cause was ever a violation of a physiological.

RECORDER. But it was a practical error which is thought important enough to be opposed by the author of the book of Job, and our Saviour in the instance of the blind man, who had "not sinned, neither his parents," to ascribe the misfortunes of an individual to the sins he did not commit personally.

MR. ALCOTT. And like all popular errors, it had an Idea at the bottom, which is what we are to seek after in these conversations.

RECORDER. But surely Mark and Luke were not intending to teach the Idea in this narrative. They merely used the language of the day, and in their minds, as well as words, it was erroneous.

MR. ALCOTT. Suppose that it be as you say. It is of small consequence to these children to appreciate Mark and Luke's degree of truth or error; but important to get the Ideas at the foundation of the circumstances, good or evil, of human life.

RECORDER. All this is perfectly true, if they only know the fact, that it is not Mark's or Luke's view that they are dwelling upon. To know that, would not interfere with their going beyond it.

MR. ALCOTT. But it is better for their minds to be possessed with the Ideas at first. And you see that they seem to apprehend these as if by a spiritual instinct. They can recur to Mark and Luke and the historical view hereafter.[51]

CONVERSATION XXXVII

* * *

SPIRITUAL INVIGORATION:

Healing

Mr. Alcott recalled the last conversation, on the casting out of the unclean spirit in the synagogue at Capernaum. He then read:

HEALING OF PETER'S WIFE'S MOTHER

And he arose out of the synagogue. And forthwith, when they were come out of the synagogue, they entered into the house of Simon and Andrew, with James and John. And Simon's wife's mother was taken with a great fever, and lay sick; And when Jesus was come into Peter's house, anon they tell him of her, and they besought him for her. And he came and stood over her and rebuked the fever, and took her by the hand, and lifted her up; and immediately the fever left her; and immediately she arose and ministered unto them. And at even, when the sun did set, was setting, all they that had any sick, with divers diseases, they brought unto him all that were diseased, and them that were possessed with devils: (and all the city was gathered together at the door:) and he laid his hands on every one of them that were sick of divers diseases, and healed them: and he cast out the spirits with his word, and healed all that were sick: That it might be fulfilled which was spoken by Esaias the prophet, saying, "Himself took our infirmities and bare our sicknesses." And devils also came out of many, crying out, and saying, Thou art Christ, the Son of God. And he, rebuking them, suffered not the devils to speak, because they knew him, that he was Christ. (Matt. 8:14-17, 4:24, Mark 1:29-34, Luke 4:38-41.)

(Mr. Alcott then asked them what they thought of it?)

GEORGE K. I was interested in the words "And she ministered unto them." I suppose the reason was, because she was glad Jesus had cured her.

MR. ALCOTT. But did you think the reason why she ministered to them was because Jesus had cured her — did she not always do so?

GEORGE K. I suppose she would not have done it with so much joy, as now that he had cured her.

MR. ALCOTT. What principle was in this joy?

GEORGE K. Love. Faith. Thankfulness.

MR. ALCOTT. Is there something else beside Love, Faith, Thankfulness, in her Joy?

GEORGE K. Gratitude?

MR. ALCOTT. Yes; Gratitude.

RECORDER. What is the difference between thankfulness and gratitude?

MR. ALCOTT. Thankfulness is less spiritual than gratitude. There is more Idea in gratitude. Is this all that you have to say about it, George?

FRANKLIN. I thought she was sleeping when he went in, and just as Jesus touched her she was dreaming that something was going to be done to cure her, and so she rose.

LEMUEL. She ministered to them because, when Jesus touched her, some of his goodness went out of him into her.

MR. ALCOTT. Can goodness be communicated in such a way in these days?

LEMUEL. No; because no one has so much virtue as he had.

MR. ALCOTT. Just as far as a person is like Jesus, does his goodness pass out of him into those about him.

LEMUEL. Yes; if they have faith, just so much.

MR. ALCOTT. Did any person's virtue ever pass into you? Did you ever feel as if it did?

LEMUEL. No; I never felt so.

SEVERAL. I have felt as if it did into me.

MR. ALCOTT. Now those, who are not aware that they have ever felt any good influence pass into them from others, may hold up hands. *(Several did.)* Will either of you who have felt this influence tell any instance?

ELLEN. I have felt it from the minister at meeting, when he looked round kindly, together with his words.

AUGUSTINE and FRANKLIN. I have felt it in kind, good looks.

MR. ALCOTT. Who of you think that faith is always necessary to cure diseases?

AUGUSTINE. I know that among father's patients, when all the physicians think they are going to die, and they think so themselves, they sometimes get well.

MR. ALCOTT. How do you think they were cured?

LEMUEL. God thought it was best.

MR. ALCOTT. What did God give them to make them well?

GEORGE K. He gave them spirit.

FRANKLIN. There is faith in spirit. I cannot conceive of any body's getting well without some faith.

MR. ALCOTT. How many of you have been sick enough to have a physician? *(Many.)* How many wanted a physician should be sent for? *(The same.)* How many believed the physician would cure them? *(Several.)*

HALES. I did not think the Doctor could cure me, and yet he did.

MR. ALCOTT. Suppose that when the Doctor came you felt a confidence that he could cure you, and you should get well, do you think you should be cured any more certainly, than if you doubted?

(Some thought they should certainly be cured more quickly if they had faith. Others hesitated, but finally agreed it might help.)

AUGUSTINE. I have no opinion about it. I know my mother was sick, and thought she should die herself, and every body else thought so, and yet she did get well.

MR. ALCOTT. Do you think the Doctor could cure as quickly, if he thought his patient was going to die, as if he thought he would get well?

AUGUSTINE. Yes, just as quick.

MR. ALCOTT. Then faith has nothing to do with curing bodies?

AUGUSTINE. No; it only cures spirits.

MR. ALCOTT. Will a little boy get well just as quick, if he says to himself, Now I never shall get well?

AUGUSTINE. Yes.

MR. ALCOTT. Will a little boy get a lesson just as quick, if he says, I shall never get it?

AUGUSTINE. No; that is very different.

LEMUEL. Augustine said faith cures the Spirit; and if it does, then it must cure the body too, because body is joined to spirit so closely.

AUGUSTINE. But people without any faith do get well of being sick.

MR. ALCOTT. Do you not know that physicians sometimes endeavour to make sick people think they are going to get well? Why do they?

AUGUSTINE. Because they do not want the sick person to give up.

MR. ALCOTT. To give up! What must he not give up — his faith and hope of getting well? You see physicians recognise our principle.

ANDREW. I think when Jesus lifted her up, he lifted up her faith which was asleep.

MR. ALCOTT. Where does faith go to sleep?

ANDREW. In the head.

MR. ALCOTT. What wakes up the sleeping faith?

ANDREW. Encouragement.

MR. ALCOTT. If any one wishes to wake up the sleeping faith of a little boy, what must he do?

ANDREW. Tell the boy he will succeed if he tries.

MR. ALCOTT. How must he look?

ANDREW. He must not look cross.

MR. ALCOTT. Love, then, is one of the encouragements. But suppose you have been so kind to a little boy that he begins to abuse the kindness, and he grows impatient with all his wants — what must be done? Must not a boy who is sluggish and dull in his faith and actions be punished to wake him up, and make him believe in some inward power? What do you think? How many of you have had your faith quickened by punishment? (*Several held up their hands.*) Who will tell an instance?

GEORGE K. My faith was waked up to justice by my own injustice —on that day when you punished us, because we thought the little boys ought not to have a longer recess than we did.

MR. ALCOTT. How many of you think virtue has gone out of you to make people better? (*None answered.*) How many think you have made people worse — your parents, or your brothers and sisters, or people who waited on you — tried and injured their tempers —made them feel unkindly, &c.? (*Almost all raised their hands.*) Whom have you made worse, Nathan?

NATHAN. Almost everybody.

MR. ALCOTT. Have I made you worse sometimes? (*No, no.*) Sometimes have not been quite loving enough — sometimes have lost my patience — sometimes have hardened your good feelings, &c.? (*He particularized further; but all protested vehemently against it.*) Have I sometimes not been severe enough? (*Several.*)

SUSAN. You have borne too much from me.

MR. ALCOTT. Why did they bring their sick "at even"?

FRANKLIN. Because they were so bad they did not wish to be seen.

MR. ALCOTT. Now, why so farfetched? Give some natural reason, close at hand.

LUCIA. Because they had more leisure then.

LEMUEL. Because they did not want the hot sun to be shining on the sick.

GEORGE K. Because they had time to get ready.

MR. ALCOTT. Why would not Jesus suffer them to speak, do you think? When there is a little child with his passion, his demon up — what is the best word to say, "Be quiet" — "say nothing"?

LEMUEL. Yes; and parents do say so.

MR. ALCOTT. How many think that, when you are angry, your demon utters many very wrong words? (*Many held up hands.*) Can you tell any instance, when you felt very angry? — it seemed as if something was in you, making you feel badly, and think naughtily, and speak unkindly. It seemed as if you were possessed. Did you ever have such feelings, such a demon? (*Many held up hands.*) Have you a demon or an unclean spirit?

JOSIAH. Mine is laziness.

MR. ALCOTT. Does it get up early? — and wash its face in the morning?

JOSIAH. No; it does not want to.

MR. ALCOTT. It is an unclean spirit then — does it ever become angry?

JOSIAH. Yes.

MR. ALCOTT. Yes; and then it becomes a demon.

ELLEN. Impatience is a demon.

MR. ALCOTT. Yes; and almost every body is possessed with that demon more or less. If that demon could be cast out of the world, we should have almost heaven on earth. Who have that demon? (*Several.*) Who are possessed with anger? (*Several.*) What other demons are you possessed with?

SEVERAL. Eating too much. Mr. Alcott, what is your fault?

MR. ALCOTT. I think I am possessed with a spirit of indolence, sometimes. What faults do you think I have?

SUSAN. You bear with us too long.

MR. ALCOTT. Do you say so? I have been particularly severe with you. That it might be fulfilled, what was said by Isaiah, "himself took our infirmities and bare our sicknesses." What does that mean?

LUCIA. That he cured them.

MR. ALCOTT. When did Jesus do this?

MARTHA. When he was crucified.

AUGUSTINE. He was crucified for our sins.

GEORGE K. I think he bore things for us when he was on earth, always; for if he had not been on earth, we should not have known so much about right and wrong, and have had more sufferings here, and required more punishments.

MR. ALCOTT. Who think he bore them only at the crucifixion? (*Alfred and Others.*) Who think he bore them all his life long? (*Most of them held up hands.*) Did he suffer most at his crucifixion, or in his toilsome life?

GEORGE K. He always suffered more at seeing people do wrong than he did in his body, even on the cross.

ALFRED. He suffered more in the garden than on the cross, I think.

FRANKLIN. He suffered to see the wickedness of the crucifiers.

MR. ALCOTT. How many think he was patient with the sins of others? (*All.*) Are you patient with the faults of others, with your brothers and sisters, with persons who are pre-occupied with care, and cannot attend to you, with boys you meet who have not been taught how to believe, &c.? (*They did not respond.*) Are you patient when people are sick, and give up play and noise that disturbs them; or when they are tired and wish for quiet? (*None thought they were.*) Jesus said, "he that believeth in me shall never die." The Body does nothing of itself; it is but the garb of the Spirit, and without it, a corrupting corpse. Faith lifts the Soul from the grave of the Body, and perpetuates it in Immortality.

CONVERSATION XXXVIII

* * *

MINISTRATION OF SPIRIT:

Philanthropy

Mr. Alcott began with the lesson for the day:

MINISTRY OF JESUS

And in the morning, rising up a great while before day, he went out, and departed into a solitary place, and there prayed. And Simon, and they that were with him, followed after him. And when they had found him, they said unto him, All men seek for thee. And he said unto them, Let us go into the next towns, that I may preach there also: for therefore came I forth. And Jesus went about all Galilee, teaching in their synagogues, and preaching the gospel of the kingdom, and healing all manner of sickness, and all manner of disease among the people. And his fame went throughout all Syria, and they brought unto him all sick people that were taken with divers diseases and torments, and those which were possessed with devils, and those which were lunatic, and those that had the palsy; and he healed them. And there followed him great multitudes of people from Galilee, and from Decapolis, and from Jerusalem, and from Judaea, and from beyond Jordan. (Matt. 4:23-25, Mark 1:35-38, Luke 4:42-43.)

(Mr. Alcott then asked the usual question.)

SUSAN. They must have felt a great deal of interest in him to have gone so far.

HALES. They followed Jesus to hear him preach, and be made better.

WILLIAM C. They were interested by seeing him cure people, both from curiosity and to be made better.

LEMUEL. I was interested in his going into a solitary place to think and pray.

SEVERAL. So was I.

MR. ALCOTT. Why do we wish to be alone when we pray?

LEMUEL. Because we do not wish everybody to be talking about it, as if we were proud of it.

MR. ALCOTT. Why do we have that feeling?

LEMUEL. I don't know.

AUGUSTINE. Jesus went away alone to pray, because he was so thronged in the city, that he had no place for it.

ANDREW. He wanted to see Nature.

MR. ALCOTT. Has Nature any influence upon prayer?

ANDREW. Yes; the works of God are more spiritual than brick houses.

MR. ALCOTT. Do the works of God ever make you want to pray?

ANDREW. Sometimes; for there is life in all the works of Nature.

MR. ALCOTT. And the morning seems an appropriate hour. Did you ever know of any person, who went out in the morning and saw the sun rise, and was led to adore the Sunmaker, and to pray that light might come into his mind, over his thoughts, just as the sun's light was spreading over things, fresh with the dews of night? I knew of a boy once, who lived in a small farm house, under the brow of a hill covered with trees, and beautiful retired coves and solitudes; and he used to rise early in the morning, and go out and choose one of these beautiful places, when the dew was on the ground and the trees, and the birds were singing, and the sun was glittering; and there he would say his prayers; and he found it was easy to be good and kind all day, when he practised this. I knew this boy very intimately.[52] Have you anything about your devotional habits of this kind? Do you have any aid from Nature? It is a misfortune to live in a city on this account, perhaps. You cannot have Nature's aids to devotion. But you may tell me, if you please, anything about your habits of devotion, at morning and evening.

AUGUSTINE. I do not have prayers in the morning, but at night.

SEVERAL. So it is with me.

MR. ALCOTT. Are there any who have no prayers, morning or evening? (*Not one.*) Now, those who have a form of prayer, and always say some particular one, may hold up hands. (*Alfred and others did.*) Now, those who are in the habit of making their own prayers.

(*Several held up hands.*)

JOSIAH. I say the Lord's Prayer always, but generally add something of my own.

FRANKLIN. I do not say any prayer in words, but in my mind.

MR. ALCOTT. In what place do you generally pray?

FRANKLIN. I pray going along to school in the morning, when I am walking.

JOSIAH. I pray in my chamber, at my bed-side. (*Almost all held up hands.*)

MR. ALCOTT. Who say their prayers to their mothers? (*Amost all the little boys.*) I hope none say words which they do not entirely understand.

EMMA. I pray in my chamber at morning and evening; and besides my father has a prayer in the parlor before breakfast.

MR. ALCOTT. You have a family prayer. (*Several held up hands.*) Do you ever pray in this school room? Perhaps I shall have prayers in words here some time. When I feel sure that you are all in earnest about prayer, I shall. But I would not have it a form merely.

FRANKLIN. Jesus went away alone to pray, because he did not like to appear like the Pharisees.

LEMUEL. I was interested in his going into the next towns; he did not mean to be partial.

MR. ALCOTT. What is that feeling named, which leads us to spread ourselves out to do good?

LEMUEL. Charity.

ANDREW. Kindness.

MR. ALCOTT. What does kindness mean? You know "kind" means "nature"; you are of the same kind as Lemuel; and what kind is that?

ANDREW. Human kind.

MR. ALCOTT. And to act kindly would be to act humanly — kindness is humanity.

JOHN D. Generosity.

LUCIA. Benevolence.

MR. ALCOTT. There is another word for love of man — Philanthropy. Name some philanthropists.

AUGUSTINE. Socrates.

FRANCIS. John — Peter.

AUGUSTINE. My mother.

JOHN D. God.

LEMUEL. God is the one who gives philanthropy.

AUGUSTINE. Don't the word mean something about brother?

MR. ALCOTT. It means lover of man, from two Greek words. There is brotherly feeling in it.

FRANKLIN. Quakers are philanthropists.

MR. ALCOTT. What did Jesus say he came forth for?

EMMA. To teach of his Father.

FRANKLIN. He came to teach people to be humane, by being a philanthropist himself.

EMMA. By knowing and doing the right.

LUCIA. By saying and acting the truth.

MR. ALCOTT. How many ways are there of showing forth truth?

FRANKLIN. By thinking and writing it.

AUGUSTINE. By feeling it.

EMMA. And knowing it.

MR. ALCOTT. Yes; you must think, feel, and know it, before you can say, do, or write it. Which is the best way, to say, do, or write it?

JOSIAH and OTHERS. To do it.

LEMUEL. And tell others how to do it.

MR. ALCOTT. What is the "kingdom of God?"

LEMUEL. It means everything that is good.

FRANK. All good things.

FRANKLIN. Humanity; he preached it.

MR. ALCOTT. Is humanity — feeling and doing for our kind — the kingdom of God?

FRANKLIN. Yes; and feeling for brutes too.

MR. ALCOTT. Is there any other object for sacred feeling but persons and brutes?

ANDREW. Nature.

MR. ALCOTT. Is there a feeling which sometimes checks you in plucking and trampling flowers, in cutting trees, in destroying any beautiful things? Or is it humane to destroy? But what else is there that makes up the kingdom of God, beside this sentiment of humanity?

EMMA. A feeling for God.

AUGUSTINE. And for Spirit.

MR. ALCOTT. What is the feeling for God called?

AUGUSTINE. Devotional spirit.

MR. ALCOTT. That approaches the subject; but did any of you ever hear the word Piety? (*All held up hands.*)

FRANKLIN. I was going to say Christianity.

MR. ALCOTT. Did you ever hear the word Religion? (*All held up hands.*) What is the nature of God called?

GEORGE K. Divinity.

MR. ALCOTT. Who think there is divinity in humanity — something divine in man? (*Some held up hands.*) Where about in man?

AUGUSTINE. In the Spiritual Faculty.

MR. ALCOTT. Have you ever felt the divine striving within you? (*Several held up hands.*) Are you willing to tell the instances?

FRANK A. I cannot remember an instance.

MR. ALCOTT. What does the word gospel mean?

EMMA. The word of God.

MR. ALCOTT. It means good news — glad tidings. How do you think Jesus healed all manner of sickness and disease?

JOSIAH. (*Stammering*) He had faith in God, that God could cure them. (*The boys laughed.*)

MR. ALCOTT. Would Jesus cure Josiah's infirmity if he were here?

ALL. Yes. (*Josiah smiled.*)

MR. ALCOTT. Would he laugh at him?

ALL. (*Ashamed*) No; and we did not laugh *at* him!

MR. ALCOTT. What does faith take hold of? (*No answer.*) Does it not take hold of the divinty — the divine in one's own spirit, in the spirits of other men, and in the Spirit of God?

ALL. Yes.

MR. ALCOTT. Suppose a person who is sick believes in the divinity within himself, and the divinity which is diffused through other men, and nature, and in God — and is allowed to breathe the fresh air, and thinks and feels about spiritual things, and never loses faith an instant?

SEVERAL. He would be cured.

ANDREW. God's Spirit is in the air; and his body feeds on Spirit, and he must breathe in the air or he will die.

MR. ALCOTT. What does "lunatic" mean?

FRANKLIN. A deranged person.

MR. ALCOTT. What does *Luna* mean?

SEVERAL. The moon.

MR. ALCOTT. It used to be thought that the moon was the cause of derangement. It is still thought that there are seasons which operate on the deranged, and indeed on all persons. Do you feel equally bright and thoughtful all the year round?

EMMA. I think more of my body in winter.

FRANKLIN. I am lazier in winter.

SEVERAL. I feel lazy in summer.

MR. ALCOTT. I feel the influence of the seasons and find I do best by yielding to this influence.

AUGUSTINE. I am not so good-natured in Spring.

RECORDER. You left the subject of curing disease too much without qualification, I think.

MR. ALCOTT. Perhaps so; but it was qualified in the last Conversation. It is the tendency of faith to lift up and restore the body from disease (and this truth is practised upon by physicians); though after a certain physiological point of decay, it is not done, as restoration is impossible.

RECORDER. Was it good advice to sanction, by your example, the yielding to the influences of the season, passively?

MR. ALCOTT. I did not mean to say that I yielded to the depressing, but to the renovating influences of the seasons. The transitions of Nature, and especially of the seasons, are, I conceive, intended to work out their influence on the Soul of man; and we should yield to them for this end. They quicken, diversify, renovate, and strengthen the Soul.

CONVERSATION XXXIX

* * *

APOSTACY OF SPIRIT:

Impiety

Mr. Alcott read the passage for the day:

CURE OF THE PARALYTIC

And again he entered into Capernaum after *some* days: and it was noised that he was in the house. And straightway many were gathered together, insomuch that there was no room to receive them, no, not so much as about the door: and he preached the word unto them. And it came to pass on a certain day, as he was teaching, that there were Pharisees and doctors of the law sitting by, which were come out of every town of Galilee, and Judaea, and Jerusalem; and the power of the Lord was present to heal them. And behold, they come unto him bringing one sick of the palsy, lying on a bed, which was borne of four: and they sought means to bring him in, and to lay him before him. And when they could not find by what way they might bring him in, because of the multitude, they could not come nigh him for the press; they went upon the house-top, and they uncovered the roof where he was; and when they had broken it up, they let him down through the tiling, with his couch, into the midst before Jesus. When Jesus saw their faith, he said unto the sick of the palsy, Son, be of good cheer, thy sins be forgiven thee: And behold, there were certain of the Scribes sitting there, reasoning in their hearts; and the Pharisees began to reason, saying within themselves, This man blasphemeth: Who can forgive sins but God alone? And immediately, when Jesus perceived in his Spirit that they so reasoned within themselves, knowing their thoughts, he, answering, said unto them, Why reason ye these things in your hearts? Wherefore think ye evil in your hearts? For whether is it easier to say to the sick of the palsy, *Thy* sins be forgiven thee; or to say, Arise, and take up thy bed, and walk? But that ye may know that the Son of man hath power on earth to forgive sins: (Then saith he to the sick of the palsy) I say unto thee, Arise, and take up thy bed, and go thy way into thine house. And immediately he rose up before them, and took up the bed that whereon he lay, and went forth before them all, and departed to his own house, glorifying God, insomuch that, when the multitudes saw it, they marvelled, and they were all amazed, and were filled with fear, saying, We have seen strange things today; we never saw it on this fashion. And they glorified God, which had given such power unto men. (Matt. 9:2-8, Mark 2:1-12, Luke 5:17-26.)

CHARLES. I was most interested in the verse, "Son, thy sins are forgiven thee." That shows that the man had done wickedly in his life, and had been stricken by God with the palsy, by way of punishment.

LUCIA. I was most interested in the verse where it speaks of their going on the house-top, and letting the paralytic down — they had such faith.

MR. ALCOTT. The houses were of one story, and there were openings from the top down into them. They were not such houses as we have; some of you are aware of that. If any of you pictured out this scene you may give your picture.

ALFRED. I thought the house was very full of people, and had a flat roof. And I imagined the young men on the roof just letting him down; and Jesus standing in the room below.

JOSIAH. I thought the house was rather small; and on the roof was a great square place where they let down the man's bed. It was not a bed, but a kind of sheet with four ropes at the four corners. I thought there was but one room in the house, and Jesus stood about the middle of it, and had a smile on his face.

ANDREW. I thought of a small flat-roofed house, and stairs on the outside up to the top. The bed was a kind of cushion about as large as a common bed. There were four ropes and two men; each man had hold of two ropes; and they let him down through a hole in the roof, which they made on purpose.

MR. ALCOTT. What was the name of his feelings?

GEORGE K. Gratitude and faith.

CHARLES. I imagined a long low building, not much higher than a man's head; and Jesus was in the largest of the two rooms in the house, two steps higher than the rest, talking to the people. Bye and bye four men bring along a very old man on a sofa — it was their father. He has a crutch — for though he expected Jesus would cure his palsy, one leg was shorter than the other, and he did not expect he would make them of equal length. When they came to the house, they put a ladder to the side of the house, and took the old man upon a piece of canvas, and opened a trap door on the roof and let him down; and there was just space enough made for him; and Jesus looked at him and smiled; and then his four sons were so transported that they jumped down from the roof.

(Others wished to give pictures, but Mr. Alcott said he could hear no more. Several said they thought of the face of Jesus.)

MR. ALCOTT. Who thinks the body is a sign of what is in the mind? *(Several held up hands.)*

CHARLES. I don't think that, when persons are perfectly well, they ought to think they have all right within them. I am in remarkably good health always; and I do a great many wrong things. I am punished, I suppose, in some other way than in my body.

MR. ALCOTT. The effect of a violated law is not immediate. You know diseases are inherited. Sometimes the effect does not come out until the children and grandchildren appear; and we may suffer from the sins of our parents.

FRANKLIN. Then it is not our fault.

MR. ALCOTT. No; but it is our duty, when we know we have any particular tendencies to disease, to check them by all the self-denial in our power. It is said by some very learned physiologists that, if mankind were perfectly faithful to every physiological as well as moral law, we might be born without giving suffering to any one, live without suffering, and die with the pleasant sensation of going to sleep.

CHARLES. I have had two really hard punishments in my life.

MR. ALCOTT. What did Jesus mean by this question — "Whether is it easier to say, take up thy bed and walk, or, thy sins be forgiven thee?"

LUCIA. He meant to show that he could do either.

LEMUEL. To show that his power could go out both ways.

MR. ALCOTT. Where does sin begin?

ELLEN. In the body. *(Several repeated this idea.)*

LEMUEL. Sin begins in the first wrong thing you do.

ANDREW. I think sin begins in the second wrong thing you do, for the first is only to show you the difference between right and wrong.

GEORGE K. Sin comes from Satan.

> *(Several others repeated this idea, some substituting the word Serpent.)*

CHARLES. Sin began with Eve — she ate the apple.

MR. ALCOTT. Why did she eat the apple?

CHARLES. Oh, she saw the serpent eating, and she thought it tasted good.

MR. ALCOTT. There are some apples before you, and you think they look good to eat. Another person eats and it seems to be very pleasant. But your mother has told you that they are not good for your constitution, and you know that your mother is wiser than you — that she is very kind to you. But you do not think of this; you will not think of it; you try not to think of it; and all the while your eyes and your appetites keep saying, eat. You eat — is it wrong?

ALL. Yes.

MR. ALCOTT. Where is the wrong?

SUSAN. In the determination — the choice.

MR. ALCOTT. Suppose there had been no such bad choice, where would be your Satan?

SUSAN. There would not be any.

MR. ALCOTT. Who then are Satan-makers? Who are the Satans?

GEORGE K. I used to think God made me do wrong.

FRANKLIN. Yes; I thought God made me do every thing.

(One more assented.)

MR. ALCOTT. And now what do you think?

LUCIA. We do wrong at first, and then that makes us do wrong again.

FRANKLIN. Eve was not punished for the first wrong, but for giving the apple to Adam.[53]

MR. ALCOTT. Suppose all the wickedness in each of you, and in all the world, were to be taken out and put into one being; what would be the name of that being?[54]

SEVERAL. Satan — the Devil.

MR. ALCOTT. But it is not all in one being. It is in Charles, and Lemuel, and Francis, and Mr. Alcott, and —

SEVERAL. No; not in Mr. Alcott.

MR. ALCOTT. What did the Pharisees mean by saying "This man blasphemeth"?

GEORGE K. They thought God alone could forgive sins.

MR. ALCOTT. What was the mistake?

SUSAN. They thought no one else ought to.

MR. ALCOTT. And what did Jesus teach on that?

LUCIA. That we must do something ourselves.

MR. ALCOTT. Suppose the persons present this morning, at this Conversation, should go away and say, these children blaspheme, they do not believe in an Outward Devil — would they have understood what we mean?

SEVERAL. No.

MR. ALCOTT. What is blasphemy?

LEMUEL. Swearing.

CHARLES. Saying false things against God.

GEORGE K. That was blasphemy (only I did not know it), when I used to say that God made me do wrong.

CHARLES. It is blasphemy, when we do wrong, to say that Eve did it.

FRANKLIN. I think it is blasphemy to say that Satan did it.

RECORDER. The Conversation today was full of good beginnings, not followed up.

MR. ALCOTT. There were so many things to be considered, that there was not time; and I felt hurried.

RECORDER. And you showed it — you suggested more than usual. You went before them with the Idea that Satan is not a person, and that it would be blasphemy to speak of evil in an infant.

MR. ALCOTT. I was conscious of this. But you know they have never believed in the Personality of Evil, except in one or two instances — that Idea has before come from themselves; and if I had pursued the question on blasphemy, they would themselves have suggested the Infant.

RECORDER. I think so, certainly, and therefore I wanted it to be so. [55]

CONVERSATION XL

* * *

IMITATION OF SPIRIT:

Discipleship

MR. ALCOTT. Have any of you ever thought that Faith alone, without any means of a material kind, would cure diseases?

MOST. No; but that it would help.

(Lucia, Ellen, Susan, George B. held up hands, as thinking that faith alone cured.)

MR. ALCOTT. Did you think so?

ELLEN. No; but I thought you did.

MR. ALCOTT. Do you remember what was said about the little infant?

CHARLES. Yes; you asked, what if you should bring a little Infant into the room, and say it was wicked, would it be blasphemy?

MR. ALCOTT. Did you think that I thought it would be? (*All held up hands.*)

ELLEN. I thought so myself, however, before I thought of what you thought.

MR. ALCOTT. What made you think I thought so?

ELLEN. From the way in which you put the question.

(*Mr. Alcott here read the lesson for the day:*)

THE CALLING OF MATTHEW

And after these things he went forth again by the sea side; and all the multitude resorted unto him, and he taught them. And as he passed by from thence, he saw a man, a publican, named Levi, named Matthew, the son of Alpheus, sitting at the receipt of custom. And he said unto him, follow me. And he left all, rose up, and followed him. (Matt. 9:9, Mark 2:13-14, Luke 5:27-28.)

(*He asked who expected to be interested, and to talk?*)

EMMA. I shall be interested; but I do not like to talk, because I never seem to have said anything when I do speak — I cannot get words for my thoughts.

MR. ALCOTT. Who prefer to hear others talk to talking themselves?

(*All held up hands, except Josiah.*)

JOSIAH. I prefer to talk myself generally.

MR. ALCOTT. Why?

JOSIAH. Because I do not think the others always say what is true.

MR. ALCOTT. But when they do say what is true, how is it?

JOSIAH. Oh! Then I like to hear them talk.

GEORGE K. and MARTHA. Others think more interesting things than I do.

GEORGE B. I never have any thing to say.

JOSIAH. Mr. Alcott, I do not know why Jesus went upon the seaside, unless it was very pleasant there, and it was hot, and he wanted to cool himself.

FRANKLIN. I think he went there because he liked to see the waves and Nature.

MR. ALCOTT. Why did he wish to see nature?

FRANKLIN. I cannot express it.

GEORGE K. Because he liked to have room enough, and perhaps there might be boats there, and if the multitude pressed upon him, he could get in and teach.

ANDREW. I think he went there to see the little fishes.

MR. ALCOTT. Why did he want to see them?

ANDREW. Because he liked to see them swimming.

MR. ALCOTT. Why did he like to look at them then?

ANDREW. Because they had such pretty skins.

ELLEN. I think he liked to go by the sea, because I like to go there.

CHARLES. He wanted to have the sea put mightiness into his words.

MR. ALCOTT. He wanted, you think, to take advantage of the influences of Nature on the Imagination?

NATHAN. He wanted to have other people learn to admire Nature.

JOSIAH. I thought Jesus looked very hot, and he went down by the sea; and you could just see the other side of the sea. And he and his disciples were together; and the multitude was on the other side of the bank, and his hand was up, teaching. (*He gave the attitude.*)

MR. ALCOTT. And what was his hand up for?

JOSIAH. Because it looked pretty. In ancient times they always did so, but they don't do so now; and they all had white robes on.

MR. ALCOTT. Why white robes?

JOSIAH. It was the fashion. And there was a bridge, not for carriages but for foot passengers, that went over the lake. Jesus and his disciples were on that at first; and when he had done teaching, he went on till he came to Matthew; and he called him, and Matthew rose up and followed him.

LEMUEL. I thought Jesus was in a boat, very near the shore, preaching; and the people were on the shore; and when he had done, he called Matthew, who was sitting there, and he went into the boat; and they sailed across, talking about spiritual things, such as God, and —

JOSIAH. He went so willingly to see him perform miracles.

MR. ALCOTT. What kind of miracles?

JOSIAH. Spiritual and material.

MR. ALCOTT. What is the difference?

JOSIAH. To change water into wine is a material miracle, but to overcome any appetite is a spiritual miracle.

MR. ALCOTT. How was curing the leper?

JOSIAH. Material, mostly.

MR. ALCOTT. What was material in it?

JOSIAH. Why, the touching was material, and the faith was the spiritual part.

MR. ALCOTT. How was it with the Paralytic?

JOSIAH. Wholly spiritual — "thy sins be forgiven thee" — yes, spiritual.

MR. ALCOTT. If you saw seed as it sprouted in the ground — the acorn out of which the oak was opening as large as the elm on the Common, should you call that a miracle?

JOSIAH. Yes; partly material.

MR. ALCOTT. And suppose you should see an egg move, then see the shell break, and a little chick come out — would that be material?

JOSIAH. Yes; partly.

MR. ALCOTT. Suppose you saw a baby dying.

JOSIAH. That would be spiritual.

MR. ALCOTT. Suppose you saw a baby being born.

JOSIAH. That is wholly spiritual — being born.

MR. ALCOTT. Did you ever see a spiritual miracle?

JOSIAH. No; spiritual miracles cannot be seen, because they are spiritual.

MR. ALCOTT. Did you ever feel a spiritual miracle?

JOSIAH. Oh yes.

MR. ALCOTT. Did you ever see a material miracle?

JOSIAH. No; there were none only when Jesus Christ was on earth.

MR. ALCOTT. But you said that a seed opening out into a tree was partly a material miracle.

JOSIAH. You asked for material miracles, and that is partly spiritual, and so was the chicken and the dying baby; but the dead baby is material.

MR. ALCOTT. Lay your hands on your hearts. (*They did so, and there was silent listening for a moment.*) Is breathing a miracle?

(*Immediately almost all raised hands.*)

CHARLES. I think it is miraculous, because you breathe without knowing it.

> (*A few thought breathing was not miraculous, because they could explain some of the phenomena and their immediate causes; but all found, on analysis, that they at last came to a link of the chain which was lost in the supernatural.*)

MR. ALCOTT. Feel your pulses. (*They did so. Mr. Alcott expressed in so many words, that breathing and birth were among the greatest of miracles. They analyzed growth in an egg — an acorn — and found that everything led up to the Supernatural.*) Which of your faculties feels the outward miracle, and which the inward?

JOSIAH. The eyes see the outward and the Spirit the inward miracle.

MR. ALCOTT. What is it to follow Christ?

FRANKLIN. He meant to follow him, to try to be good like him, and to go with him too. (*Many agreed.*)

CHARLES. He meant to follow his spiritual path, and his material path. (*Many.*)

JOSIAH. Mr. Alcott, what was done with the table Matthew left?

MR. ALCOTT. Perhaps he did not leave it immediately.

JOSIAH. Why yes; he rose up, immediately, "and he left all and followed him." I have a picture of it in my mind. I think Matthew had a table before him, with a white cloth over it; and he had all his money counted out in piles, the dollars in one place, and the cents in another, and the bills in another.

MR. ALCOTT. It was rather an early age for dollars and bills.

JOSIAH. And when Jesus called him he arose up immediately and left all. He never thought of staying one moment after Jesus called him.

MR. ALCOTT. Do the rest of you think Matthew went as soon as he was called? (*All held up their hands.*)

JOSIAH. Oh! Mr. Alcott, I have another thought now. I think that Matthew was expecting to be called at first, as soon as he saw Jesus coming, and might have gathered up all his money to go as soon as he spoke.

MR. ALCOTT. Why did he think Jesus was going to call him?

JOSIAH. Why, when they set out, Peter and the rest of them did not know where Matthew was gone, and that was the reason he was not among them now, and Matthew knew that Jesus would call him as soon as he saw him.

SAMUEL R. I think Matthew was not already a disciple — this was the first time he was called; but he had already gathered up his bags and money, and was preparing to go home when Jesus called him. (*Several held up hands in assent.*)

JOSIAH. It is all the same thing, even if he did not go that minute — he began to prepare to go perhaps, and did not actually go, till Jesus had passed some time.

MR. ALCOTT. No; it was of very little consequence. Now tell me what it is to follow Jesus, how can you follow him?

NATHAN. I must be good and mind his example.

MR. ALCOTT. But I want a real action — something that you can live, today.

CHARLES. To be temperate when I eat my dinner today.

ELLEN. To be patient, as Jesus was with people, when my little sister troubles me.

MR. ALCOTT. Do you trouble her ever?

ELLEN. Yes; I know I do; but she troubles me when I am getting her to sleep; sometimes she will not go to sleep, and she often cries when I take care of her. I must be patient and kind.

GEORGE K. When my brother plagues me and strikes me, instead of striking back again, I must forbear.

LEMUEL. When my mother asks me to go an errand — to go down to a shop and get some cloth, because the man is engaged, and I am at play, I must go willingly, I must obey her cheerfully.

SUSAN. I must bear with Frank.

LUCIA. I must bear with my little brother, when I put him to bed — very often he cries and will not be good.

MR. ALCOTT. Are you kind to him when he cries?

LUCIA. Yes; yet he will cry, and not do as I want him to; then I must be patient.

JOSIAH. I think that Jesus meant that Matthew should follow him and hear him preach; and when he was crucified, that he should follow his example and preach, and should tell others about it, so that when he died they should preach, and then those persons should preach, and so on till now.

ALFRED. I think like Josiah, and that Jesus wanted Matthew to follow him till he died, and then be an apostle till he was himself crucified, or something else, like Jesus.

MR. ALCOTT. Josiah, did you ever follow Christ yourself?

JOSIAH. Yes; I did today. My little sister this morning had a withered flower, which she seemed to think a great deal of, and my mother asked me to put the faded leaves, that had fallen off, into the fire; and when I did, my little sister cried excessively, and I went up to her and told her a story, which seemed to please her very much, so that she forgot the disappointment about the withered flower and its faded leaves.

MR. ALCOTT. Have all been interested today?

MANY. Very much interested.

JOSIAH. I have been interested, because I have had a chance to talk so much.

MR. ALCOTT. Do you think some others were not interested, because they had no chance to talk?

JOSIAH. The next time I will not speak till recess.

MR. ALCOTT. We wish to have you talk, Josiah, and all others, when you have thoughts of your own to give. We want your own thoughts and feelings. We want you to tell what goes on in your mind while we are reading, and while you are conversing one with the other. That is one way by which we can understand what good the conversations do you. Put your thoughts into words, and then we know what you are, and what you intend. By words and actions we judge of all intentions.

CONVERSATION XLI

* * *

SPIRITUAL INSTINCT:

Superstition

Mr. Alcott began by inquiring about the last Conversation. They remembered Josiah's illustration of the withered flower, and Andrew's image of Jesus' looking at the beautiful fishes; also the discussion of the difference between material and spiritual miracles, and Josiah's long conversation thereon. Each recalled the thoughts of others. Then the lesson of the day was read:

HEALING OF THE INFIRM MAN AT THE POOL OF BETHESDA

After this there was a feast of the Jews; and Jesus went up to Jerusalem. Now there is at Jerusalem, by the sheep market, a pool, which is called in the Hebrew tongue Bethesda, having five porches. In these lay a great multitude of impotent folk, of blind, halt, withered, waiting for the moving of the water. For an angel went down at a certain season into the pool, and troubled the water: whosoever then first, after the troubling of the water, stepped in, was made whole of whatsoever disease he had. And a certain man was there, which had an infirmity thirty and eight years. When Jesus saw him lie, and knew that he had been now a long time in that case, he saith unto him, Wilt thou be made whole?

The impotent man answered him, Sir, I have no man, when the water is troubled, to put me into the pool: but while I am coming, another steppeth down before me. Jesus saith unto him, Rise, take up thy bed, and walk. And immediately the man was made whole, and took up his bed, and walked: and on the same day was the Sabbath.

The Jews therefore said unto him that was cured, It is the Sabbathday; it is not lawful for thee to carry thy bed. He answered them, He that made me whole, the same said unto me, Take up thy bed, and walk. Then asked they him, What man is that which said unto thee, take up thy bed, and walk? And he that was healed wist not who it was: for Jesus had conveyed himself away, a multitude being in that place. (John 5:1-13.)

The children asked Mr. Alcott the meaning of the words "halt," "wist," "impotent."

GEORGE B. I don't see why the man could not step in, when the other men did.

MR. ALCOTT. Can either of you explain that?

LUCIA. It was the man who stept in first that was to be cured; because he would render the water impure.

FRANKLIN. Only one had room to go in at once, and that one would impurify the water.

GEORGE B. Perhaps it was a steep place, and only one could go down at once.

SUSAN. They had different diseases, and when the water was stained with one disease, they had to wait till it had settled down to the bottom of the pool, and the clean water had come up.

CHARLES. I was interested in this verse, "For an angel went down at a certain season." I thought of the angel as coming down and putting his hand in and moving it about to make it pure. I think it is all an emblem. The pool, you know, has stagnant water and is not very pure. It represents the mind of a sick person. And the angel represents goodness coming into the mind, and purifying it; and when the mind is perfectly pure, it purifies the body and makes it well.

MR. ALCOTT. Can you describe the angel?

JOSIAH. I can, Mr. Alcott. It was not visible to the people; and they only saw the water troubled and thought of an angel.

ELLEN. I thought of an angel with a white robe, all unspotted, to represent purity. It was the angel of purity because it purified the water, and the angel had light hair, and a wreath of lilies round his head to represent purity. The wings were light blue.

CHARLES. I thought of a white robe, but a red mantle to represent warm zeal — the zeal to do good. I thought the hair was black, so as to make a fine contrast; and he had a trumpet with which he blowed upon the waters to trouble them. He comes on the wind because that is high and strong and invisible. At first there was a very slight expression of doubt upon his countenance, whether he could do what he was going to do, when he found that he had done it, he smiled and flew away. He had two wings on his head, two on his sides, and two on his feet.

FRANKLIN. I think he had a long golden wand to touch the waters with, and not a trumpet; and a wreath of flowers on his head, and on his forehead, in golden letters the words "Angel of Purity," and he had golden slippers. (*The rest laughed.*)

MR. ALCOTT. How many would dispense with the golden slippers? (*All held up their hands.*) Who think a visible angel literally troubled the water? (*All.*) Are there any such pools now-a-days?

ELLEN. There are none we can see with our eyes.

LEMUEL. I thought that a pool could be seen.

MR. ALCOTT. Yes; it can be seen now, I believe. Did it differ from all other pools that you have heard of?

CHARLES. An angel was in the pool to make it cure, and they believed it could; but there is no faith in such things now.

MR. ALCOTT. Did you never hear of pools that cured?

CHARLES. Oh, yes I have. Virginia Springs.

OTHERS. And Saratoga.

FRANKLIN. And I think the pool of Bethesda was a mineral spring; and they believed it could cure, and so it could.

MR. ALCOTT. How did the porches round the pool look?

NATHAN. They were places to stay in while they were waiting; they were built on the banks of the pool — five of them, and seats were all round, and a room to go in and put on another dress.

JOSIAH. I think they were little houses with slanting roofs on one side. Mr. Alcott, in the country I wonder whether you have ever seen those sheds near churches; people are in the habit of driving their chaises under them. I think there were five like those, or one all round, divided into five parts, and little doors on the back part, where they could go in, and one was for the lepers exclusively.

HALES. I thought of small houses on the banks of the pool, and there were little rooms to dress in.

LEMUEL. I thought there were arches, like that one under the Franklin Library; and within the arches, after you had passed through, you came to steps of granite that led down to the pool.

NATHAN. I thought of tents only, made of wood.

CHARLES. I thought there was a little round house that enclosed the whole pool, and there was a little narrow entry all round large enough for two persons to walk; and the roof of the house made five inclined planes supported by two pillars each. Between each of these was a small window from the entry, except one place where there was a door into the entry, and opposite that door, on the other side of the entry, there was another to go down into the pool.

MR. ALCOTT. Did you ever see such a house?

CHARLES. Yes, my uncle has one at his farm.

MR. ALCOTT. What made the bubbling?

CHARLES. Why, the spring bubbled.

MR. ALCOTT. What made the spring bubble? (*Several attempts but no answer.*)

NATHAN. The angel made the bubble.

CHARLES. The angel moved the waters on the top, but the bubbling below went on all the time.

LEMUEL. The water ran through the rocks with so much force, it made the bubbling below.

HALES. I thought it was full of rocks down at the bottom.

FRANKLIN. I think it was rain that filled the springs at a distance and run through the rocks, that made the lower bubbling.

MR. ALCOTT. Then there were two forces?

FRANKLIN. Yes; the spring below and the angel above.

MR. ALCOTT. Who made the spring from below?

FRANKLIN. God.

MR. ALCOTT. Who sent the angel?

FRANKLIN. God.

MR. ALCOTT. There was one source; might there not have been but one force — one agitation?

FRANKLIN. Oh yes! I suppose they were superstitious; they saw the water moving, and they thought an angel did it.

MR. ALCOTT. What does superstition do?

FRANKLIN. It makes us suspect and imagine.

CHARLES. I suppose the Pharisees had taught them that there were angels, and angels were great things; and when they saw the water moving, they thought that was a great thing, and so they thought an angel did it.

LEMUEL. I think it was the prophets who told them of the virtues of the Spring, and they said it was an angel.

FRANKLIN. But even the prophets only saw the angel in their spirits.

MR. ALCOTT. When a little infant sees a leaf twirling and shaking in the wind, and sees no hand move it, what do you think he thinks?

LUCIA. He wants to know why it does so.

CHARLES. He thinks it is God.

SAMUEL R. No; he does not think it is God, exactly — he thinks it is something above himself, but he does not know what.

MR. ALCOTT. When a very little child is hurt by a stick, what does he think?

FRANKLIN. He thinks it is a bad stick.

MR. ALCOTT. What does he make of the stick and the quivering leaf?

FRANCIS. He thinks the leaf quivers of itself.

ELLEN. He thinks it is a living creature.

FRANCIS. Yes; because it moves, as he does.

MR. ALCOTT. What did these people at the sheep-market think, when they saw the waters moving? (*No answer.*) A child sees a carriage and horses in the sky — they seem to be galloping down —the carriage is all on fire — the horses go very swiftly — oh, mother, see it! — it is coming down! — it will carry me off! — it will burn the world up! My dear, it is only a cloud. What is all that?

SEVERAL. Imagination — fear.

FRANKLIN. Superstition.

MR. ALCOTT. Have any of you superstition — fear of the unknown? (*Many.*) Tell me an instance. (*Several declined, though they said they remembered.*)

GEORGE B. Once I was in bed and heard the creaking of a door, and I thought it was a robber.

MR. ALCOTT. Is there always fear in superstition? Can any other sentiment make it — can love? (*Most doubted.*)

FRANKLIN. Yes.

CHARLES. Hope can make superstition; people desire good and find good signs.

MR. ALCOTT. Do you think there was any superstition about this pool? *(Some held up hands.)* Who among you really think an angel came down and troubled the waters — that these people understood the whole matter right? *(All rose.)* The subject of superstition will come up again; we will return to the text. Are you sure that they thought no one but Jesus could do such miracles?

LEMUEL. It would have been very ungrateful for that man to have told it was Jesus, to expose him to danger; but I think he did not know that it would.

CHARLES. I think he thought it would make the Jews believe in Jesus, to tell them what he had done.

FRANKLIN. Yes; he thought they would love Jesus for it, but they only wanted to know it that they might accuse Jesus.

MR. ALCOTT. How accuse him?

FRANKLIN. About the Sabbath day; they did not understand that doing good was not work.

MR. ALCOTT. But carrying a bed through the streets — was that work?

HALES. Not when Jesus told him to.

MR. ALCOTT. Do you think they really thought either Jesus or the man did wrong?

NATHAN. I don't see why they should.

FRANKLIN. I think that man was very sorry afterwards that he told of the cure.

MR. ALCOTT. We should think before we tell of our friends, things that cannot be understood or appreciated. According to their law it was wrong to carry a bed on the Sabbath day.

CHARLES. I think if Jesus had come with a king's crown, and sceptre, and royal robes, and bringing a great deal of money and honors, they would have let him do anything on Sunday that he wished, and said not a word about it.

FRANKLIN. I don't think he would have done so much good if he had come so.

MR. ALCOTT. Can you tell me of any example in modern times of a mistake, such as these Jews made about the Sabbath day?

LEMUEL. Some people think it is wrong to go and see sick people on Sunday.

JOSIAH. I have heard people say it was wrong to go to an apothecary's shop on Sunday.

GEORGE B. People think it is always wrong to sew on Sunday; but it would not be wrong to sew a shroud.

W. AUGUSTUS. People think it is wrong to go and buy medicine on Sunday, but it is not.

HALES. Some people think it is wrong to eat on Fast day, but we do.

ANDREW. Some think it wrong to ride out on Sunday, or to take a walk. *(Franklin and Corinna agreed.)*

MR. ALCOTT. Do you think those things are wrong?

ELLEN. I think it is wrong to go out on a visit, because it will be likely to take your mind from what you ought to be thinking of yourself; but it is not wrong to visit the sick, or to go out to talk on interesting subjects.

EMMA. If they were going to take a ride for mere pleasure, I think it would be as well to take another day; for though you might think or talk of anything wrong, and the riding would not be wrong, yet other and different kind of people would do so.

JOSIAH. A friend of mine was sick, and the doctor thought it would be well to go and ride on Sunday — and that was right.

GEORGE B. It is wrong to go and sail on Sunday.

ELLEN. Yes; I know that it is wrong, because boats almost always get upset that go and sail on Sunday. *(The children laughed.)* I have very often heard so; I have often heard of pleasure boats being upset on Sunday; and I should think it would be so — that God would make it so on purpose as a punishment.

MR. ALCOTT. Would the same wind upset it on any other day? What is meant by Jesus conveying himself away?

CHARLES. Why, he walked away as any man would. I suppose the lame man was so delighted at finding himself well that he did not take notice.

MR. ALCOTT. Have any of you been more interested than usual

today? (*Several said yes.*) How many have been as much interested as usual? (*Many.*) How many not so much? (*Hales.*) Those who have tried as much as usual today may stand up. (*Many.*) Sometimes I ask a question, and you look as if you were going to say some-thing, and I wait, and nothing comes; how is that?

SAMUEL R. I can't express my thoughts. (*Several agreed.*)

ELLEN. I have no thoughts to express.

(*So several.*)

CHARLES. I don't have either difficulty; but sometimes my attention is diverted, and I do not hear what is going on.

JOSIAH. I cannot always remember the words I want to use. I sometimes have to wait; and I try to remember my words by saying them over to myself; but very often, while I am doing it, my words, and thoughts, and all, are forgotten!

MR. ALCOTT. Sometimes I do not express myself well, or so that you can understand me. How many feel that? (*Some raised their hands.*) Whenever that is the case, you should say that you do not understand the question. Do you always have thoughts? (*All rose, and some said, "almost always."*) How long do you think we have been conversing today?

(*The judgment varied from ten minutes up to two hours. It was two hours.*)

CONVERSATION XLII
• • •
RESURRECTION OF SPIRIT:
Spiritual Revival

Mr. Alcott began by recalling the miracle at the pool of Bethesda, and asked what else they remembered.

NATHAN. We talked about the porches.

FRANK. And about the angel pictures.

LUCIA. And why the first man only was cured.

MR. ALCOTT. What principle did the conversation lead us to think of? You know we spoke of people's ascribing things to wrong causes — of a little infant's thinking a twirling leaf was alive.

CHARLES. Superstition.

(Mr. Alcott referred to the Dutch superstition about the Stork's protecting houses.)

CHARLES. That is because Storks are kind.

(Various other superstitions were mentioned, some beautiful and some not so, both by Mr. Alcott and the children. But so many associations of this kind, signs, &c. came thronging, that he arrested the subject, and said that it was too great a subject to take up now.)

ELLEN. I wish we could have a whole forenoon's conversation on superstition.

MR. ALCOTT. We will at some time. It was introduced now, as you remember, by there having been a superstition about this pool of Bethesda — they thought an angel made it bubble. It really bubbled. Now look over while I read.

THE CONVERSATION OF JESUS WITH THE JEWS ON THE CURE OF THE IMPOTENT MAN

Afterward Jesus findeth him in the temple, and said unto him, Behold, thou art made whole: sin no more, lest a worse thing come unto thee. The man departed, and told the Jews that it was Jesus, which made him whole. And therefore did the Jews persecute Jesus, and sought to slay him, because he had done these things on the Sabbath day. But Jesus answered them, My Father worketh hitherto, and I work. Therefore the Jews sought the more to kill him, because he not only had broken the Sabbath, but said also that God was his Father, making himself equal with God. Then answered Jesus and said unto them, Verily, verily, I say unto you, The Son can do nothing of himself, but what he seeth the Father do: for what things soever he doeth, these also doeth the Son likewise. For the Father loveth the Son, and showeth him all things that himself doeth: and he will show him greater works than these, that ye may marvel. For as the Father raiseth up the dead, and quickeneth *them;* even so the Son quickeneth whom he will. For the Father judgeth no man, but hath committed all judgment unto the Son: That all *men* should honor the Son, even as they honor the Father. He that honoreth not the Son honoreth not the Father which hath sent him. Verily, verily, I say unto you, He that heareth my word, and believeth on him that sent me, hath everlasting life, and shall not come into condemnation: but is passed from death unto life. Verily, verily, I say unto you, The hour is coming, and now is, when the dead shall hear the voice of the Son of God: and they that hear shall live. For as the Father hath life in himself; so hath he given to the Son to have life in himself; And hath given him authority to execute judgment also, because he is the Son of man. Marvel not at this: for the hour is coming, in the which all that are in the graves shall hear his voice, And shall come forth, they that have done good, unto the resurrection of life; and they that have done evil, unto the resurrection of damnation. I can of mine own self do nothing: as I hear, I judge; and my judgment is just; because I seek not mine own will, but the will of the Father which hath sent me. (John 5:14-30.)

MR. ALCOTT. Now tell me, what has been most interesting in this reading? What is the feeling about the past?

GEORGE K. Repentance about wrong.

MR. ALCOTT. Did you ever hear the words "a humble and contrite heart"? As many as have had the feeling of contrition, not fear of punishment, but of contrition, may rise. (*Several rose.*) I will tell you a story of contrition in a little girl, three years old, who was the other day being prepared for dinner by her mother, who was in a hurry to go to her little baby, the little girl's sister. The little girl does not like to be washed, and was displeased because her mother was in a hurry; and when she heard her little sister cry, and felt that it made her mother more in a hurry, she was angry and said, I don't love little sister, I wish she was dead, I will throw her out of the window! Her mother said, Why, my little girl! not your little sister! Wish she was dead! And when the little girl heard what she had said, though her mother did not say another word, or speak of punishment, she looked very much shocked, and said, Oh, mother, I am very naughty; I want to go and lie down; I feel bad; I want to be alone. And her mother said, you had better, and think of it. And she put her on the bed and left her. And bye and bye the little girl's father went into the room, and he did not know what had happened, and he said, What are you lying there for, my little girl? And she said, Oh, father! I feel very bad — I am very naughty —I am not fit to be seen (and she hid her face in the pillow). What have you done? said he. Oh, I have said I did not love little sister; I wished she was dead; and I would throw her out of the window. I am very naughty; I feel bad; I want to be alone (and she hid her face again and cried). In a minute she said again, Father don't love me, mother don't love me, little sister don't love me, God won't love me. And her father said, I love you, and am very sorry for what you have done; and God is sorry; but he will love you again, if you are really sorry — are you sorry? Yes, father; and I love you, and I love God, and every body. And her father said, will you go and kiss little sister? And she said yes; and she got up and went and kissed everbody in the room.[56] Was that contrition? (All assented.) But to return —

CHARLES. I think "the grave" here means the state of those who have been led into wrong by others, and who have stifled their consciences. And "the hour that is coming" is when Jesus shall have been killed, and they shall be awakened by that to think; and when their consciences will either punish them or make them happy.

MR. ALCOTT. Such of you as think that you have not risen from the grave of appetite and passion, may rise. (None rose.) Such as have not risen fully? (All rose.) What is the grave of the soul of each particular one of you? Each one of you think within yourself, into what particular grave your spirits are most liable to fall. I shall require an answer from each.

ELLEN. Temper — love of vexing. I sometimes love to say things to plague my little sister.

MR. ALCOTT. Oh, Ellen! To try to give pain! It will need the voice of the Son of God to lift you out of that grave.

GEORGE K. My grave is something like Ellen's. (*This very unwillingly, as if ashamed.*)

HALES. Mine is passion, I think.

MARTHA. I don't know the principal one, but impatience is one of mine.

FRANCIS. The appetites are mine, and I like to thump and hurt. To-day I only mean to eat a piece of ham for my dinner, so big. (*Showing his two fingers.*)

CORINNA. My grave is passion.[57]

ANDREW. Mine is anger.

NATHAN. Laziness and eating are mine.

MR. ALCOTT. You mean eating more than you ought. How does your head feel afterward; does it not feel heavy? How is it with you, Lucia? (*Lucia did not speak.*) Perhaps there is not any.

WILLIAM. Mine is anger.

MR. ALCOTT. Anger is more than the grave. The raging of anger is like fire; it originated the pictures of hell. Hell is the state of raging passions.

LEMUEL. My grave is appetites and passions.

CHARLES. Passions. Anger is a hot grave.

SAMUEL R. Tantalizing — a love of playing unkind tricks; and I have a great many more.

MR. ALCOTT. I should like to have the deepest grave told.

SUSAN. Disobedience and thoughtlessness.

MR. ALCOTT. Disobedience is the spade that digs the graves; and sometimes it digs very deep graves.

W. AUGUSTUS. Passions and appetites.

SAMUEL R. Love of tantalizing is the deepest in me.

(*All the rest confessed to this sin, and Mr. Alcott made some observations upon the malignity that has its germ in this habit of tantalizing.*)

MR. ALCOTT. But Lucia, you have not told.

LUCIA. (*Hesitating*) Impatience, I believe.

MR. ALCOTT. What is meant by "passed from death unto life"?

MARTHA. Awakening of Conscience.

MR. ALCOTT. Why did the Jews seek to persecute Jesus?

GEORGE K. I think they really thought he had done wrong. (*Some agreed.*)

ELLEN. I don't — I think they hated him because he was so good.

(*Others.*)

MR. ALCOTT. Who think as George does, that the Jews really thought it was wrong to cure the man on the Sabbath day? (*Charles, Samuel R., George, Martha, and Andrew.*) How many think they knew it was not wrong? (*The rest.*) What was the feeling within them, do you think?

ELLEN. Jealousy, and malice, and spite.

CHARLES. And envy.

MR. ALCOTT. Who among you have felt spite? (*Many rose.*) Who have felt jealousy? (*Some.*) Who have felt malignity — a love of hurting? (*Many.*) What did Jesus mean by "My Father worketh hitherto, and I work"?

ONE. God works all the time.

CHARLES. On Sunday as well as at other times.

GEORGE K. God works in our Faculties.

MR. ALCOTT. What did Jesus mean by saying God was his Father?

CHARLES. The Father of his Spirit. God made Jesus — He was a part of God.

GEORGE K. It don't seem to me that Jesus was equal with God exactly.

CHARLES. Jesus had a decaying body on him — that was all the difference.

MR. ALCOTT. Was not the body God's, and has not God the Universe on him? Are you in God, or is God in you?

CHARLES. I had rather think of myself in God, because it seems as if we should be taken better care of.

ALL. So I think.

ANDREW. I think "resurrection unto life" means that, if we are good, we are carried into God; but if we are bad we are not.

MR. ALCOTT. What does it mean by "the Son can do nothing of himself," &c.?

LEMUEL. The "Son" means our Spirits, and our spirits can do nothing without God's help.

MR. ALCOTT. What does it mean by saying "I will show you yet greater things"?

SUSAN. Raise the dead bodies of people.

CHARLES. It is a greater thing to raise men's spirits out of wrong things and feelings, into right thoughts.

GEORGE K. I think the crucifixion was a greater thing.

SAMUEL R. I think the birth of a little child is greater than to do the miracle of raising the dead.

CHARLES. I think it would be a greater thing to raise us out of our appetites and passions.

MR. ALCOTT. What does it mean by "The Son quickeneth whom he will"?

GEORGE K. Puts Spirit into men.

MR. ALCOTT. What is meant by "The Father judgeth no man, but has committed all judgment unto the Son"? When you have done wrong, do you first condemn it yourself, before you feel that God does?

CHARLES. Yes; our conscience condemns us.

MR. ALCOTT. What does it mean by "Honoring the Son even as you honor the Father"?

CHARLES. Conscience is just like God, and if we do not mind conscience, we shall not honor God.

MR. ALCOTT. What does it mean by this, "Of myself I can do nothing"?

LEMUEL. The body can do nothing alone.

MR. ALCOTT. What is Will?

CHARLES and LEMUEL. Your determination.

ANDREW. Your desire.

ELLEN. Your wishes are your will.

MR. ALCOTT. The will wishes, desires, determines, chooses, acts; the will is the Spirit in action, even when we are determining to do something.

LEMUEL. Yes; determining is an action.

MR. ALCOTT. Thought is will in the mind, Love is will in the heart, Lust is will in the body.[58]

CONVERSATION XLIII

* * *

UNITY OF SPIRIT:

Conscientiousness

Mr. Alcott read the lesson:

CONTINUATION OF THE CONVERSATION
ON HEALING THE IMPOTENT MAN

If I bear witness of myself, my witness is not true. There is another that beareth witness of me; and I know that the witness which he witnesseth of me is true. Ye sent unto John, and he bare witness unto the truth. But I receive not testimony from man: but these things I say, that ye might be saved. He was a burning and a shining light: and ye were willing for a season to rejoice in his light. But I have greater witness than *that* of John: for the works which the Father hath given me to finish, the same works that I do, bear witness of me, that the Father hath sent me. And the Father himself, which hath sent me, hath borne witness of me. Ye have neither heard his voice at any time, nor seen his shape. And ye have not his word abiding in you: for whom he hath sent, him ye believe not. Search the scriptures; for in them ye think ye have eternal life: and they are they which testify of me. And ye will not come to me, that ye might have life. I receive not honor from men. But I know you, that ye have not the love of God in you. I am come in my Father's name, and ye receive me not: if another shall come in his own name, him ye will receive. How can ye believe, which receive honor one of another, and seek not the honor that cometh from God only? Do not think that I will accuse you to the Father: there is *one* that accuseth you, *even* Moses in whom ye trust. For had ye believed Moses, ye would have believed me: for he wrote of me. But if ye believe not his writings, how shall ye believe my words? (John 5: 31-47.)

ANDREW. I like the "I am come," &c. I think his coming in his Father's name means that he came to tell them there was a God, and to teach about God; and they would not receive him because they did not care about such things; but those who come in their own names are kings and people, who only think of themselves and only talk about themselves.

CHARLES. They did not like Jesus because he was so plain, and did not pretend to anything, and talked about spiritual subjects, instead of about battles, and conquest, and worldly honors, and such things.

GEORGE K. The reason they did not like Jesus was, that he was so simple and meek. He was not an outward, but an inward man, who talked about God.

CHARLES. They would have been glad of a man who would feast them; they did not understand what he meant, so they thought it was very dull and dry.

MR. ALCOTT. Why did they not understand?

CHARLES. Because their minds were darkened by temptation.

MR. ALCOTT. How is it when Charles's mind is darkened by temptation?

CHARLES. Then I am as stupid and dull —

MR. ALCOTT. What unfits us for receiving spiritual truth?

LEMUEL. Intemperance — Self-indulgence.

CHARLES. We are blinded. I do not understand what is meant by "If I bear witness of myself, it is not true." I should think it meant that one should not rely on one's own views of one's self, and that others should not. Jesus could rely on himself, but he wanted to teach the people generally to get impartial witnesses, like John and others.

GEORGE K. I think he did not choose to bear witness of himself, because that would seem like boasting; but that John's witness would not seem so.

MR. ALCOTT. Why did they think John's witness was true?

ELLEN. Because he was a prophet, and they believed in him.

MR. ALCOTT. Suppose a man should come and say with great earnestness, that he was Jesus Christ, and so that you knew he believed it himself; what would be in your mind?

CHARLES. That he was insane.

MR. ALCOTT. Is there no internal evidence of the truth or false-hood of anything?

CHARLES. Yes; Reason.

MR. ALCOTT. Is Reason unerring?

GEORGE K. Conscience.

MR. ALCOTT. How many think it is Conscience that testifies to the truth? (All held up hands.)

RECORDER. Is there no such thing as a morbid or mistaken conscience?

MR. ALCOTT. A little while ago I heard two persons discussing the subject; one said Conscience never erred; but that Reason mistook its decisions; the other that Conscience erred. What is your opinion — is it your conscience that errs, or your other faculties? (Most said Conscience never erred.)

CHARLES. I know your opinion; for you often tell us that Conscience should be obeyed.

MR. ALCOTT. Yes; I hope that I have always told you to obey Conscience. Do you think that Jesus' Conscience always spoke, and that his Reason always understood it; and that he always obeyed it? (*All held up hands.*) How is it that some people do not hear the Conscience?

CHARLES. Because they leave off obeying it, so that they cannot understand it. Intemperance dims the perception of Conscience.

MR. ALCOTT. Tell some instance.

GEORGE K. Conscience does not speak to me when I am doing a thing, but afterwards.

MR. ALCOTT. Does it not speak, or do you not hear? Do you suppose you could hear it before, or when you were doing it, if you listened?

GEORGE K. Yes.

EMMA. Mr. Alcott, I very often do wrong things; but I always hear my conscience; it speaks low even at first, and while I am doing wrong.

MR. ALCOTT. Those boys, who hear the voice of Conscience sometimes speaking loud and of punishment, may rise. (*Many rose.*) Why does it speak loud?

SUSAN. Because it wants to keep us from doing wrong.

GEORGE K. When you first begin to do wrong, it begins to speak low; then it becomes loud; and at last it gets tired, and the voice dies away.

MR. ALCOTT. What makes the voice die away?

CHARLES. Because you get deafened.

MR. ALCOTT. There is a friend at a distance, whose lips are moving, and I hear him speak low words of warning; I approach him and he grows louder, clearer, and more distinct. Again I see him speak to me, and I turn away from him. He raises his voice to make me hear, but I walk away, and away, till at last his loudest voice can no longer be heard. Is Conscience your friend?

CHARLES. Yes, it is our friend, though we are sometimes its foe.

MR. ALCOTT. Have you all heard the voice of Conscience?

CHARLES. I might as well pretend not to hear a cannon.

MR. ALCOTT. How many are near Conscience?

ANDREW. I am getting nearer and nearer; and when I get up there I stay a good while.

MR. ALCOTT. You linger a while around it. (*Others said they sometimes went up to it and sometimes ran away from it.*) Where is Conscience?

LEMUEL. In the Spirit.

ANDREW. I think a little of it is in every faculty.

MR. ALCOTT. Yes; I suppose that you cannot think, cannot study, cannot remember, unless you use your Conscience; that every lesson you learn without the Sense of duty is in vain. It never becomes any part of your mind. But only earnest love makes it one with your mind. What bore witness in Jesus, that he was good?

MANY. God.

MR. ALCOTT. What bears witness in you?

SOME. Conscience.

OTHERS. Your actions.

MR. ALCOTT. Your actions prove you come from God? Why do you love?

LEMUEL. Because I cannot help it.

GEORGE K. Because Conscience tells me.

MR. ALCOTT. What does it mean by saying "Ye have not seen God," &c.?

LEMUEL. It means by the outward eyes.

MR. ALCOTT. How many of you think that God has a shape?

LEMUEL. God is not a thing.

NATHAN. God is nothing.

MR. ALCOTT. Do you mean there is no God, or that God is not a thing?

NATHAN. God is not a thing, he is a Spirit.

MR. ALCOTT. How do you know that he is?

LEMUEL. Because he holds everything together.

MR. ALCOTT. What does it mean by "And ye have not his word abiding in you"?

MARTHA. The Bible is his word; and the Bible prophesied there would be a Saviour; and they did not believe. They were not conscientious.

FRANCIS. Conscience did not stay in them, because they did not mind it.

MR. ALCOTT. It says in the Bible, "All things are double." What does that mean?

CHARLES. Body and spirit.

MARTHA. Reason and Conscience.

CHARLES. What is there double about God?

MR. ALCOTT. Spirit and Matter. Nature and Man double God, and thus present him in appreciable forms to the senses.

CONVERSATION XLIV

* * *

SABBATH OF SPIRIT:

Holy Time

After a review, Mr. Alcott read the lesson for the day:

THE DISCIPLES PLUCKING THE EARS OF CORN ON THE SABBATH DAY

And it came to pass on the second Sabbath after the first, that he went through the corn-fields: and his disciples were an hungered, and began to pluck the ears of corn as they went, and to eat, rubbing them in their hands. But when the Pharisees saw *it*, they said unto him, Behold, thy disciples do that which is not lawful to do on the Sabbath day. Why do they on the Sabbath day that which is not lawful? And certain of the Pharisees said unto them, Why do you that which is not lawful to do on the Sabbath days? And Jesus, answering them, said unto them, Have ye never read so much as this, what David did, when he had need, and was an hungered, he, and they that were with him? How he went into the house of God in the days of Abiathar the high priest, and did take, and eat the show-bread, and gave also to them that were with him, which was not lawful for him to eat, neither for them that were with him, but only for the priests? Or have ye not read in the law, how that, on the Sabbath days, the priests in the temple profane the Sabbath and are blameless? But I say unto you, that in this place is one greater than the temple. But if ye had known what *this* meaneth, I will have mercy, and not sacrifice, ye would not have condemned the guiltless. And he said unto them, The Sabbath was made for man, and not man for the Sabbath: Therefore the Son of man is Lord also of the Sabbath. (Matt. 12:1-8, Mark 2:23, Luke 6:1-5.)

MR. ALCOTT. What interested you?

LUCIA. What is the showbread?

MR. ALCOTT. The showbread was prepared for the priests, and for them alone.

CHARLES. I liked the second verse. It was not lawful according to their law. They made their own law.

MR. ALCOTT. That law was made by Moses.

CHARLES. They did not understand it right.

MR. ALCOTT. What was their mistake? Was it in the nature of the work?

CHARLES. They thought everything was work.

MR. ALCOTT. What distinction is there in work?

CHARLES. Work of the hands, and work of the spirit. The Pharisees did not consider.

MR. ALCOTT. What was their mistake, as to the nature of work?

GEORGE K. They were mistaken — they thought they ought to think on the Sabbath day, and not to do anything else.

LEMUEL. I think the Pharisees did not understand.

MR. ALCOTT. What part of their nature was wrong?

LEMUEL. I don't know.

MR. ALCOTT. What is the proper work for Sunday? That will explain your ideas.

HERBERT. Going to church.

NATHAN. Reading.

ANDREW. Going to church, and not playing all the time as on week days. We may read other books beside the Bible, such as Psalm books.

CORINNA. *Watt's Hymns.*

EDWARD J. *Pilgrim's Progress.*

NATHAN. I read any book I can get.

MR. ALCOTT. Such as German Popular Tales?

NATHAN. Yes; if I could get it.

MR. ALCOTT. Would it be right?

NATHAN. No; but I do.

MR. ALCOTT. All who think it right to select their reading on Sunday, may rise. *(Almost all rose.)* All who read what they please — anything they can get, may rise. *(Nathan and Edward J.)*

ANDREW. I generally read in the Bible, when I read on Sunday; and sometimes I draw.

MR. ALCOTT. What other ways of spending Sunday are there?

W. AUGUSTUS. Going to Church.

CHARLES. We should go to Church to hear, and understand, and think about the sermon; but if we go because other people go, it is better to stay at home.

FRANKLIN. I think so too.

GEORGE K. I think it is not the going to Church, but the hearing, and thinking, and improving.

MR. ALCOTT. What is Sunday for?

FRANKLIN. To learn and think about moral subjects — to make resolutions, &c.

MR. ALCOTT. Which of our faculties is Sunday for?

FRANKLIN. The Spiritual.

MR. ALCOTT. How is the body to be used that day — should you indulge your appetites — should you eat and drink a great deal on Sunday?

ALL. No.

MR. ALCOTT. Should you be disobedient to your parents?

ALL. No.

MR. ALCOTT. Should you get angry, and be unkind to your brothers and sisters?

ALL. No.

EMMA. I should not think that it would be right to be disobedient, or to do any of those things on any other day.

MR. ALCOTT. Would it be worse to do those wrong things on Sunday than on any other day?

CHARLES. Yes; for it is a day especially set apart for thinking about right and wrong, and all the reasons for doing right.

MR. ALCOTT. I should like to have some of the little boys tell me what Sunday is for — I want a little boy's Sunday, not a grown up person's.

SEVERAL. To make us better.

MR. ALCOTT. Oh yes; everybody has said that always; but I want to know what is to be done.

EDWARD C. We should go to Church.

MR. ALCOTT. What is the object of going to Church?

EDWARD C. Goodness.

MR. ALCOTT. Whose goodness, the Church's?

EDWARD C. The person's who goes to Church.

WILLIAM C. To learn about Spirit, and to go to Church, and read, and think, so as to learn.

CHARLES. I think the Church does a great deal of good by supporting the minister.

GEORGE K. And it holds the people.

LEMUEL. We go to Church to learn how to keep our spirit pure, and to repent.

MR. ALCOTT. Describe repentance.

LEMUEL and OTHERS. I cannot.

GEORGE K. It is brought about by Conscience speaking; you listen and feel you do wrong.

CHARLES. I think the use of Sunday is to take us from outward things, and carry us inward — to think about God. Thinking is an action.

MR. ALCOTT. What makes a thought good?

CHARLES. What you think about. It does good to think, at any rate. It always does yourself good.

LEMUEL. You must practise what you think.

MR. ALCOTT. Give me a description of a Sunday, for a little boy.

GEORGE K. He should get up early, after he has rested; he should pray thanks.

(I lost the rest, because three spoke together. I only retained Lemuel's.)

MR. ALCOTT. Is getting up the first thing? I want you to begin while he is asleep.

LEMUEL. He should wake up, and pray to be made good; he should go down and read his Bible; and should eat but little breakfast so as not to be dull and unable to think; and then he should study his Sunday School lesson, think about it, and behave very well at Sunday School, and walk still, and not play, because there should not be noise. And when he is in Church, he ought not to whisper, but try to understand the sermon; and if he cannot understand, ask his parents; then he should not eat any meat for dinner; and should keep very still at intermission; and then if he does not go to Church, he should read and think about it; and then at supper, he should eat bread and milk; then he ought to read in the evening.

MR. ALCOTT. Where are father and mother — brothers and sisters?

LEMUEL. He should be kind to them.

GEORGE K. If you have younger brothers and sisters, and they do not know how to read, you should read to them spiritual stories.

CHARLES. Then just before going to bed you should say your prayers.

MR. ALCOTT. Say your prayers?

CHARLES. Think your prayers.

GEORGE K. Act your prayers.

CHARLES. You should think of the baby, and then you will get good. And, that thing puts me in mind about the right way of passing Sunday; that it should be easy, and you should smile. A little baby smiles, and you should smile back again; for a little baby is perfectly good, and would not smile if it was wrong.

MR. ALCOTT. And if your neighbour were sick?

CHARLES. And should get well, you should smile.

MR. ALCOTT. You spoke of saying prayers — what prayers are best, those learned by heart, or those which you make yourself?

SEVERAL. Those you make yourself.

CHARLES. I should not think it made any difference, if you understood them.

LEMUEL. And if you felt them.

MR. ALCOTT. Would you say the same prayer if you had been good or bad?

LEMUEL. You can say the prayer of repentance, when you are bad.

MR. ALCOTT. How do you say a prayer of repentance?

LEMUEL. You feel sorry, and resolve to do so no more.

MR. ALCOTT. How many of you are in the practice of saying a prayer that has been taught you?

(Almost all rose.)

CHARLES. I say Jesus' prayer — but something else besides.

MR. ALCOTT. How many say prayers of your own entirely? *(All sat down, and none rose.)* How many add a little to the prayers that they have learned? *(Almost all rose again.)*

CHARLES. There is one thing I do not understand. In the evening you cannot say, "Give us this day our daily bread," because it is not day. I generally alter it and say "night rest" instead of bread.

WELLES. You can say "day by day".

GEORGE K. I have heard it said that that sentence of the prayer showed that it was to be said every day.

MR. ALCOTT. Now let us return to the text. What do you say about the disciples' going through the cornfields and plucking the ears of corn and rubbing them in their hands?

CHARLES. Why it is only a plain fact; there is nothing to be said about it. They were hungry and wanted corn; they rubbed it in their hands, because they had no other way of getting it out.

MR. ALCOTT. What is meant by a greater than the temple?

CHARLES. Himself.

LEMUEL. It means that a Spirit is greater than a Temple.

MR. ALCOTT. What is meant by its being greater?

LEMUEL. It is not greater in space, but greater in goodness; the temple had no goodness.

MR. ALCOTT. Are there any other Spirits, than that of Jesus, greater than a temple?

LEMUEL. Yes; anybody is.

ANDREW. A body is not greater than the Temple, but a spirit is.

MR. ALCOTT. In what sense is the spirit greater than the temple?

SEVERAL. In goodness.

MR. ALCOTT. How are you greater than the temple we are in?

FRANKLIN. In goodness.

CHARLES. And in imagination; for we can spread our thoughts wider and higher than the temple.

MR. ALCOTT. Is a drunkard greater than a temple?

SEVERAL. No.

FRANKLIN. Yes; I think he is a little greater; for the smallest particle of spirit is greater than the largest temple.

LEMUEL. Even a drunkard is not all bad. (*The rest assented to these last ideas.*)

MR. ALCOTT. What is the holiest temple to worship in?

LEMUEL and OTHERS. The body.

FRANKLIN. The drunkard's body is the temple of the appetites.

MR. ALCOTT. Do the appetites have so holy a thing as a temple? Do they always make a temple of the body?

ONE. No; a market-house, sometimes.

LEMUEL. A distillery.

FRANCIS. A pig-stye.

ANOTHER. A grog-shop.

MR. ALCOTT. Is a drunkard's body a temple in ruins, telling of former greatness?

CHARLES. Oh yes! That is a beautiful way to express it!

MR. ALCOTT. Is a proud man greater than the temple?

LEMUEL and OTHERS. Yes.

FRANKLIN. A proud man may be good in other things.

CHARLES. He is a peacock — the greater he thinks himself the smaller he is.

MR. ALCOTT. What does the seventh verse mean?

ANDREW. It means that if they had known what Jesus meant and understood him, they would not have thought him guilty of any thing wrong.

MR. ALCOTT. How is the Son of man Lord of the Sabbath day?

CHARLES. Goodness governs the Sabbath, and Jesus was goodness.

FRANKLIN. The Sabbath is an emblem of holy time.

LEMUEL. The Sabbath day was time, and Jesus was better than time.

CHARLES. The Sabbath day is time, and Jesus is eternity.

MR. ALCOTT. What does Son of Man mean?

LEMUEL. Jesus — he was the son of Joseph.

MR. ALCOTT. Are any of you Lord of the Sabbath day? (*None*

thought so.) Which is the inferior, the time in which we worship, or the worshipper?

ALL. The time is inferior.

MR. ALCOTT. What is the subject of this day's conversation? Now all wait and think before you speak.

NATHAN and EMMA. What Sunday is for.

SAMUEL R. How to spend Sunday.

MR. ALCOTT. Can you take the subject out of Sunday? Have we not said something about forms?

NATHAN. Oh yes; to avoid outward things has been a part of the subject.

FRANKLIN. How to avoid forms.

CHARLES. Will not that answer do?

MR. ALCOTT. Nothing will do, but to have you think. I expect the truth from you, because I deem it within you.

CHARLES. You always keep asking and askng, till you get some particular word for the subject, and then you say, Yes, I understand that.

MR. ALCOTT. Yes; I ask and ask, till I get something fit and worthy; but I am not thinking, generally, of any particular answer. Sometimes I ask because I do not think myself, and hope that you will find some word that will embody the spirit of the conversation. Sometimes, always, indeed, I seek to assist you by my questions in finding the answer, by the free exercise of your own minds. All truth is within; my business is to lead you to find it in your own Souls. Your YES and NO, when you think freely, declare the fact that you have found it, or have failed in your quest of it. The spirit says yes, or no; implying that the truth *is* or is *not* made conscious to its vision. We never know nor see all of ourselves.[59]

CONVERSATION XLV

* * *

SPIRITUAL AND CORPOREAL RELATIONS:

Appetites and Passions

MR. ALCOTT. Why do I commence the conversation by asking what we talked about last?

LEMUEL. Because the conversations are joined together.

ANDREW. Because, to understand one helps us to understand the next — because they are all one.

MR. ALCOTT. Where did we leave Jesus?

CHARLES. In the cornfields near Jerusalem.

MR. ALCOTT. He was near Jerusalem, and I shall now read.

THE HEALING OF THE WITHERED HAND

And when he was departed thence, it came to pass also on another Sabbath that he entered again, went into their synagogue, and taught. And, behold, there was a man whose right hand was withered. And the Scribes and Pharisees watched him, whether he would heal him on the Sabbath day: that they might find an accusation against him. But he knew their thoughts, and said to the man which had the withered hand, Rise up and stand forth in the midst. And he arose, and stood forth. And they asked him, saying, Is it lawful to heal on the Sabbath days? That they might accuse him. Then said Jesus unto them, I will ask you one thing; Is it lawful on the Sabbath days to do good or to do evil? To save life or to destroy it? But they held their peace. And he said unto them, What man shall there be among you, that shall have one sheep, and if it fall into a pit on the Sabbath day, will he not lay hold on it, and lift it out? How much then is a man better than a sheep? Wherefore it is lawful to do well on the Sabbath days. And when he had looked round about on them with anger; being grieved for the hardness of their hearts: he saith unto the man, Stretch forth thine hand. And he stretched it forth; and it was restored whole, like as the other. Then the Pharisees were filled with madness, and they went forth with the Herodians, and straightway held a council against him; and communed one with another, how they might destroy him. (Matt. 12:9-15, Mark 3:1-7, Luke 6:6-12.)

CHARLES. I don't think it is right for the Evangelist to say that he looked round with anger — I don't think he ever was angry. I think it means indignation.

GEORGE K. He looked angry.

LUCIA. He felt indignation.

FRANKLIN. I think they mistook the indignation for anger.

MR. ALCOTT. Is the look of indignation different from that of anger?

EMMA. The look of indignation is not like that of anger.

CHARLES. No; there is disdain in indignation — contempt for meanness. I don't think you can feel indignation without something of contempt.

MR. ALCOTT. Can anger be mistaken by the good?

SOME. Yes.

MR. ALCOTT. Are they likely to do so, unless they are easily angry themselves?

SOME. No.

MR. ALCOTT. Did Mark mistake?

CHARLES. Perhaps Mark was angry himself, and so thought Jesus was angry.

RECORDER. The word "anger", in the time this translation of the Scriptures was made, did not mean anything wrong. It merely meant trouble, agitation. Thus St. Paul says, "Be angry and sin not"; and in another part of the Bible it says, "God is angry with the wicked every day."

MR. ALCOTT. Anger generally refers to persons, and indignation to principles. I do not think any degree of anger is right on any occasion.

GEORGE K. I like the tenth and eleventh verses; "And behold there was a man, &c." I was interested in their asking whether it was lawful to heal on the Sabbath days? It was a catch.

MR. ALCOTT. Why did they wish to do this?

GEORGE K. They wanted to hear what he could say.

LEMUEL. They wanted to accuse him before Pilate.

FRANKLIN. When Jesus asked his questions, they held their peace, because they felt awe, they felt that they were in the wrong.

CHARLES. That shows some good in them.

FRANKLIN. I used to think they were struck dumb, but now I see that they felt awe.

MR. ALCOTT. Who has felt this awe sometimes among you? (*Several.*) Two little girls were standing in the parlor with their mother; and their father, looking over his papers, found a beautiful picture, and gave it to the oldest little girl; and her sister, who was younger, in a moment of jealousy, said, "I don't like father." And her father said, "I will give you a picture;" and he found another and gave it to her. And she said that it was not so pretty — that she did not like her sister. And their father said to the oldest, "Will you give your beautiful picture to your little sister?" and she gave it to her immediately; but the younger sister did not look pleased. She held her head down, and looked unhappy. Bye and bye her father said to her, "Which is the best girl, the one who gives away her picture, or the one who takes it?" She replied, "The one who gives it away." Soon the father went out of the room; and the little girl followed him, and said, "Father, I am going to give this picture back again;" and so she went and gave it back to her sister. Why was this?

FRANKLIN. She was overawed.

CHARLES. I should think that she would not have taken it in the first place.

MR. ALCOTT. She is a very little girl, not four years old. How many of you understand the movements of that little girl's mind? (*Several held up hands.*) Do you think that the generosity of the sentiment expressed by Jesus, about saving the body on Sunday or any day, and the illustrations he used, overawed them? (*They held up hands.*) What do you think of the questions of Jesus, "Is it lawful to do good or to do evil on the Sabbath day"?

GEORGE K. By asking that question they could answer their own.

MR. ALCOTT. Do you observe that he often talked in this interrogative way?

CHARLES. Yes.

MR. ALCOTT. How was he able always to strike at the state of their minds? Why was it that he knew their states of mind?

LUCIA. He knew about Human nature by having studied himself.

MR. ALCOTT. Do you think that you have some of this knowledge, by which you can discover what is going on in other people's minds? (*George K. held up his hand.*) What is the innermost feeling in me now?

GEORGE K. That we should attend. Sometimes I answer a question by asking another.

MR. ALCOTT. And so you understand this method of Jesus? Who knows something of Human Nature, and can tell what is going on within others' minds? (*Not many.*) I will see whether I know.

(*He went on and made personal remarks, as to the present state of their minds, and asked whether he was right. Most acknowledged that he was right.*)

MR. ALCOTT. Now what is my thought?

SEVERAL. You want us to attend.

MR. ALCOTT. How could Jesus know people's thoughts? By the same method of discovery that you would, if you discovered them?

GEORGE K. Yes; he learnt it as we learn that people are happy by their smile.

CHARLES. He thought first of their words, then their manners, then their faces.

MR. ALCOTT. Why is it that faces mean more to some people than to others?

CHARLES. Because they understand — they examine faces.

MR. ALCOTT. What is it that tells?

CHARLES. The Spirit — the judgment.

LEMUEL. Other people's spirits were like his; and he knew his own, and so he knew others'.

MR. ALCOTT. Why don't we know?

FRANKLIN. Because we do not choose to try.

MR. ALCOTT. What gives the face its expression?

FRANK. Mind. Spirit.

LEMUEL. Thoughts and feelings.

MR. ALCOTT. What effect does self-indulgence give to the face?

FRANKLIN. It makes people's faces pale.

LEMUEL. It makes the face red.

MR. ALCOTT. Who think that the shape of the face is made by the predominant feelings and thoughts? (*Almost all.*) Who think the appetites and passions do not affect the face? (*Some.*) Who think that your faces are as expressive as they would have been, had you lived as you ought? (*None held up hands.*) You may give me some emblems of indignation, when it shows itself forth in the face. (*No answer for a long time.*) How did Jesus look?

FRANCIS. He looked sorrowful.

LUCIA. There was some degree of contempt.

MR. ALCOTT. Can you give an emblem of anger?

CHARLES. A tiger.

FRANKLIN. The elephant is indignant.

ANDREW. The hyena is the emblem of anger.

MR. ALCOTT. Give an emblem of love.

GEORGE B. An angel.

LEMUEL. A dove.

MR. ALCOTT. An emblem of revenge.

GEORGE B. An Indian.

CHARLES. A lion.

FRANKLIN. Apollyon.

MR. ALCOTT. That is factitious.

FRANKLIN. No more so than an angel.

CHARLES. Certainly not.

MR. ALCOTT. Your emblems this morning do not seem to come; there is little imagination in them. Could you paint Jesus looking round on the multitude?

LUCIA. I can describe how he stands, but cannot describe his look. (*Others expressed the same.*)

LEMUEL. I think he had a slight scowl.

CHARLES. Oh no; Jesus never had a scowl; he was looking down upon them.

MR. ALCOTT. Why did Jesus speak of raising a sheep out of the pit?

CHARLES. He knew that they valued their property, and he gave that as an emblem.

MR. ALCOTT. What two objects was he trying to value?

EMMA. A sheep and a man.

MR. ALCOTT. And if they would save a sheep on the Sabbath day —

CHARLES. Why should they not save a man?

(*Later.*)

MR. ALCOTT. Is the body the eater and drinker? (*Several said yes.*)

NATHAN. No; the Spirit.

CHARLES. Does the spirit eat and drink?

MR. ALCOTT. Does a dead body eat and drink?

FRANCIS. No; because the spirit is not there to move the body.

LUCIA. I think the spirit eats and drinks through the body.

MR. ALCOTT. How?

FRANCIS. The will moves the body.

CHARLES. The spirit does not eat and drink, I am sure.

ANDREW. The spirit makes the body eat, and gets all the good; but it could not eat without a body.

MR. ALCOTT. Which is the eater?

ANDREW. The body eats, but the spirit sets it in motion.

GEORGE K. The spirit does not eat, it makes the body eat.

FRANKLIN. When the spirit leaves the body, the spirit does not eat.

MR. ALCOTT. What hungers?

SEVERAL. The Body.

SOME. The Spirit.

MR. ALCOTT. Does a dead body hunger?

GEORGE K. No; then the spirit must.

MR. ALCOTT. Which is the hungerer and thirster and eater?

GEORGE K. Why, I suppose it must be the spirit then.

MR. ALCOTT. Does the eye see?

FRANCIS. Yes; but the spirit makes it see.

MR. ALCOTT. Does the hand touch?

SEVERAL. Yes; but the spirit moves it.

MR. ALCOTT. Does the knife cut?

SEVERAL. Yes; but the hand uses it.

LEMUEL and LUCIA. No; it is the spirit uses it.

MR. ALCOTT. Do you think, that the organs used for mastication have any power of their own?

CHARLES. No; but the spirit gives them power.

MR. ALCOTT. Why is it that you think the body sees and hears, eats and drinks?

CHARLES. The spirit sees and hears, but does not eat and drink.

MARTHA. The spirit eats and fixes the food and builds it upon the body.

MR. ALCOTT. Has your spirit the appetite?

CHARLES. No; the body has the appetite.

MR. ALCOTT. What organ of your body?

SEVERAL. The mouth.

MR. ALCOTT. What moves the mouth?

SEVERAL. The spirit.

MR. ALCOTT. What is the connexion between the spirit and the mouth?

CHARLES. I do not think any one can tell that.

MR. ALCOTT. It is very simple, if you will think. What makes the spirit act on the body?

SEVERAL. Hunger.

MR. ALCOTT. Where is hunger, in the soul or the body?

SEVERAL. In the soul.

CHARLES. In the body. The soul does not hunger for food.

MR. ALCOTT. What acts in hunger?

CHARLES. The stomach wants something to do.

MR. ALCOTT. Does the hunger begin to act on the stomach, or the stomach act on the hunger?

CHARLES. We are so made that we hunger at times; and the spirit directs the action of the body when it hungers, and makes it eat; but the spirit does not hunger for food. The spirit hungers for inward things, and directs the body and makes it eat; it does not get the food into itself.

MR. ALCOTT. But the spirit surely gets the good from the act of eating, does it not?

CHARLES. The spirit causes the body to eat, and the effect of the body's eating is good on the spirit; but the effect is not the cause.

MR. ALCOTT. The effect is always involved in the cause. Did you ever hear these words — "Blessed are ye, when ye shall hunger and thirst after righteousness"?

CHARLES. I said the spirit hungered after inward things, but the body after material things. I think there is something low in making the spirit hunger after food.

MR. ALCOTT. Yet the spirit must take care of the body, supply its waste and build it up, as it tends to decay.

ANDREW. Mr. Alcott, I do not think that the soul hungers, because it makes the body hunger, any more than that the man is the house, because he builds it.

MR. ALCOTT. Those, who agree with Charles, may hold up their hands. *(One or two did.)* Those who think that the Spirit hungers, may hold up their hands. *(Several did.)* I am unable to decide this question.

CHARLES. Then why do you reason against me, and bring up every argument that you can against what I say?

MR. ALCOTT. I do not reason against you; I am endeavouring to bring out what you think, and also the other view.

CHARLES. What is your object then?

MR. ALCOTT. I will ask Lemuel — What is it that I am trying to do? *(Lemuel hesitated.)*

MARTHA. I think you wanted to show Charles that the spirit eats, and not the body; for Charles seems to think that the body can do things without the Spirit.

CHARLES. Well, if I do seem to think so, I do not; I think the body hungers, but the spirit shows it how to satisfy its hunger; but you wanted to make me think that the Spirit hungers.

MR. ALCOTT. Do any of you think that I wanted to make Charles think so?

SAMUEL R. I thought you wanted to make Charles see as you did about this.

MR. ALCOTT. I do not usually tell my opinion — but it is true that I cannot conceive of the body hungering, any more than I can conceive of the body's seeing, or hearing, or touching, or running, or walking.

CHARLES. So it does run, and walk, and all; but the Spirit makes it.

MR. ALCOTT. It is my opinion that the Spirit itself hungers after food for the body, as well as after spiritual things — that the Spirit sees, hears, walks.

CHARLES. I think the Spirit sees and hears, but that it only makes the body hunger and walk.

MR. ALCOTT. I see how it is in your mind and where the difficulty lies.

CHARLES. Well, I wish you would make me see how it is, for I cannot see that the Spirit hungers after food.

MR. ALCOTT. So I perceive; but we must now drop the subject, and bring the conversation to a close. It will come up again hereafter. What has been the subject?

FRANCIS. Spirit acting through the body.

(Several repeated the idea in several modifications.)

MR. ALCOTT. The conversation has been long today. — We have had more than usual of argument, if argument it can be called.

CHARLES. I don't think it has been much of an argument on your side, for your side was only asking questions.

MR. ALCOTT. No; it is my object to make you argue — make you reason, by giving the terms. I have not sought in these conversations to present my own views of truth, but to call forth yours; and by so doing make you conscious of your own powers of finding it. It is the part of a wise instructor to tempt forth from the minds of his pupils the facts of their inmost consciousness, and make them apprehend the gifts and faculties of their own being. Education, when rightly understood, will be found to lie in the art of asking apt and fit questions, and in thus leading the mind by its own light to the perception of truth.

CONVERSATION XLVI

· · ·

FORESIGHT OF SPIRIT:

Prophecy

MR. ALCOTT. What was the subject of the last conversation?

NATHAN. Whether it was right to heal on the Sabbath day.

(Mr. Alcott then read the lesson for this day.)

MULTITUDES FOLLOW JESUS

But when Jesus knew it, he withdrew himself from thence, with his disciples to the sea: and great multitudes followed him. And he spake to his disciples, that a small ship should wait on him, because of the multitude, lest they should throng him. For he had healed many; insomuch that they pressed upon him to touch him, as many as had plagues. And unclean spirits, when they saw him, fell down before him, and cried, saying, Thou art the Son of God. And he straightway charged them that they should not make him known. That it might be fulfilled which was spoken by Esaias the prophet, saying, Behold my servant whom I have chosen; My beloved, in whom my soul is well pleased: I will put my spirit upon him, and he shall show judgment to the Gentiles. He shall not strive nor cry; Neither shall any man hear his voice in the streets. A bruised reed shall he not break, And smoking flax shall he not quench, Till he send forth judgment unto victory. And in his name shall the Gentiles trust. (Matt. 12:15-22, Mark 3:7-13.)

MR. ALCOTT. Why did the multitudes go and seek Jesus?

HERBERT. Because they wanted to hear him preach.

MR. ALCOTT. Did you ever go to hear anyone talk about right and wrong?

HERBERT. No.

NATHAN. Yes; you do, whenever you go to church.

LEMUEL. The multitudes followed Jesus to see his miracles.

MR. ALCOTT. Could you see a miracle? Did you ever see a miracle?

GEORGE K. Yes; a great many.

MR. ALCOTT. What?

GEORGE K. Why, breathing — the motion of the pulse.

CHARLES. It can be proved that miracles are not in sight, but in feeling; for whatever you might see, you could not know it was a miracle, unless you thought and felt — all the miracle is in the meaning.

MR. ALCOTT. What is a prophet?

ANDREW. I think only a good man can be a prophet, because he keeps his Spirit pure.

MR. ALCOTT. Are there any prophets now?

ANDREW. I don't know of one.

LEMUEL. I think there may be one whom God tells; and that he can assist others to be good. God tells a good man more than a wicked man.

MR. ALCOTT. Does God make a man a prophet, or does he make himself?

LEMUEL. Himself.

MR. ALCOTT. How does a prophet find out things?

GEORGE K. God tells him.

MR. ALCOTT. Is a prophet born, or does it depend on himself to be a prophet?

GEORGE K. It depends all on himself.

CHARLES. I think good people, who hope to make others good, are thus made to prophesy, and believe that it will come to pass.

MR. ALCOTT. Hope then is the prophet?

CHARLES. Yes; Hope and Faith.

MR. ALCOTT. Are there any prophets now?

CHARLES. No; because people are not so good now; they have not hope and faith; but if all the babies could speak right off there would be prophets enough.

MR. ALCOTT. What is it that despoils these little ones of their prophetic power?

CHARLES. Oh, they learn outward things, and it takes up their attention, and the bad begins to come in.

MR. ALCOTT. Suppose the father and mother had the prophetic power, and should guard it in their children.

CHARLES. It would be necessary to have a great many parents join and arrange things, so that the babies should not be tempted too much by outward things; they should make a society, a prophetic society. Besides, there is another reason why babies cannot be prophets immediately — it takes them some time to get acquainted with their bodies, and get their organs used to speaking; and they are not able to speak till it is too late. It is important that the child should be taught to keep on good terms with the body; should feed it right, and take right care of it.

MR. ALCOTT. Can there be a prophet among you?

(Some thought there might, and some not.)

CHARLES. I think every one can be a prophet; everyone has the small germs of the prophet within him.

MR. ALCOTT. Are there other creatures beside men that prophesy?

GEORGE K. Quails prophesy rainy weather.

CHARLES. Cows in Switzerland go under fir-trees before there are storms; and storms always come soon after, though there is not the slightest cloud in the sky before. I saw that in a well authenticated account.

MR. ALCOTT. Do you believe these things?

CHARLES. Yes.

MR. ALCOTT. What believes?

CHARLES. My prophetic power, I suppose.

MR. ALCOTT. How is it with birds of passage?

GEORGE K. What we call prophecy in animals is generally called instinct.

MR. ALCOTT. What is instinct?

CHARLES. I do not like to think that animals that prophesy, and birds of passage, &c., when they prophesy, act as machines. I like to think they know.

MARTHA. I used to think that prophets were never babies; but thought they came into the world grown up.

MR. ALCOTT. Do you think so now?

MARTHA. Yes, rather.

CHARLES. But if they were born grown up, they would still be young.

MARTHA. But their Spirits might be old.

CHARLES. What would a mother say, if God should give her a great man for a child!

MARTHA. I did not think they had parents, but came from God.

CHARLES. I used to think so too; for it says in one place, that two prophets went up to heaven in chariots of fire; and I supposed that, if they could go off so, they might have come so.

MR. ALCOTT. What do you say to this verse, "Behold my servant," &c.?

NATHAN. "My beloved" means Jesus. God was pleased with him because he was good — full of spirit.

MR. ALCOTT. Have you ever felt that thoughts were given you, that you were full of spirit?

GEORGE K. Yes; all our thoughts are given us; I think that God chose Jesus from out of his angels.

MR. ALCOTT. What are angels?

LEMUEL. Spirits without bodies.

MR. ALCOTT. How did God put his Spirit upon him?

GEORGE K. God gave some of his Spirit, not all of it, upon him —but a great deal.

LEMUEL. You should not say a great deal.

NATHAN. He gave him a little at first to see if he would use it well, and then more.

CHARLES. I wish you would let me say that God is up in the sky; for I like to think of God up there, though I know he is in my thought and inspires it. For I like to have a place; and that is so pure, so blue, and handsome, with such beautiful stars!

MR. ALCOTT. But there is danger of mistaking the forms for the thoughts themselves.

CHARLES. Oh, I don't think I should ever go so far as that.

MR. ALCOTT. What is meant by judgment and victory here?

CHARLES. Oh, when a person is all wrong and has injured his body very much — increased its appetites, and filled it with bad habits, and his strength is almost gone, and it is very hard to repent and have pure thoughts, and get right ideas, and do right all the time, and not indulge, then it is a very great victory for him to be as he ought, and understand the words of Jesus, and do as he directs.

MR. ALCOTT. Who are the Gentiles?

CHARLES. I suppose the rest of the world thought the Jews, who were the only people that ever had prophets, were a great deal better than they. God had seemed to send everything to them; and there were no prophets anywhere else. But when Jesus came to the whole world, then they found they were something themselves, and trusted in him.

MR. ALCOTT. We have now followed Jesus through the varied and successive scenes of his life, to the time when he is preparing to enter upon a more public course of action. In our next conversation we shall see him preparing to preach his celebrated Sermon on the Mount.[60] But we shall leave him for the present; and after Vacation, during which I hope you will refresh your minds, and renovate your bodies, by healthful sports and beautiful scenery, resume our conversations at this place. Before we close, however, let us dwell a moment on the principal events that have interested us. At our last general review, we left Jesus, *whom we regard as the Symbol of Spirit,*[61] about making disciples. We have now seen this same spirit, of which he is the type to our outward senses, gaining Disciples; sanctioning Marriage by its presence; anouncing the glorious doctrines of Immortality, of Spiritual Renewal, and spiritual Worship; the Efficacy of Faith, its power over Physical Nature, and its Divine Sympathy with Suffering and Sorrow.

FOOTNOTES

Conversation I

1. This seems like a direct appeal to what Jung termed the Collective Unconscious. Jung, like Alcott, believed the child had the closest access to it. AOH

2. So did Rene Descartes! This is his *Cogito ergo sum.* AOH.

3. The reader may be struck with the fact of a child of six years of age giving *self-government,* as a proof of the existence of spirit independent of matter. This boy undoubtedly owes much to nature, but the measure cannot easily be determined, because his education, thus far, had been admirable. I refer to the training of the *mind* and *moral nature,* and to nothing more outward; for he was not so much advanced as many others in the mechanical faculty of reading and writing; he was backward in arithmetic, and in those things in which there is often a very deceptive precocity; and, in general, he evinced no extraordinary ardor to acquire. He had always been exclusively under the instruction of his mother, whose principles and methods, as far as Mr. Alcott has been able to discover, were singularly in unison with his own. His eye had been educated by pictures; his mind cultivated by self-inspection, and conscientious stimulus, and his taste for beauty met and sympathised with. His mother had read to him a great deal, and taught him the use of words by conversation with herself, in which he peculiarly delighted, but which he could not enjoy much, except with the grownup and the gentle, on account of a natural impediment in his speech. It is also worthy of remark, that the only books, which he had ever been induced to read by himself, were Gallaudet's Books of the Soul, in which, in fact, he learned to read. He had, however, in his memory a good deal of poetry, learned by rote, and he was in the habit of dictating, himself, a sort of measured, unrhymed composition which he called poetry, the subject of which was generally the beauty of nature, and which always expressed religious feeling. REC.

4. This child had been in the school a year, without often speaking. Evidently unused to having his intellect addressed, he had only been remarkable for his faithfulness, and the expression of sentiment, that glowed in his face, whenever an interesting subject was under discussion. He was always very attentive, yet when Mr. Alcott asked him a question that required words in answer, all his soul flew into his face, but he was dumb; and Mr. Alcott would generally say, well, it is no matter, I see how you feel; to which the child would reply, with a look of gratitude. It was evident that his mind was not idle; for he constantly seemed full of attention, and intelligence, and he always expressed himself by a silent vote, when a question was to be answered by raising the hand. From this day, in which his tongue was for the first time loosed, he became one of our most ready speakers, and in some departments of thought was always remarkably lucid. I have been thus particular, because I think that, in this instance, Mr. Alcott's sagacity is strikingly proved, and his example of patient waiting is worthy of consideration. If George's parents had felt the uneasy ambition of seeing immediate effects produced; and thus lost their confidence in Mr. Alcott, as many others have done, because he would not force a mind, whose progress was real in its own way; he would not have

come the second year, but have carried into another school the flower of the seed Mr. Alcott had planted; — a thing which has not unfrequently been done, as Mr. Alcott has painfully felt. REC.

5. This is a remarkable insight concerning intuition. AOH

6. This child is deaf. His seat was always close by Mr. Alcott, and he fixed his eyes always on Mr. Alcott's lips, and then would follow his eye to the speaker among the children. Sometimes Mr. Alcott would tell him what the children said. His remarks are very characteristic throughout. REC.

7. The word "conscience" is frequently used as we would use "consciousness" today. The idea of a moral implication is sometimes implied, but not always. It is something for the reader to differentiate. AOH

8. This is a spontaneous recognition of the Self (as defined by Jung psychologically) and which religions have variously defined as the Christ Within, the Atman (Hinduism), and the Beloved (Sufi). AOH

9. Psychologically, this bears out Erich Neumann's theory of the "uroboric" phase of the development of human consciousness, both at the collective level in history and the individual in infancy. AOH

Conversation II

10. Many theological debates have revolved around this question. AOH

Conversation III

11. This is an image found in The Upanishads. AOH

Conversation IV

12. Those who think Mr. Alcott systematically teaches pre-existence, should mark this answer of a boy who has been his scholar longer than any other and lives in his house. REC.

13. "The spirit of Man is the candle of the Lord." Proverbs

14. The concept of our spirits being the "sons of God" implies the Christ Within, the Atman. AOH

Conversation V

15. A remarkable observation. AOH

16. This remark is very characteristic of the child who made it. His mind was, in many respects, of a precocious development. His physical organization seemed to cast him early in life upon the religious sentiment for happiness; and he had become somewhat mature in religious experience. He was very serious in disposition, and had the germs of very fine reasoning powers, as will be remarked in much that he says. But an ardent temperament, together with his feeble physical organization, exposed him to great inequalities of spirits, and gave him great moral difficulties to master within himself. He was deeply sincere, and every

one of his words may be depended upon as a perfect transcript of his mind for the time being. REC.

[17]. It is hard to believe that with this conversation Bronson Alcott was heading for disaster. AOH

Conversation VII

[18]. Resolution and faith, lead to success. Faith brings out what is planted in the spirit into the external world. ED. (from original)

Conversation VIII

[19]. This is the conversation that scandalized Boston! Edward B's remarks were omitted from the original text. AOH

[20]. This remark echoes the ancient Egyptians. AOH

Conversation IX

[21]. This speech was omitted at Miss Peabody's request, but put back by Bronson Alcott. See Miss Peabody's letter in the introductory Commentary. AOH

[22]. It will be observed that Mr. Alcott does not decide between such differing views. All opinions seem to be represented by the different children, and there is something characteristic in the views which they take. Very few seem indoctrinated at home. The same original difference of mind, which originates different creeds, originates them here. They have formed their own creeds; and these sometimes differ from those of their parents. Mr. Alcott leads them to express their views, and then leaves these to make their own impression, confident that truth will prevail in the end. REC.

[23]. The dialogue here is reminiscent of the Council of Nicea! AOH

Conversation X

[24]. This conversation demonstrates Bronson Alcott's cultivation of his pupils' imagination. AOH

[25]. Josiah takes off in this conversation! AOH

[26]. In Mr. Alcott's school-room is an "Angel of Silence" in a plaster cast.

Conversation XI

[27]. This last remark is at the heart of Alcott's belief. AOH

Conversation XIII

[28]. Editor of the *Moral Reformer, House that I Live In, The Young Mother,* and other popular books.

Conversation XVI

[29]. Luke 3:23-38, Matt. 1:1-17. Here Mr. Alcott read 36 verses of "begats" tracing the lineage of Jesus back to Adam.

[30]. A remarkable observation for a six-year old. AOH

[31]. The reader will observe that this conversation is more connected, and satisfactory, than most of those which precede it. It may have been more so, in reality. Yet the impression, which it leaves in the mind, arises, chiefly, from the fact, that the record is fuller and more complete. ED.

Conversation XVII

[32]. The mind of this child is altogether unique. When it acts entirely of itself, it follows the highest law of imagination. All his thoughts "body" themselves forth; and all the forms of nature speak to him. He never abstracts; yet he is always in the spiritual.

Connected with this intellectual structure, he has a fine eye for drawing, and an obedient hand; and thus seems armed at all points, for communicating with his race, through the canvass or marble. His character was once given by the children, in the most natural way. Mr. Alcott was reading over a list of the disciples, and saying, like Lemuel, like Josiah, &c., of each name. When he came to Nathaniel, he hesitated, and the boys spoke out, all round the class, "like Andrew!" It was a coincidence confirmatory, that I had anticipated them in my own mind, some minutes before, and hoped Mr. Alcott would be reminded of him, by "the Israelite in whom was no guile."

The reader loses a great deal of natural commentary on the conversation, in losing the manner of the children, which cannot be printed; but in no case is the loss more unimaginable, than in that of Andrew. It would be impossible to describe the difference of manner between the two last answers. REC.

[33]. Conversation XVII from the original is omitted since it consists of review and repetition. The subsequent chapters are renumbered. AOH

Conversation XVIII

[34]. This comes close to what Jung calls the Collective Shadow. AOH

Conversation XX

[35]. The vocabulary of this ten-year-old is astonishing! AOH

Conversation XXVI

[36]. In Conversation XXXI Josiah recalls this remark.

Conversation XXVII

[37]. A confirmation of left and right brain? AOH

Conversation XXVIII

38. This Conversation has all the elements of a theologians debate in the early days of the Church Fathers! AOH

39. Conversation XXIX in the original text is omitted. It contains mostly review and repetition. The subsequent conversations are renumbered for consistency. AOH

Conversation XXX

40. John is under 7! AOH

41. In this Conversation, Bronson Alcott is clearly teaching the children the handicaps of literalism. It is amazing to see how easily the children are able to think symbolically. AOH

Conversation XXXI

42. Many might agree with Josiah! AOH

43. Footnoted in Conversation XXVII. — a remark of Mr. Alcott's.

44. This improvisation is preserved in its words. REC.

45. Here I was obliged to pause, as I was altogether fatigued with keeping my pen in long and uncommonly constant requisition. I was enabled to preserve the words better than usual, because Josiah had so much of the conversation, whose impediment of speech makes his enunciation slow, and whose fine choice of language and steadiness of mind, makes him easy to follow and remember. REC.

46. In this Conversation, Josiah wins hands down. It is truly difficult to believe that this child is under seven years of age. One wonders how he would fare in a public school today and in which direction his fervent intuition and enthusiasm would lead him. AOH

Conversation XXXII

47. Conversation XXXIV in the original text is omitted since it contained much review and repetition. The subsequent conversations are renumbered. AOH

48. The anticipation of psychosomatic psychology is interesting in view of the beliefs of holistic medicine today. AOH

Conversation XXXIV

49. "A Description of the Person of JESUS CHRIST, as it was found in an Ancient Manuscript, sent by Publius Latilus, President of Judaea, to the Senate of Rome."

"There lives at this time in Judaea, a man of singular character, whose name is Jesus Christ. The barbarians esteem him a prophet, but his followers adore him as the immediate offspring of the immortal God. He is endowed with such unparalleled virtue, as to call back the dead from their graves, and to heal every kind of disease with a word or touch. His person is tall and elegantly shaped; his aspect amiable and reverend; his hair flows into these beauteous shades which no aspect amiable and reverend; his hair flows into these beauteous shades which no united colors can match, falling into graceful curls below his ears, agreeably couching on his shoulders, and parting on the crown of his head, like the head dress of the sect of Nazarites. His forehead is smooth and large, his cheeks without a spot, save that of a lovely red, his nose and mouth are formed with exquisite symmetry, his beard is thick and suitable to the hair of the head, reaching a little below the chin, and parting in the middle like a fork; his eyes are bright, clear and serene. He rebukes with majesty, counsels with mildness, and invites with the most tender and persuasive language; his whole address, whether word or deed, being elegant, grave, and strictly characteristic of so exalted a being. No man has seen him laugh, but the whole world beholds him weep frequently; and so persuasive are his tears, that the multitude cannot withhold their tears from joining in sympathy with him.

He is very modest, temperate, and wise; in short, whatever this phenomenon may turn out in the end, he seems at present a man of excellent beauty and divine perfections, every way surpassing the children of men."

This letter has had an extensive circulation through the country, but of its history or authenticity we know nothing more than this, that it was found in Rome, and was published a few years since with the caption here affixed to it.

Conversation XXXVI

50. The Recorder commented elsewhere that to her amusement, the children mentioned the creatures that they themselves sometimes resembled. A "shadow projection," in Jungian terms. AOH
51. This spat could not have occurred between Elizabeth Peabody and Bronson Alcott as Elizabeth had left the Temple School. It most probably was the high-spirited Margaret Fuller. Alcott was almost a fanatical vegetarian and purist in matters of food and drink. AOH

Conversation XXXVIII

52. It was Alcott himself.

Conversation XXXIX

53. In this place, as in several others, this morning, an opportunity to go deeper was omitted. There were many persons present, and the children kept on the surface, because they were diverted from going into their deepest thoughts by the interest, which their more superficial ones seemed to excite in the company. This did not seem to be from the idea of display on their part; it was merely the physical effect, if I may so express it, of the presence. The children do really conceive so much of these subjects, that they are in no danger of being elated with their feeble power of expressing what is much more adequately thought than worded. REC.
54. The Collective Shadow is hinted at in this remark. AOH
55. Conversation XLII from the original is omitted and the subsequent chapters renumbered. AOH

Conversation XLII

56. This anecdote is a true one of Louisa May and her little sister May. AOH

57. Hales and Corinna are under 7! AOH

58. By today's standards this Conversation sounds almost like an "Inquisition," with Mr. Alcott relapsing into a most puritanical mode. However, his aim was always self-knowledge and awareness. The psychological integrity of the children and their free responses indicate their trust in their teacher's tenderness.

Any study of Bronson Alcott's Journals will reveal that he was every bit as hard on himself in trying to become more conscious of his faults and shortcomings, or his personal Shadow. Benjamin Franklin, as a young man, listed his faults and proceeded to attempt to eradicate them one by one. Yet one eluded him to the end of his days: sloppiness. In his autobiography he tells of giving up the attempt on the grounds that he should leave some imperfection handy for others to criticize! The closest Alcott came to accepting his shortcomings was his confession that he simply could not and preferred not to make money. AOH

Conversation XLIV

59. This last paragraph is an apt summary of Alcott's philosophy of spiritual education. AOH

Conversation XLVI

60. As we now know, this was never to take place. A pity. AOH

61. Italics mine. AOH

APPENDICES

APPENDIX ONE

* * *

GENERAL MAXIMS

By Which to Regulate
The Instructor's Practice in Instruction

I. To teach, with a sense of the accountableness of the profession.

II. To teach, with reference to Eternity.

III. To teach, as an agent of the Great Instructor.

IV. To teach, depending on the Divine Blessings, for success.

V. To teach, as the former of character, and the promoter of the collective happiness of man.

VI. To teach, to subserve the great cause of philanthropy, and benevolence.

VII. To teach, distinctive from all sinister, sectarian, and oppressive principles.

VIII. To teach, with charitable feelings toward all rational and animal beings.

IX. To teach, distinct from prejudice, from veneration of Antiquity and from excess of novelty.

X. To teach, to improve the Science of Instruction, and of Mind.

XI. To teach, duly appreciating the importance of the profession.

XII. To teach, unawed by the clamours of ignorance, yet governed by the dictates of wisdom.

XIII. To teach nothing, merely from subservience to custom.

XIV. To teach with unremitted solicitude, and faithfulness.

XV. To teach, appreciating the value of the beings to whom Instruction is given.

XVI. To teach, regarding the matter as well as the manner of Instruction.

XVII. To teach that, alone, which is useful.

XVIII. To teach, in imitation of the Saviour.

XIX. To teach, by exact, uniform example.

XX. To teach in the Inductive method.

XXI. To teach gradually, and understandingly, by the shortest steps, from the more easy, and known, to the more difficult and unknown.

XXII. To teach by the exercise of Reason.

XXIII. To teach, illustrating by sensible and tangible objects.

XXIV. To teach, by clear, and copious Explanation.

XXV. To teach, by a strict adherence to System.

XXVI. To teach, by simple, and plain, unambiguous language.

XXVII. To teach, by short, and perfectly obtained, Lessons.

XXVIII. To teach, by Encouragement.

XXIX. To teach but one thing at the same time.

XXX. To teach interestingly.

XXXI. To teach principally a Knowledge of things, not of words; of ideas, not of names.

XXXII. To teach, by consulting in the arrangement of lessons, that proportion of variety, which is adapted to the genius and habits of the young mind.

XXXIII. To teach, by keeping curiosity awake.

XXXIV. To teach nothing that pupils can teach themselves.

XXXV. To teach, as much as possible by Analysis.

XXXVI. To teach, by exciting a laudable ambition for excellence, guarding against its opposite.

XXXVII. To teach, endeavouring to make pupils feel their importance by the hope which mankind placed in their conduct.

XXXVIII. To teach, endeavouring to preserve the understanding from implicit belief, and to secure the habit of independence of thought and of feeling.

XXXIX. To teach, endeavouring to invigorate and bring into exercise all the intellectual and moral and physical powers.

XL. To teach, attempting to associate with literature the idea, and perception of pleasure.

XLI. To teach, attempting to induce the laudable ambition of progressive improvement.

XLII. To teach, by consulting the feelings of scholars.

XLIII. To teach, with animation and interest.

XLIV. To teach, by furnishing constant, useful, and as much as possible, pleasing employment.

XLV. To teach, treating pupils with uniform familiarity, and patience, and with the greatest kindness, tenderness, and respect.

XLVI. To teach, by cultivating the moral and sympathetic feelings and affections.

XLVII. To teach, by consulting the collective happiness of the school.

XLVIII. To teach, by persuasion, not coercion.

XLIX. To teach, by Comparison and Contrast.

L. To teach, by allusion to familiar objects, and occurrencies.

LI. To teach, without Indolence, and discouragement.

LII. To teach pupils to teach themselves.

LIII. To teach, by intermingling Questions with Instruction.

LIV. To teach, with relation to the practical business of life.

LV. To teach, endeavouring to fix things in the understanding — rather than words in the memory.

LVI. To teach, without bringing pupils in comparison with one another, or touching the spring of personal emulation.

LVII. To teach, with reference to Habit.

LVIII. To teach, with independence.

APPENDIX TWO

* * *

ORIGINAL EDITOR'S PREFACE

A. Bronson Alcott

The work now presented to the reader, forms the introduction to a course of conversations with children, on the Life of Christ, as recorded in the Gospels. It is the Record of an attempt to unfold the Idea of Spirit from the Consciousness of Childhood; and to trace its Intellectual and Corporeal Relations; its Temptations and Disciplines; its Struggles and Conquests, while in the Flesh. To this end, the character of Jesus has been presented to the consideration of children, as the brightest Symbol of Spirit; and they have been encouraged to express their views regarding it. The Conductor of these conversations has reverently explored their consciousness, for the testimony which it might furnish in favor of the truth of Christianity.

Assuming as a fact the spiritual integrity of the young mind, he was desirous of placing under the inspection of children, a character so much in conformity with their own, as that of Jesus of Nazareth. He believed that children would as readily apprehend the divine beauty of this character, when rightly presented, as adults. He even hoped that, through their simple consciousness, the Divine Idea of a Man, as Imaged in Jesus, yet almost lost to the world, might be revived in the mind of adults, who might thus be recalled into the spiritual kingdom. These views, confirmed by long intimacy with the young, as well as by the tendency of his own mind to regard the bright visions of childhood, as the promise of the soul's future blessedness; as the loadstar to conduct it through this terrestrial Life, led him to undertake this enterprise, and to prosecute it with a deep and kindling interest, which he feels will continue unabated to its close.

The Editor will not, meanwhile, conceal the fact, that it is with no little solicitude that he ventures these documents before the eye of others. He feels that his book should be studied in Simplicity. It is, in no small measure, the production of children. It is a record of their consciousness; a natural history of the undepraved spirit. It is the testimony of unspoiled natures to the spiritual purity of Jesus. It is a revelation of the Divinity in the soul of childhood. Like the Sacred volume — on which it is, indeed, a juvenile commentary — of which it is an interpretation, it cannot be at once, apprehended in all its bearings, and find its true value.

There may be those, however, who, unconscious of its worth, shall avail themselves of the statements, views, and speculations, which it contains, to the detriment of religion and humanity; not perceiving, that it is a work, intended rather to awaken thought; enkindle feeling; and quicken to duty; than to settle opinions, or promulgate sentiments of any kind. Whoever shall find its significance, will scarce treat with disrespect these products of the sacred being of childhood. For childhood utters sage things, worthy of all note; and he who scoffs at its improvisations, or perverts its simple sayings, proves the corruption of his own being, and his want of reverence for the Good, the Beautiful, the True, and the Holy. He beholds not the Face of the Heavenly Father.

It has been a main purpose of the Conductor of these conversations, to tempt forth, by appropriate questions, the cherished sentiments of the children on the subjects presented to their consideration. It was no part of his intention to bring forward, except by necessary implication, his own favorite opinions as a means of biassing, in the smallest degree, the judgments and decisions of the children. He wished to inculcate only what was the universal product of our common nature. He endeavoured to avoid dogmatizing. He was desirous of gathering the sentiments of the little circle, in which it is his pleasure and privilege to move as teacher and friend. He believed that Christianity was in Childhood, and he sought the readiest and simplest means to unfold it, and bring it into the light of day.

That he has withheld his own sentiments from the children in all instances, he can scarce hope. It was next to impossible. He has doubtless led them, in some instances, by the tenor of his questions, and his manner of disposing of replies, to the adoption or rejection of sentiments, foreign to their nature. But he believes that he has seldom erred in this way. He preferred to become the simple Analyst of the consciousness of the children, and, having no opinions of his own to establish against their common convictions, he treated with reverence whatever he found within it, deeming it, when spontaneous, a revelation of the same Divinity, as was Jesus.

He is aware that the work which he has assumed is one of great difficulty. He feels that it is not easy to ascertain the precise state of a child's mind. He knows that much of what a child utters has been received from others, that language is an uncertain organ in his use; that he often endows words with his own significance; that he is liable to mistake the phenomena of his own consciousness; and, moreover, that his scanty vocabulary often leaves him without the means of revealing himself. Still some certainty is attainable. For a child can be trusted when urged to ingenuous expression; and when all temptations to deceive are withdrawn. A wise and sympatizing observer will readily distinguish the real from the assumed; penetrate through all the varying phases of expression, and do him justice.

Yet, while so little is done to guard children against servile imitation, by a wise training of their minds to original thought, we are in danger of not giving them credit for what is their own. So little confidence, indeed, do we place in their statements, and so imitative do we deem them, that, when a wise saying chances to drop from their lips, instead of regarding it, as it of right should be, the product of their own minds, we seek its origin among adults, as if it must of necessity spring from this source alone. We greatly underrate the genius of children. We do not apprehend the inward power, that but awaits the genial touch, to be quickened into life. The art of tempting this forth we have scarce attained. We have outlived our own simple consciousness, and have thus lost our power of apprehending them. We have yet to learn, that Wisdom and Holiness are of no Age; that they preexist, separate from time, and are the possession of Childhood, not less than of later years; that they, indeed, often appear in fresher features, in the earlier seasons of life, than in physical maturity. In Man they are often quenched by the vulgar aims of the corporeal life.

To a child, all questions touching the Soul are deeply interesting. He loves his own consciousness. It is a charmed world to him. As yet he has not been drawn out of it by the seductions of the propensities; nor is he beguiled by the illusions of his external senses. And were he assisted in the study and discipline of it, by those who could meet his wants, and on whom he could rely, his spiritual acquirements would keep pace with his years, and he would grow up wise in the mysteries of the spiritual kingdom. The Divine Idea of a Man, the vision of Self-Perfection, would live in his consciousness; instead of being, as now, pushed aside by the intrusive images, and vulgar claims, of unhallowed appetite and desire. Christ would be formed in the Soul the Hope of Immortality.

In the original copy of this record, the names of the speakers were preserved, as necessary to identify their different views and statements. It is feared that some persons may regret the insertion of these in the printed volume, from a regard to the effect on the speakers themselves. Yet to have used assumed names would have impaired the identity of the record, and have diminished its value, of course, as an historical fact. No serious evils, it is believed can arise from retaining them. The children expressed themselves in simplicity; there is nothing in their remarks, to flatter their vanity; and they have no desire to see their names in print. The Editor would regret extremely, to be the means of wounding the feelings of those of his patrons, who have expressed their sympathy with his views, and who, amid much to try their faith in the practicability of his attempt to renovate education, have continued their children under his care. Much less, would he wantonly do ought to injure, in the slightest degree, that simplicity and meekness, which he has sought to cherish in those, for whose spiritual and intellectual culture, these conversations were primarily intended.

The Editor would remark, in conclusion, that he deems his labors valuable, not only to those children, who were present at these conversations, and to the general reader, but he ventures to hope that they will commend themselves, also, to those parents and teachers, who deem the spiritual growth and discipline of those committed to their care, of unspeakable and primary importance. He trusts that he has given, in these specimens of his intercourse with children, a model, not unworthy of imitation, of the simplest and readiest mode of presenting religious truth to the young. He believes that he has shed some light over the path of Human Culture. He feels, that for children, if not for adults, he has delineated, and in a form which they can apprehend, the Divine Life of Jesus; and has urged upon them, through the mouths of his little ones, considerations and motives, fitted to inspire them with the noble ambition to strive to imitate his Example.

APPENDIX THREE

• • •

SOME PERSONAL NOTES AND OBSERVATIONS

Alice O. Howell

Not long after the two books about Bronson Alcott fell into my hands, the headmistress of the small school that two of my children attended dropped dead of a heart attack. Not only had she been administering, but she also had taught the sixth grade and even done some of the cooking. I volunteered to help, expecting to work in the kitchen, but I was asked to hold down the class of eleven-year olds until another teacher could be found.

It was an early May morning when I walked into the class, saw the wistful faces of my pupils, and felt I had come home. This was it! But only for a short while, since school closed for the summer the first week of June. I will never forget that last day of school and the shock of it. Almost every child walked out and dumped the year's notebooks into the trash! I went home and cried, and I vowed to change this if ever I had a chance. I am happy to report that the following June several students complained that school would be over. Why, they wanted to know, could they not continue at my house? Why not, indeed? So about six to eight of them came twice a week in the afternoons, and we read history one summer, plays the following, and studied the history of art the next. We sat under the trees in the small backyard and called it "the Grove." They studied geometry and drawing with my husband, and drank lemonade and ate cookies in between. I got so caught up in Greek history that I can remember going to the local supermarket and reading a banner as proclaiming POP-sic-lees, 10 cents! Pericles and Popsicles must have been brothers. That summer confirmed for me that we learn so much more when we want to learn than when we have to.

I would love to share some of the observations that were so helpful to me as a teacher — the "practical philosophy" that I extracted from those books which spoke to my heart and proved so helpful. One of the first things that impressed me was the time and space Mr. Alcott gave every child for self-expression. Most teaching is instruction — building in — rules, disciplines of the subject, and facts, all essential. But e-ducation (e-ducere) means drawing forth what is already within. This Alcott did supremely well. He listened. And by judicious questioning, he provided what I have called in my other books "occasions for attacks of insight" — those "Aha! I get it!" outbursts which are the teacher's delight.

Setting aside a few minutes in every class for a miniconversation pays off. It establishes trust and mutual respect. Like the eye of a camera, the lens of the psyche opens wider, so that more information can subsequently flow in. Having attended so many schools in several different countries in my own childhood, I learned quickly to "psych" out my teachers and noticed what made some of them good and some even bad at teaching. You can also slam the door in a child's mind. I learned that fear closes the lens of learning. Fear of punishment, fear of mistakes, fear of ridicule, fear of criticism and rejection. There was no fear in Mr. Alcott's schoolroom, and I hope there was none in mine.

My good teachers, and I had three, all had two things in common: they loved what they were doing, and they made learning exciting. Over the years I have been privileged to observe several colleagues who had the same gifts, and I have read of many others. It is evident from Miss Peabody's records that the children greatly enjoyed the Conversations.

Why are these conversations interesting? said Mr. Alcott. Because they give us new ideas, said a boy. Many others said they liked them for the same reason. Mr. Alcott then said, conversations are the most perfect transcript of the mind. Could all the conversations of great minds be recorded, it would give us a better idea of them than the history of their lives. Why is the New Testament so interesting? Because it is full of the conversations of Jesus. Conversations of Socrates make the next most interesting book. Conversation is full of life. The spirit's workings come out in conversations, fresh and vivid. Why, if I thought I only gave you knowledge and could not lead you to use it to make yourselves better, I would never enter this schoolroom again!

Further on, Miss Peabody tells of a five-year old boy bursting out: "Oh, Mr. Alcott, I never even knew I had a mind until I came to this school!"

The first day of school, therefore, one can make a point of stressing that the year's work ahead is not for the purpose of passing exams and getting ahead a grade; it is for life.

* One can explain that mistakes are allowed here and that we often learn better for having made them.

* One can have ungraded "pretests" which are not handed in, so that students can check out what they don't quite know.

* To alleviate fear, numbered quizzes can have two extra questions, so that it is possible to get 25 out of 25 and even a bonus.

* Every now and then one can have a "teacher test" to see how well the teacher has taught. Students love these the best and knock themselves out to prove one has done a good job!

In the ninth grade, I copied Alcott's idea of the journal. Each student was given a Commonplace Book into which he or she could write thoughts, gripe or rejoice, copy out poems or jokes or lyrics of pop songs or whatever. The rule was that I would never correct either the writing or the spelling, I would simply write back. And whatever was confided would be held sacred and private. I remember having an ongoing philosophical, if not religious, correspondence with two girls. Week after week, we wrote one another, but never once discussed it out loud! Years later, I received a touching letter from one of them, then attending seminary to become a priest. She told me that her parents had been divorcing and that the Commonplace Book had become her lifeline to sanity. Naturally, composition was taught separately, but even there, it seemed wiser to give a grade for mechanics and a comment for creativity, because we really cannot grade creativity in children. So I was happy to come across these words by Miss Peabody just recently:

> He made no criticisms on the language or even on the spelling; knowing that courage is easily checked, in these first efforts, by criticism and wishing to produce freedom as a condition of freedom of expression. . . . Premature criticism mildews the flower and blasts the promised fruit.

Mr. Alcott, as one reads on, spent much time on giving each child the chance to visualize the *mis en scène* within his mind's eye. This was to encourage the powers of imagination and to make them conscious and meaningful.

> Does the eye see? [asked Mr. Alcott] A boy of five said, When we look at any picture, there is a picture reflected into the inside of our eyes, and the mind sees it. But you know, said Mr. Alcott, that there are some pictures which we see in our imaginations? Well, said the child, the way that is I will tell you: the pictures we look at out of us go into our minds, and change and mix up, and come before our minds in new forms. Do these pictures come into our outward eyes, said Mr. Alcott. Oh no! our mind looks into itself and sees them.

Television today externalizes so much of the imagery that we once had when limited to books, but imaging still can be encouraged in class. This takes patience, as we can see when Mr. Alcott listens to the numbers of descriptions surrounding the actual location and arrangement of people, buildings, and so forth at the healing of the leper or at the Nativity; but this was the purpose. In view of what we know about left and right brain modes today, I suspect that Alcott was instinctively balancing out linear and imaginal thinking in his pupils. Over the years that I taught, I noticed a decrease in visual memory in my students and an increase in auditory memory, so that the spelling and reading scores decreased on entrance tests (as, according to statistics, they continue to do nationwide.) I believe that television has something to do with this, since we watch it with our right brain. Perhaps there is a connection even between this more "feminine" or holistic vision and the peace movement and the flower children of the sixties — these were the first generation of television's children. Linear or "masculine" thinking separates and discriminates.

Education continues to demand and reward linear thinking or left brain endeavors far more than imaginal thinking. How many children have lost all interest in poetry, for example, due to the relentless analysis of poems! Perhaps the increased use of computers will redress the balance at the level of the brain, but nothing surely can take the place of "that inner eye which is the bliss of solitude."

Alcott also had an unusual approach to the teaching of words. He handed them out as we would jewels, using each to take off on speculations and discussions. This is an idea we find carried out on "Sesame Street" in a delightful way, though not quite at the same level.

They were led to consider how words bodied forth thoughts signing external objects and suggesting internal facts of the spirit . . . To learn to use words is a ready way to appreciate their force. Everyone knows that a technical memory of words and of rules of composition gives very little command of language, while a rich consciousness, a quick imagination, and force of feeling seem to unlock the treasury.

Etymology was frequently included, and children would often write about which word was their favorite on a particular day. Here are two examples, taken from the Record:

Meek was defined and Mr. Alcott described a meek character and said there were some meek ones in school, and asked if they knew who they were; but they need not say. He should like each to think for himself, if he was meek. One boy said, if I thought I was meek I would not say so, lest the other boys should say I was proud. [A quick lesson in the perils of inflation!]

The word veil led to a consideration of the body as the veil of spirit, and of the earth as the veil of many of the ideas of God. When was the veil of sense wrapped around the soul? When we were born, said one. When will it be taken away? When we die, said several. Could the veil be raised before we die? After a while, it was seen that being born again out of sense into thoughts or spirit; by insight [intuition].

This is a far cry from "See Spot. See Spot run."

Oddly, as gifted as Mr. Alcott was in introducing simple words with profound meanings to his students, he so often forgot this simplicity when writing himself! But his introduction to grammar was brilliantly thought out in terms of the functions of the parts of speech; only later were the pupils given the formal nomenclature. That grammar can be fun, I know for a fact. So much depends on using amusing sentences for examples. I remember my grandfather quoting the following sentence overheard in a trolley-car on Boylston Street. Said one girl to another in an unmatchable sequence of double negatives: "Well, Mabel, if I ain't never had no good time, 't ain't cause I ain't never went none!" To rephrase that is a struggle.

A teacher can write a composition involving and naming all the pupils in the class, leaving out all the adverbs and adjectives modifying them and their actions. Calling upon the students to supply — unwittingly — the description of themselves and their actions can result in hilarity when the composition is read aloud. I remember the headmaster escorting some parents of a prospective student down the hall as shrieks of laughter were pouring through the closed door. When somewhat shamed, we confessed that we were having a grammar lesson, they shook their heads in pleasured disbelief.

Mr. Alcott's discipline was always linked to social awareness.

In many of the punishments — in the pauses in his reading, for instance, the innocent were made to suffer with the guilty. Mr. Alcott wished both parties to feel that this was the inevitable consequence of moral evil in this world, and that the good, in proportion to the depth of their principle, always feel it to be worthwhile to share the suffering in order to bring the guilty to rectitude and moral sensibility. [A tall order!]

One cannot fail to observe in reading the Conversations that the purpose of the strict discipline was mainly to provide a secure framework for an astonishing democracy of thought and opinion. The children were completely free to disagree or dispute or contradict the master in their search for their own view of the truth. This process delighted him and sometimes frustrated them because they wanted to know his opinion of the matter. This he was most reluctant to give, convinced as he was that the psyche of the child would intuit when a matter was right, even that of a five-year-old. For him there could be no age, no time, no space at that center, only truth, love, and beauty. This instilling of self-awareness and inner confidence breaks down the differences in age, and in power, and in authority. Miss Peabody includes a priceless example in the appendix to the Record — witness the grave condescension exhibited in this 1834 letter to Mr. Alcott from an eight-year-old Philadelphia boy:

Dear Sir: I received your letter with great satisfaction; the good advice you gave me I will try to remember and profit by. That inward ray of immortal life which you have so minutely described, I understand to mean conscience, though I do not always obey its influence. The comparisons in your letter, I think were very good — the one that struck me most forcibly and which I have before mentioned in my journal, was the Looking

Glass of Circumstance, which I think meets the subject. In this letter you have fully convinced me, that we should not too often commit the dreadful sin of seeking all good without, and not beholding it within our imagination.

Today, it seems incomprehensible that children that young were able to express themselves in such a manner, but these books include other examples that (with apologies for uncorrected spelling and punctuation) are equally impressive.

Another of Alcott's helpful practices was to summarize the lesson of the day most concisely and then to ask for its recapitulation at the next session. To make sure a point was understood, he often paused during the lesson and asked the child to paraphrase what he had said. Having pupils paraphrase poetry or excerpts of literature was still another of his devices, probably common to most education of the period.

Today our ever-increasing body of knowledge may contribute to a sense of urgency in education — to a sense that interesting as they may be, we do not have the time to implement ideas like Alcott's. I believe we need to take the time. As Muhammad said: "An unwise man is just a donkey with a load of books on his back." We need to help our students reconnect with the purpose of learning; to help children to think and to make connections between what they are learning and who they are themselves. I had a recent conversation with an eleven year old girl who was studying ancient history. She was struggling with Greek names, spelling, and memorizing. I asked her if she liked the subject. She said, "No," with a shrug of her shoulders, "it's just something we have to do." What a far cry from the "Symposium" on Mt. Olympus we held in fifth grade when we had a contest to see which Greek had contributed the most to the world. Thirty students fanned out to research and write a short monograph on their person. Came the day given over to the contest, they all dressed up in sheets, and the three teachers dressed up as gods and goddesses (Zeus had a mop for a beard; Athena arrived with a stuffed owl.) Ambrosia was served before recess, and Olympic games were held at sports time. Socrates, Eratosthenes, Archimedes, Hipparchus, Anaxagoras, Sophocles, Aeschylus, Euripedes, and twenty-two more attended. Photon took pictures. The gods had a dreadful time deciding, but came to the conclusion that the "Greek woman" probably deserved the prize, because without her none of the others would have come into being or lived to make their contributions. This decision was accepted with a collective humorous groan. The Symposium was such a success, that the next year we held a Renaissance "colloquium." History had come to life a wee bit more, I do believe. For the girl I had my recent conversation with, the glories of ancient Greece remain shut in the pages of a school text. But my fifth grade Symposium students, years later, still remember who they were — for in their preparations they had busily told and taught each other about their subjects. I fondly remember two little boys racing inchworms in a Marathon on my front stoop: one worm was called Phaeton and the other Pheidippides!

Again, in teaching a high school course on the "History of Cultural Civilization" we encouraged each student to pick a subject of special interest to him or her to follow through the year. Each then would write a short monograph on that topic for the time and area being studied. Thus a student picking "writing," or "medicine," or "epics" would do research in primitive, Egyptian, Mesopotamian, Indian, Chinese, or Norse writing and alphabets or in methods of healing or in early literature. They could use sources appropriate to their level of capacity: the slower students using below grade resources, the more apt students, college level resources. A week would then be set aside during which the students became teachers themselves, sharing their expertise with enthusiasm (and teaching me besides!). By the end of the year, each pupil had become a mini-expert in one area, and all had benefited from the informal sharing of information as they had done their research. The religious expression, the mythology, and the contributions of each civilization were studied, and the students learned much about archetypes, symbolism, and the collective unconscious at the same time. Much of the groundwork laid by Jung and by Joseph Campbell was well within the grasp of the students. The basic text was covered, tests dealt with, but the emphasis was — thanks to Bronson Alcott — "To teach, endeavoring to make pupils feel their importance, by the hope which mankind placed in their conduct."

If there is more in the world than we possibly can learn about, and there is, then it behooves us 1) to teach our students the skills of how to find out what they need to know and 2) to enjoy the quest. But the most important thing of all is to make education relevant and meaningful at the level of the psyche, to demonstrate that there is, as Bronson Alcott and Elizabeth Peabody so devoutly believed, an inner reason for learning that in order to love and understand more about the world and the people in it, one must learn who one is.

Mr. Alcott was glad to hear that one of the scholars had said out of school, that it was impossible to remain in Mr. Alcott's school and not to learn one's self.

We come again to the similarity between Alcott's outlook and what Jung later proposed concerning the psyche. Alcott's statement — "Do you understand this? The spiritual world is the inward life of all things — " comes very close to Jung's view of the Collective Unconscious. And Elizabeth Peabody's observation — "It was very striking to see how much nearer the kingdom of heaven were the little children than those who had begun to pride themselves on knowing something," —comes close to Jung's idea that with the necessary development of the ego (the center of consciousness) a separation from the Self (the center and totality of the psyche) takes place, with the ensuing temptation for us to identify with the ego and to think that that is all we are. Jung goes on then to see our sufferings and neuroses as promptings from the unconscious for us to turn inward in order to find more consciously what we have become separated from. This is the most profound aspect of analysis, a step Jung felt to be successful only when accompanied by a spiritual experience in the depths of the individual psyche. "Theologically understood," he wrote, "individuation is incarnation."

To accomplish this incarnation, Jung insisted, means to lead a symbolic life which opens for us a way of being more deeply connected to the underlying unity, the unus mundus, hidden within the seemingly dualistic world of outer and inner, matter and spirit. The two most powerful aids for developing this unifying vision are the ability to use symbols and the ability to read myths and dreams (our personal myths.). The word "symbol" (symbollein) means literally to throw or put together. (Its antonym is diabollein which sheds light on our word "devil" and means to throw apart, to separate.) Throughout the Conversations Alcott uses the words "emblem" and "emblematic" in the sense of "symbol" or "symbolic," and it is obvious that the children understand how to use the concept to an astonishing degree. Alcott set out to teach his pupils this wonderful secret game, this way of thinking. He knew instinctively that if we are initiated into this skill, life will always be meaningful.

Emblems I have found to be extremely attractive and instructive to children. I could not teach without them. Their universal spirit flows into nature, whether material, or human, through faculties that receive the divine stream — the one from without and the other from within — and pour it upon the soul. The manner of Jesus and Plato . . . show what the mind requires in order to be quickened and renewed. "Without a parable spake he not unto them." From neglecting this mode of instruction we have shorn the young mind of its beams. We have made it prosaic, literal, worldly.

Compare Alcott's statement with the following ones by Jung:

Now we have no symbolic life, and we are badly in need of the symbolic life. Only the symbolic life can express the need of the soul — the daily need of the soul mind you! And because people have no such thing, they can never step out of this mill — this awful, grinding, banal life in which they are "nothing but" . . . and that is the reason people are neurotic.

When the intellect does not serve the symbolic life, it is the devil; it makes you neurotic.

I really suppose that these ideas of Alcott's and Jung prompted the writing of my book *The Dove in the Stone: On Finding the Sacred in the Commonplace.* That book is devoted to developing this very theme as a function of Hagia Sophia (the original Third Person of the Trinity). She is the delightful archetype of feminine Holy Wisdom and her process shows how to unlock the messages of things and everyday events and how to find meaning all about us. It really does help to view the outward and visible world as full of inward and spiritual meaning. Children do this quite easily — for them it is like looking at those puzzles that challenge us to see how many hidden animals we can find included; for them it is easy to find "tongues in trees, books in running brooks, sermons in stones, and good in everything." As one of the little scholars told Mr. Alcott: "The body's eye cannot see what it wants to, but the spirit's eye can." Alcott seems to have had that in mind:

In the subsequent lesson the word tale came up; it elicited a good deal of conversation. It was seen that a tale might be the medium of conveying truth. Mr. Alcott went to show that the things we see tell us a tale all the time. And he asked what the things that happened in the outward world were tales of? It was answered

334 / How Like an Angel Came I Down

that there was not a thing that happened that had not existed in some mind or God's mind. He then said, the world was a tale, and life is a tale.

Any object around the house can be the center of a cosmic tale without end if you have to explain where the object came from and how you came to it, and all the associations that well up from it, and so forth. This makes for a good conversation with children. I remember a lively discussion arising when I held up a Bible and asked the children to imagine all the people involved in the book standing in one place. How big a place would that have to be? Pretty big, they thought. Then a child added all the people involved in producing the book, the type, and the paper, and the children traced back through history the inventions of the materials involved. We all had to agree that just one book, and especially a history book, was like an implosion of cosmic energy.

Mr. Alcott also had some thoughts on the Bible. He said:

The Bible is God in words. But the Bible is not the only Revelation of God. There are many Bibles to those who think. Nature, the outward world is a Bible. Its objects typify God's thoughts. The soul is a Bible.

Summing up, it is my heartfelt hope that others will be inspired in their own way by the thought and work of Mr. Alcott. As one of his descendants, Alcott Allison, has observed — of the great triumverate of Concord, Emerson prevailed in the nineteenth century; Thoreau in the twentieth, and surely Bronson Alcott will be recognized in the new century to come. "He does not need our praise, but we need his wisdom," writes Allison. I would only add that the time for Bronson Alcott is already at hand and we are ready for him. A blessing on him!

APPENDIX FOUR

* * *

BIBLIOGRAPHY

Alcott, A. Bronson. 1835/1836. Conversations with children on the Gospels. 2 vols. Boston: Munroe

—. 1938. The journals of Bronson Alcott. Ed. Odell Shepard. Boston: Little, Brown and Company.

Alcott, Louisa May. 1980. Transcendental wild oats. Boston: Harvard Common Press.

Bedell, Madelon. 1977. The Alcotts: Biography of a family. New York: Clarkson N. Potter, Publishers.

Brooks, Van Wyck. 1941. The flowering of New England. New York: E. P. Dutton and Company.

Bunyan, John. 1904. Pilgrims's progress. New York: R. F. Fenno and Company.

Cremin, Laurence A. 1980. American education: The national experience 1783-1876. New York: Harper and Row.

Ellenberger, Henry. 1970. History of the unconscious. New York: Basic Books.

Emerson, Ralph Waldo. 1926. Essays. New York: Thomas Q. Crowell Company.

Frothingham, Octavius Brooks. 1972. Transcendentalism in New England. Philadelphia: University of Pennsylvania Press.

Harwood, A. C. 1940. The way of a child. London: Rudolf Steiner Press.

Hochfield, George, Ed. 1966. Selected writings of the American transcendentalists. New York: Signet Classics.

Holbrook, Stewart H. 1957. Dreamers of the American dream. Garden City, NY: Doubleday.

Howell, Alice O. 1988. The dove in the stone: Finding the sacred in the commonplace. Wheaton, IL: The Theosophical Publishing House, Quest Books.

Jung, Carl Gustav. 1957-1979. The collected works. Trans. R. F. C. Hull. Bollingen Series. 20 vols. Princeton, NJ: Princeton University Press.

Koepke, Hermann. 1989. Encountering the self. Hudson, NY: Anthroposophic Press.

McCuskey, Dorothy. 1940. Bronson Alcott, teacher. Boston: The Macmillan Company.

Miller, Perry. 1957. The American transcendentalists: Their prose and poetry. Garden City, NY: Doubleday Anchor Books.

Muses, Charles A. 1951. Illumination on Jacob Boehme: The work of Dionysius Andreas Freher. New York: Columbia University Press.

Neumann, Erich. 1973. The child. New York: Harper and Row.

Peabody, Elizabeth Palmer. 1984. Letters of Elizabeth Palmer Peabody. Ed. Bruce A. Ronda. Middletown, CT: Wesleyan University Press.

—. 1835. The record of a school. Boston: William Monroe.Pearce, Pearce, Joseph Chilton. 1977. Magical child: Rediscovering nature's plan for our children. New York: E. P. Dutton.

Saxton, Martha. 1977. Louisa May: A modern biography of Louisa May Alcott. Boston: Houghton Mifflin Company.

Shepard, Odell. 1937. Pedlar's progress. Boston: Little, Brown and Company.

Shepard, Odell, Ed. The journals of Bronson Alcott.

Steiner, Rudolf. 1974. The kingdom of childhood. London: Rudolf Steiner Press.

Taylor, Thomas. 1969. Thomas Taylor the Platonist. Eds Kathleen Raine and George Mills Harper. Princeton, NJ: Princeton University Press.

Tharp, Louise Hall. The Peabody sisters of Salem. 1950. Boston: Little, Brown and Company.

Von Heydebrand, Caroline. 1942. Childhood: A study of the growing soul. Letchworth, Hertfordshire: Rudolf Steiner Press.